Call the Mothers

California Series in Public Anthropology

The California Series in Public Anthropology emphasizes the anthropologist's role as an engaged intellectual. It continues anthropology's commitment to being an ethnographic witness, to describing, in human terms, how life is lived beyond the borders of many readers' experiences. But it also adds a commitment, through ethnography, to reframing the terms of public debate—transforming received, accepted understandings of social issues with new insights, new framings.

Call the Mothers

SEARCHING FOR MEXICO'S
DISAPPEARED IN THE WAR ON DRUGS

Shaylih Muehlmann

UNIVERSITY OF CALIFORNIA PRESS

University of California Press
Oakland, California

© 2024 by Shaylih Muehlmann

Cataloging-in-Publication data is on file at the Library of Congress.

ISBN 978-0-520-31457-3 (cloth)
ISBN 978-0-520-31458-0 (pbk.)
ISBN 978-0-520-97398-5 (ebook)

33   32   31   30   29   28   27   26   25   24
10   9   8   7   6   5   4   3   2   1

Contents

Illustrations

Introduction

The first thing Leticia told me when we reunited at a café in Mexico City, two years after we had first met, was, "I found her!" I jolted with joy as I rose to hug her. I had been following Leticia's courageous efforts to find her daughter and we had been communicating sporadically from a distance since we last met so this was unexpected and wonderful news. But I then watched as Leticia's face became more severe and her eyes teared over as she registered my misunderstanding. She then clarified. "I found her *sin vida, sin vida . . .*" ("lifeless"). I realized with a sinking feeling that she had found her daughter's body. It was her characterization of finding her as "good news" that led me to misunderstand and to react in a way that now seemed offensively disproportionate to the news. I sat down across from Leticia, shaken, as we ordered some coffee, and I tried to recalibrate to her situation. While Leticia's deepest hope had certainly been that her daughter might still be alive, she did indeed exude positive energy and relief about reaching some type of closure in finding her daughter *sin vida*. Leticia is not alone in navigating these fraught, contradictory emotions. She is part of a vast network of people all over Mexico who are organizing to find relatives who disappeared in the context of the "war on drugs."

While they search with the hope, and conviction even, that their loved ones are alive, often they must come to terms with more difficult outcomes.

People in Mexico have been subjected to immense violence over the past decades by the state and drug trafficking organizations in the context of the US-backed "war on drugs." Since former Mexican President Felipe Calderón launched his military offensive against the drug cartels after taking office in 2006, over 360,000 people have been killed nationwide.[1] According to the Mexican government, over 100,000 people have disappeared or been registered as missing since 2006.[2] Some cases, referred to as "enforced disappearances," have involved the complicity or direct involvement of state security forces. Disappearances are also undercounted. The actual number of people who have disappeared is much higher, since many are not officially registered by the state. Indeed, Mexico has become "a country of the disappeared."[3] In 2013 Human Rights Watch declared that Mexico had "the most severe crisis of enforced disappearances in Latin America in decades," and a decade later, the situation has only worsened.[4] In fact, between 2022 and 2023 the record of disappearances reached its highest yet: the national registry recorded 10,064, which means that in that year twenty-seven people disappeared a day.[5]

The pattern is recurring. A son leaves his home in the morning but never arrives at work; a young daughter walks back from school but never makes it home; a husband leaves for a business trip and is never seen again. This book explores how family members cope with those disappearances and the tremendous lengths to which many go to try to find their missing loved ones. For the families, what makes this even more difficult is the indifference with which the police and government officials often meet their predicaments. As a result, increasingly, the work of investigating these disappearances falls solely on the victims' loved ones, including women like Leticia who are often mothers or wives rather than agents of the state. They do the work because, as I will show, often no one else will.

As Leticia and I sipped our coffees, she filled me in on how she found her daughter's body in a communal grave in May 2013, two years after she had disappeared. The details of this discovery were, in themselves, disturbing and indicative of how flawed the systems that victims must navigate are. She found her daughter after searching all over the country. In the end, it turned out that her daughter's body had been found and reported to the police only three hours after Ivonne was killed by an unknown suspect, under circumstances that are still not understood. Ivonne was taken to a morgue where her body was tagged and numbered and her clothing was itemized. The police and officials never publicized the news of the discovery, nor did they connect the news to Leticia's campaign publicizing the image of her missing daughter. Leticia says she even went to that very morgue asking about bodies that might have matched the description of her daughter only months after she had disappeared. She stood there, in that morgue, not knowing that her daughter was only a dozen feet away from her, and was told unequivocally that no one fitting her daughter's description was in the database.

As I was listening to her story, I thought back to when I first met Leticia. We met on the Caravan for Peace organized by Mexican activists in 2012 to protest drug war policies in the United States. The caravan of 125 people, mostly from Mexico, who had been affected by the war on drugs traveled through twenty-seven cities to raise awareness about the impacts of drug war violence in Mexico. I joined the caravan for some of this journey and sat beside

Leticia on the bus for several stretches. I remembered her telling me that she scanned the faces of every crowd, at every event, even out the window of the bus in the United States as we rode, looking for her daughter. At the time, it was hard for me to imagine a scenario by which her daughter would show up in a crowd in the United States. But Leticia explained that one of her working theories was that Ivonne might have been kidnapped by a sex trafficking ring and perhaps taken north. When Ivonne disappeared, she had been working in a casino and Leticia said she knew that many "*gringos*" frequented the place. While it still seemed unlikely that she would happen upon her in the United States, over the years I have come to understand that for people whose loved ones are missing, it is a reflex to look for them everywhere, in every crowd, in every city, in every situation.

But to remember Leticia scanning crowds in the United States now, knowing that all that time her daughter was just miles from her home in Mexico, is sobering. In the time that she had searched, she had been subject to continuous bribe attempts, threats, and harassment from the Mexican police, and during the first few months of her search, the majority of the legwork she did was completely on her own. She went to dozens of morgues and flipped through registries with photos of hundreds of unidentified corpses. Her journey searching for Ivonne was long and circuitous and seemed even more so in hindsight, knowing that Ivonne had actually been in one of the first places she looked.

We had been sitting for a long time at the café and ordered more coffee and a piece of cake to share. Leticia told me she used to love chocolate but that she had lost her love of it during her search. "While I was searching for her, I would lay awake every night wondering where she was, wondering if she was cold, wondering if she was safe," she said. Not knowing was distressing for Leticia: her every waking moment was unsettled by the uncertainty. Again, I remembered the sleeping conditions while Leticia was on the caravan. Through dozens of cities the members of the caravan slept wherever their community hosts could offer them a place to lay their heads. They slept on gymnasium floors, in churches, often with sleeping bags and mats on the ground. In all of these scenarios Leticia would have been imagining how much worse her daughter's sleeping conditions were. Leticia waved the chocolate cake on her fork and said: "Even this, even eating delicious food or any food, I couldn't enjoy." She explained that eating would fill her with anxiety wondering whether Ivonne had enough to eat wherever she was. For these reasons, finding her daughter's remains had been transformative for her and had helped her heal, despite the fact that she had fervently hoped to find her alive.

Most of the activists I know and follow in this book have yet to find even this much resolution to their searches. What they have found, however, are others. Like Leticia, a vast network of activists and increasing numbers of civic and nongovernmental organizations (NGOs) and collectives are committed to supporting families in their searches. These diverse actors have come together to say *Basta!* ("enough") to the war on drugs and the violence and impunity it creates.

The War on Drugs

The war on drugs is one of the primary causes of violence and suffering across the world and one of the most heatedly contested issues of the twenty-first century. The very concept of the "war on drugs," as noted by many scholars, frames the "drug problem" not as a public health or education issue but rather as a *military* problem, requiring state violence against groups loosely framed as "the enemy," including traffickers and people who use drugs. This militarization has been particularly dramatic in countries such as the United States, Mexico, Afghanistan, and more recently the Philippines, where a brutal antidrug campaign waged by the state and paramilitaries has led to the murder of thousands of alleged drug users and traffickers.

The impact of these policies has had a profound influence in North America, in part because the United States has had one of the most coercive and punitive prohibition policies on record. The militarized prohibition of drugs has been one of the most dominant doctrines guiding US domestic and foreign policy since the 1970s, when President Richard Nixon officially launched the drug wars.[6] At the same time the United States is the main source of demand for illegal drugs in the world. As a result, this country has directly impacted the rise of drug trafficking and its associated violence in neighboring Latin American countries, first in Colombia and more recently in Mexico. Over the past fifty years, the United States has also pushed Mexico towards a more prohibitionist stance on drugs and US authorities have maintained close control of the appointment of Mexico's drug policy officials.[7] This has had disastrous consequences on Mexico, where "drug-related" violence has reached staggering dimensions.[8]

But contemporary Mexico arrived at this point of crisis because of several intersecting processes including not only drug war policies but also processes of neoliberalization and democratic transition. While prohibition policies have provided the rationale for funding the militarization of the country and have created increased impunity and human rights violations, neoliberal reforms have facilitated both illegal and legal commerce, strengthening the drug trade and weakening the government bodies charged with dealing with its associated violence.

The escalating violence in modern Mexico is also, in part, an unintended consequence of neoliberal policies and their interplay with various economic and social processes. This relationship is perhaps most evident in the effects of free trade agreements, especially those with the United States. These agreements, promoted under the umbrella of neoliberalism, have invigorated international trade, but they have also facilitated drug smuggling by opening numerous commercial channels that can be exploited as trafficking routes. Additionally, these neoliberal policies have spurred a boom in the export of high-value goods, such as avocados and limes. The profitable nature of such products has caught the attention of criminal enterprises, eager to profit through the extortion of these burgeoning industries.[9]

Another way that violence in Mexico has been exacerbated by neoliberalism is related to one of its central tenets: the reduction of state expenditure on public services. This leads to underfunded law enforcement and judicial systems, resulting in an increase in impunity, fostering an in environment in which illegal activities thrive. Finally, there's been a documented trend of private corporations aligning their interests with organized crime. These partnerships often target local and environmental activists who stand in the way of their interests.

Together, these factors create a complex narrative of how neoliberalism has inadvertently fueled an increase in violence in Mexico. These processes have also taken place during times of significant political shifts in power, and in particular, after the end of the seventy-year reign of a single party, the Institutional Revolutionary Party (PRI), which was in power between 1929 and 2000. This confluence created deep connections between criminal organizations and the state, the most glaring evidence of which is almost total impunity for cases of deaths and disappearances.[10]

According to state information only between 2 and 6 percent of the deaths and disappearances that take place in Mexico are ever investigated.[11] Mexican officials have justified their unwillingness to investigate the majority of these disappearances and murders by claiming that they consist simply of criminals killing each other off. But this book will show that the persistence of such widespread impunity has more to do with the likely perpetrators of this violence than its victims, for state agents are often involved in disappearances either as direct perpetrators or through support or acquiescence.

The term "disappeared" has a long history in Latin America and generally refers to people who have been kidnapped by government security forces and whose whereabouts, and survival, remain unknown to family members, friends, and acquaintances.[12] The concept of *"los desaparecidos"* emerged as a political term during the 1970s when protestors against state terror in Chile, Brazil, Argentina, and Uruguay adapted the Spanish verb "to disappear," *desaparecer,* to name the condition of "forced disappearance," *ser desaparecido.*[13] The concept was originally used to designate individuals who had been disappeared as part of a deliberate effort to eliminate political opponents. The practice of state forces "disappearing" citizens grew out of the Cold War when governments throughout the world instructed their security forces to covertly eliminate individuals deemed subversive: students, teachers, labor or rural activists, and those who were perceived as threats to the social order.[14]

But while disappearances have been a public phenomenon for a long time in Mexico, it was only after 2006 that they became part of the crisis associated with the war on drugs, where the practice adopted distinct features. Disappearance in contemporary Mexico is deployed in a more depoliticized manner, victims do not have a clear or single profile, and disappearances are often carried out by an opaque network of state and nonstate actors involving drug trafficking organizations, often in collusion with state forces.

It is difficult to estimate how many disappearances directly involve state agents because prosecutors and police routinely neglect to take basic investigative steps to identify those responsible. Sometimes the involvement of the state is obvious: soldiers or police in official uniforms and vehicles detain people either in public (security checkpoints, workplaces, bars) or from their homes in front of their families. These detentions are arbitrary, with no reasons or explanations given, and when the victims' relatives inquire about their detained family members whereabouts (at public headquarters or prosecutors' offices) they are often told the arrests never took place.

Data by the Mexican government does not disaggregate disappearances perpetrated by state actors and those committed by nonstate actors.[15] But we can glimpse the scope of the phenomenon of enforced disappearance from data provided by NGOs. Human Rights Watch investigated 249 disappearances between 2007 and 2013 and found that the Mexican police or military were involved in 149 of them.[16] More recently a study by the Observatory on Disappearances and Impunity in Mexico analyzed 548 cases in the state of Nuevo León, and found that, from 2005 to 2015, 46.76 percent of reported disappearances were carried out by state agents, 46.04 percent by criminal organizations, and 7.19 percent by individual or private actors.[17]

As for the victims, rather than being "criminals" it appears that they come from a variety of diverse groups.[18] Mandolessi and Olalde Rico have analyzed this variation and argued that the majority of disappearances are of men between the ages of fifteen and forty, and that some are members of professional groups who can provide specialized forced labor (doctors, architects, engineers). Others are vulnerable groups such as migrants in transit to the United States, or other marginalized populations, including Indigenous people and women, whose disappearance is sometimes linked to trafficking or gender-based violence. Journalists, social activists, and human rights defenders are also frequent victims.[19] The one thing that holds the phenomenon of contemporary disappearance in Mexico together is the pervasive impunity that allows for these crimes to go unpunished.

Women and the War on Drugs

Men are more likely to work for the drug trade, and the deaths and disappearances created by drug violence are overwhelmingly those of young men. Indeed, the lifespan of Mexican men has fallen due to the increase in murders.[20] However, the violence has both directly and indirectly affected women and trans and nonbinary people in a range of ways. One result of this violence, for example, is that tens of thousands of women have been left widowed or searching for information on missing or murdered children, siblings, or spouses. Since most drug-related deaths are not legally investigated, women who lose family members increasingly take a more political stance in demanding justice and protesting the devastating impact of drug war policies.

The chapters that follow examine how some women have been politicized by this experience. But what is particularly striking about the case of relatives of the disappeared in Mexico is the extent to which they have taken up roles that go far beyond those of traditional activists. The book shows how citizens, especially women, are increasingly taking on the roles of the state in investigating what happened to their loved ones. In the face of government corruption and negligence, it is women who carry out most of the functions involved with dealing with missing persons, kidnapping, and extortion cases and who have become the network to which other mothers of the missing turn.

The rising violence created by the war on drugs in Mexico, as well as the high incarceration rates that drug policies have produced in the United States, has generated a rich and ever-growing body of literature. Some of this scholarship has exposed the material and ideological effects of the war on drugs by analyzing the skyrocketing profits it provides to the military industrial complex, the US and Mexican financial sectors, and government agencies and corporations.[21] Other authors emphasize the important role of the war on drugs in the extension and maintenance of racial hierarchies and relations of exploitation between the United States and Latin America.[22] This line of analysis is central to exposing the elite beneficiaries of drug war policies and to destabilizing common-sense notions which too often re-entrench neoliberal ideologies— for instance by blaming the victims of violence for allegedly participating in drug trafficking.

This book adds to these literatures by examining how the war on drugs is experienced by people in Mexico in their everyday lives and by focusing on the gendered dimensions of drug war politics and how women-led activism serves as an increasingly important political force. This book will examine how this activism has emerged and taken shape, specifically around the experiences of grieving mothers. The articulation of the maternal voice by activists is particularly important because it unites several strains of protest against government violence and impunity, which increasingly bring to light the very high levels of violence against women in Mexico. The book, in this regard, historicizes women's protests against the war on drugs in Mexico within the legacy of mother-led movements against state terror in Latin America. These activists draw on a long and powerful lineage of women's activism against state violence, epitomized by the Mothers of Plaza de Mayo in Argentina and by Nobel Prize-winner Rigoberta Menchú in Guatemala.

The political space that has narrowly opened up to women in Mexico in relation to the activism around violence and the disappeared is not a space that has opened equally to all women. Queer and trans women and femmes as well as cisgendered women whose children are not direct victims of this violence are not generally public faces of these organizing efforts. Indeed, the public emphasis on these women's roles as "mothers" tends to silence other kinds of subjectivities mobilized by this activism. While women who position themselves as mothers have the most audible voices in this form of activism, other women make sense of their agency in their roles as sisters, daughters, aunts, or partners, or indeed through their experiences of violence not expressed through an affiliation with kin. These activists are part of these movements, though their voices are less audible.

One of the paradoxes of the local and national impact of drug war policies, therefore, is that the politicization of women both essentializes and potentially redefines traditional gender roles in Mexico, where the patriarchal figure of the mother is highly revered. As I explore in chapter 1, this essentializing of gender roles becomes particularly evident in a cross-cultural perspective, for the ways that women's voices have emerged in Mexico's drug debate differ from the experiences of women in the drug debate in the United States. This creates both challenges and opportunities for building a binational movement with activists in both countries.

The Caravan and the Beginning of a Longer Journey

Many people from Mexico and with connections to Mexico, myself included, have faced the heart-wrenching experience of a friend or relative disappearing without a trace. As anthropologist Claudio Lomnitz points out, there is hardly a town in Mexico that hasn't been affected by this phenomenon. The "emptiness we associate with disappearance spreads in society, like a stain."[23] For me, finding solace in the strength and resilience of the mothers and activists who have taken up the cause of seeking answers and justice was my way forward and this book is my effort to support and bring attention to their important work.

I came to this project in 2012, while I was completing research for a previous book on how the drug economy shapes rural life in northern Mexico. The book, *When I Wear My Alligator Boots,* examined how mostly working-class men in rural villages were entrapped by the pervasiveness of the drug economy in northern Mexico, often working in low-level and exploited positions as mules, and how this was affecting their lives and families.[24]

After nearly a decade conducting fieldwork among some of the most vulnerable people in the drug trade in Mexico, I felt discouraged about scholarship's potential to be part of any change to a system so profoundly entrenched in forms of neoliberal exploitation. I was also discouraged by how dangerous fieldwork had become and by the violence and deprivation so many of the people I cared about in northern Mexico had experienced. A sense of fear had increasingly permeated my research just as it had discussions and critiques about drug war policies in Mexico more generally.

Therefore, when I began attending protests against the war on drugs it was not in my role as a researcher, but as an activist. Protesting was a way of working through the impact of that decade of research and of communicating what I had learned from that experience in a simple and direct manner. On the streets, activists united in calls for an end to the drug war, with chants like "No more drug war!" or *"Hasta la madre!"* ("Enough!"). These phrases, echoing powerfully among a diverse crowd of hundreds from Mexico to the United States and Canada, offered a stark but satisfying contrast to the subdued and precise language typical of academic critique.

But as I got to know these activists, they challenged me with a persistent question—why wasn't I planning to write about their experiences and the growing political movement? With my background in writing and research, it was clear that writing was the best tool at my disposal to assist in the movement to get the word out about their tragedies. But beyond that encouragement, meeting these activists was a turning point for me, shifting my previously discouraged outlook on the war on drugs. These activists, mostly *amas de casa* or "housewives," spoke out with a fierce and unwavering political stance against drug war policies and impunity. They were fueled by anger and determination, and were not intimidated, even in the face of violence and loss. Many shared that they were unafraid because they had already faced their greatest fear—the loss of their loved ones. Their stories were both devastating and empowering.

Inspired by the bravery of these activists and a new sense of place for my work and that of other scholars and allies of the disappeared, I traveled to San Diego in August 2012 to join the Caravan for Peace, organized by Mexican activists protesting US drug war policies. During the caravan, I started collecting stories and life histories, focusing on women who were part of the activism. When I arrived at the border where they had organized a press conference officially launching the caravan, I met many family members of the disappeared. María Elena Herrera, a woman from Michoacán who had lost four sons, was the first to capture my attention. Two of her sons had disappeared on a business trip in 2008. She and her family searched for them with no help from the state and without success. In 2010, another two sons went missing. María and her remaining sons are still searching for them. María was a member of the Movement for Peace with Justice and Dignity (Movimiento por la Paz con Justicia y Dignidad, MPJD), which was a loosely organized group of activists that demanded an end to the war on drugs. The 2012 caravan where I met María, organized by MPJD in several cities in the United States, was particularly significant as it sought to target public opinion in the main country supporting and encouraging the war on drugs in Mexico: the United States.

The MPJD was organized in April 2011 after the famous poet Javier Sicilia lost his son, Juan Francisco Sicilia, who was kidnapped and killed the month before in the state of Morelos.[25] Sicilia called on the people of Mexico to protest the war on drugs and its associated violence and wrote an open letter to Mexican politicians that he closed by stating, *"Estamos hasta la madre!"* ("We've had it up to here!").[26] The next month, in May 2011, a caravan of families and members of civil society marched from the city of Cuernavaca, in Morelos, to Mexico City's main plaza, the Zócalo.[27] While that first caravan was small in numbers when it began, by the time it reached Mexico City and marched on the Zócalo, close to two hundred thousand people had joined the protest. In the speech Sicilia made in the Zócalo, he called on then Public Security (SSP) Secretary Genaro García Luna and then President Felipe Calderón to resign over their mishandling of the violence associated with the war on drugs during their time in office.

The MPJD was the first major social movement to organize in search of Mexico's disappeared. It quickly expanded beyond Morelos. Over the coming year and a half, the MPJD would organize an additional three caravans: one to Ciudad Juárez in the state of Chihuahua, one to Chiapas with the Zapatistas (EZLN), and the one on which I met María, which went through the United States.[28] The movement gained a significant following through these caravans and was vocal in articulating protests against both drug war policies and the government's responses to the violence.

The caravan to the United States brought together more than 120 people and 60 civil society organizations. Traveling on several buses, the caravan started in San Diego and ended in Washington, DC, stopping in twenty-seven cities along the way.[29] During their meetings in Washington, DC, the MPJD presented the Inter-American Commission on Human Rights with a report of 291 testimonies of kidnapping, disappearances, and homicides.[30]

Following the end of these caravans, the MPJD eventually lost some of its momentum. But the movement had succeeded in raising support for the cause and bringing people together over a shared grief, rage, and impetus for change. Most importantly, many of the women brought together by this movement would go on to create their own collectives or otherwise to work in support of the victims and their families in Mexico in the coming years. The MPJD, in many ways, helped spur a broader social movement for the disappeared on both national and local levels.

Researching the Impacts of Violence

In the decade after the Caravan for Peace, I continued to research the activist network that had emerged from the MJPD. In following up with these activists after the caravan, I also met more activists who were engaged in other forms of organizing, resistance, and mobilization across the country. For example, in 2014 I met Araceli Salcedo at a press conference in Mexico City. Araceli's daughter, Fernanda Rubí Salcedo Jiménez, disappeared in Orizaba, Veracruz, in September of 2012.[31] Rubí had just turned twenty-one when she was abducted from a bar where she was chatting with friends. A group of six men came in and grabbed her, dragging her out of the bar. "There was nothing we could do" was what the bartender told Araceli later. They do not know why this happened. But friends of Rubí theorized it was retribution for her having refused a flower from a prospective and powerful suitor the week before.

In April of 2022, I attended a talk that Araceli Salcedo gave for a Christian youth group just outside of her hometown of Orizaba, Veracruz. She was presenting a book of testimonies and photographs created by her search collective but the main purpose of the talk was to raise awareness among the youth and talk about prevention.[32] Before the talk she told me how important it is to approach the issue of violence and disappearances with young people in ways that will not potentially upset or trigger them. Araceli added, "For example, we try not get into the details of searching for graves. Instead, we try to stick to our own personal experiences and then discuss the problem more generally while also making sure the focus is on prevention strategies." Daniel, the photographer and her copresenter, whose cousin had disappeared several years before, is a teacher and he described being well versed in strategies for the mitigating potential harms created by raising difficult topics in a classroom.

I was struck by this conversation because I realized that Araceli and Daniel were struggling with some of the same representational issues that confounded my research and writing about these topics. The challenge is to write about violence in ways that do not sensationalize it but also don't dilute the reality of the pain and suffering it creates. Foremost though, my concern throughout this research has been to avoid potentially retraumatizing my research participants by, for example, asking questions that could cause them pain or harm. So I was riveted by the realization that Araceli and Daniel were consciously navigating these dilemmas themselves, mindful not to cause harm to their interlocutors.

I sat down to watch their presentation, curious to see how they would proceed, especially as some of the youth were quite young, ten or eleven years old, and I wondered what it would be like for these young people to hear about Daniel and Araceli's experiences. They began by saying, "We are here to talk about a sensitive but very important issue." Then they both, in turn, described their journeys and their efforts to find their loved ones. Their talking points were careful and measured and the audience was quiet and serious.

But the tone of the conversation changed and became livelier and more engaged during the question period. The first few questions were raised gingerly, but the youth became increasingly emboldened by Araceli and Daniel's honesty and comfort sharing their stories. At one point, a young boy, of about eleven or twelve, raised his hand and asked a question about unmarked graves, a topic that, as planned, Araceli and Daniel had tactfully glazed over. The boy asked, "Aren't the bodies that have been there a long time rotten and unrecognizable? How can you tell if it's your family member?" I flinched hearing this question, worrying about how it would sound to Araceli, or what images it would push into her thoughts. But Araceli responded generously without even a hint of discomfort. "Yes, you are right," she said. "Sometimes there are just bones." And then she said, "The first thing I look for is the fracture on Rubí's clavicle." She said that's why it's important that the families search themselves because they know these details. And then she said that the boy had raised an important issue because often ultimately you need to rely on scientific technologies like DNA testing. "Do you know about DNA testing?" she asked, and then Araceli explained, to some shaking heads, what that is and how it is done. She went into impressive detail. Rather than being uncomfortable, Araceli was eager to share her experience and proud to be able to detail the immense knowledge that she had acquired from her forensic training.

It was striking to note how much Araceli had learned in the last decade; we were coming up on the tenth anniversary of Rubí's disappearance. Araceli had gone from being a professional party planner before Rubí disappeared, decorating event rooms and organizing catering, to advising on ransom negotiations and leading substantive forensic investigations of clandestine graves. She had also received forensic training and learned all about the process of using technologies such as DNA testing. It made sense that she was eager to share this knowledge. When the question period was over

Araceli and Daniel handed out copies of their book of photos and testimonies and were approached by many of the youth with hugs and more questions and words of support and encouragement.

Because talking to people about events that are traumatic requires caution and care, I was very sparing with my questions. The family members I met who were searching for loved ones shaped the contours of our conversations almost entirely. But because my research focused on families who were already politicized, they were—like Araceli and Daniel—intent on sharing their stories. I usually met these activists at press conferences and marches. Just standing with a camera and a notebook was enough to draw people who would come to tell me what had happened to their loved one and what they had gone through in their search. Researching this topic among activists came with a clear set of expectations about my role. Family members of the disappeared who have become involved in activism largely want their stories to be heard and shared beyond national borders, so that people elsewhere learn what is happening in Mexico.

It is critical to recognize, however, that most of the people in Mexico whose loved ones have disappeared do not become activists and are not comfortable sharing their stories. It is common, and understandably so, for family members not to speak about their experiences at all out of fear for their lives and those of their remaining family members. Among my own long-term friendships in Mexico, in predominantly working-class areas of the north, this was most families' principal response. The silence that falls over many disappearances profoundly shaped the nature and focus of my research. For every account that was shared with me by activists, I knew there were many others that remained untold, and I have kept these other families in my mind as I have carried out this research. This background awareness allowed me to maintain a larger perspective on how skewed a focus simply on activism is. A study such as this does not show us what is typical about the way drug war violence tears up communities and devastates families but, rather, shows us some of the extraordinary responses to that violence.

This awareness also prompted my interest in how some people came to be politicized amid the trauma and confusion of their experiences searching for a loved one. I found that long-term ethnographic research was particularly important to tracing a process of politicization over time because this time frame provided a vantage point from which to observe a shift in the subjectivities of some activists. Sometimes I met activists early in their process of politicization, soon after a family member had disappeared, when they were ready to urgently tell the world but not yet sure how to explain or make sense of their own stories or put them in a political context. Other activists I worked with were fully engaged in the public sphere by the time I met them. It was important to see how family members of the disappeared transitioned from identifying mostly as victims to becoming vocal activists. In the process, they came to find a platform from which to understand and share their interpretation of events, as I explore in chapter 1. This arc of politicization served as the initial focus of my research. But I discovered that many of the women whose journeys I followed became much more than simply politicized, for they came to take on the roles of the state in their searches.

Throughout my research, my principal method was participant observation: spending long periods with activists, attending meetings, and accompanying them to protests and planning events. Through interviews and life histories, I also gathered accounts of how violence affected people's lives and changed their perceptions of drug war policies, with specific emphasis on how family members of the disappeared interpret the changing political climate in Mexico. In contrast to more traditional anthropological approaches, including my own in past projects, this research is not an in-depth ethnography of a single place or even one community of people. Instead, I followed a group of mostly women from various parts of Mexico who were only loosely connected to each other through their arc of politicization. I knew them in and out of different kinds of political organizing and collectives in which they were involved over a period of ten years; following their stories led me to many parts of Mexico including Mexico City, Chiapas, Veracruz, Oaxaca, and Baja California. This multisited approach highlighted how complex the phenomena of disappearances are. The range of experiences I document here shows the unique sets of local circumstances that both allow for disappearances to happen in the first place and shape the experiences that relatives have when they seek out their missing loved ones. Ethnographers who have conducted in-depth local case studies have also underscored that these specificities of location also change over time.[33]

Here I hope to highlight something that these regional specificities have in common, which is how civil society, ordinary people, and particularly relatives have mobilized across class and regional divides not only to seek out the disappeared but also to resist and protest a larger context of impunity that has allowed for these human rights abuses to proliferate. The networks that have emerged in this context have ventured outward, searching streets, morgues, and prisons, scouring deserts, mountains, and rivers. They investigate, collect evidence and information, and request and independently analyze reports. They do so also by forging alliances with civil organizations, government officials, academics, and journalists. Sometimes they weave ad hoc alliances with cartels and criminal actors willing to share information. They go to any lengths to find their loved ones.

Introductions and Organization of the Book

During my research on this project, I came to know dozens of families who were searching for a disappeared family member. But there were several women whom I came to know more closely and whose stories are the guiding lights of this book. In addition to María, described above, there is Leticia, whom I introduced briefly at the beginning of this chapter. I first met Leticia on the Caravan for Peace in the United States in August and September of 2012. At the time, her daughter had been missing for over a year and she had no idea what had happened to her, nor whether she was alive or dead. She had quit her job and devoted herself full time to finding her. "I had a good life," she said, "but I was totally oblivious." In retrospect, she describes her life as existing in a pleasant orbit of family and neighbors, with time spread out over dinners at home, cooking, and taking care of her grandchildren. She had heard things about the government being corrupt but never experienced this firsthand, other than in the more mundane reality of low-level bribes. And prior to her daughter's disappearance, Leticia said she was hardly aware of the violence associated with the war on drugs. It was only after Ivonne's disappearance that Leticia began to be aware of the immense scope of the problem of corruption and violence enveloping the nation.

But Leticia did recall that two months before her daughter disappeared, they had both been sitting in the living room watching the news when there was some coverage of Javier Sicilia. He was being interviewed about the first march organized by MPJD and talking about the people whose children had been killed or disappeared. Leticia remembers turning to Ivonne and saying, "This is horrible what is happening. Maybe we should join the march." Leticia did join the march two months later but without Ivonne, who by then was already missing. She marched not just in solidarity, as she had imagined that day in the living room with her daughter. "Instead, I marched alone, as a mother of a disappeared daughter."

Leticia spent two years investigating her daughter's disappearance and finally found her body in 2014. Since then, she has been a vocal advocate for other women in her situation and even started a network of women supporting other victims. What is striking about Leticia's story is not just that she has become such a vocal advocate for other women, but also that she took on roles generally associated with law enforcement. Nothing about her former life prepared her for this role. As a petite, well-dressed, and mild-mannered woman, the stories she recounts are often unexpected, like the numerous times she went in person, clad in bullet-proof gear, to negotiate ransoms on behalf of other families.

Another major figure in the book is Lucía, whose son disappeared from the coastal town of Xalapa, Veracruz, on June 28, 2013. Lucía has devoted all of her time and resources since then to finding her son and organizing other parents who have been searching for their own children. On Mother's Day of 2016, Lucía received a tip from members of a drug cartel that provided the coordinates for what looked like a mass grave. Tired of waiting for support from the government, Lucía and some other members of the Solecito collective decided to go to the desert themselves and dig for signs of the missing. Over the next few months, they uncovered what would become the largest mass grave ever discovered in Mexico. Though she still hasn't found her son, she hasn't stopped searching. Then there is Araceli, whose daughter, as mentioned above, disappeared in Orizaba, Veracruz, in September of 2012. I first met Araceli at a press conference in Mexico City in 2014. She has been active in organizing families in Orizaba, but what struck me most about her was how fearlessly she confronted the government powers, including individual politicians, who obstructed her search. Her experience is also emblematic of the ways that victims of disappearance are often blamed for what has happened to them.

Leticia, Araceli, Lucía, and María are some of the women who are central to the book's narrative. This book is organized around five core chapters. Each chapter follows the story of one or more women and their families navigating the fraught political and affective terrain plotted by their search for the disappeared in Mexico.

In chapter 1, "They Started Off as a Busload of Victims," I describe how, in the attempt to forge a transnational activist movement with the United States and Canada, one of the primary challenges that emerges for activists from Mexico is their imperative to proclaim the "innocence" of their missing children: that is, that their disappearance is not linked to involvement in drug trafficking. In this chapter, I argue that this pressure to foreground innocence is partially generated by the constraints of a gendered activist platform that highlights their roles as women and as "mothers" in particular. And I analyze how women who articulate their agency as sisters, daughters, or through experiences of violence not expressed through an affiliation with male kin are often less audible than those who position themselves as mothers.

Chapter 2, "Until We Find Them," follows the stories of Leticia and Lucía in their struggles to find their missing children. I analyze the Kafkaesque bureaucracy that mothers navigate in their searches and argue that gendered perceptions of agency and transgression significantly shape their interactions with the state. Lucía's and Leticia's cases confirm what other activists experienced elsewhere in Mexico when looking for missing family members: an opaque and terribly slow bureaucracy barely equipped to process even the most basic requests, in which, for instance, these women are made to wait for letters to be sent via regular snail mail through agencies sometimes located in the same building as each other. This chapter shows how this slow-motion nightmare of waiting for help from the police or other officials leads many women to forego state agencies altogether and begin the dangerous project of investigating on their own.

Chapter 3, "Call the Mothers, Not the Police," explores how many women who have been vocal about their searches have become *de facto* support networks for other victims. This chapter examines the role that women have come to take in the absence of state support for victims of drug war violence. I trace Araceli, Romina, and Leticia's experiences working to negotiate ransoms and extortions and to advise families on how to navigate the complexities of engaging with the Mexican state in registering missing people. These women have, in effect, become agents of the state, providing the kind of services that citizens of liberal democracies in the global North have come to expect from their governments. I analyze this assumption of state roles by these women as an effect of the gendered downloading of neoliberal governance strategies onto individuals.

Chapter 4, "A Rage So Fierce She Didn't Notice Her Feet," follows the case of Araceli and her confrontations with local politicians who impeded her search for her daughter. Araceli's experience forms the basis of a wider discussion about the history of collusion between the government and criminal organizations that have fortified the drug trade and influenced the nature of associated violence in Mexico. I trace these relationships to three overlapping processes in Mexico: neoliberalization, militarization, and the democratic transition away from the PRI.

Chapter 5, "Without a Body There Is No Crime," begins with Lucía's experience of receiving a tip in Veracruz from a drug cartel on Mother's Day in 2016. The information she and a group of other mothers received led to the discovery of a mass grave, which they eventually dug up with only minimal support from the state. Using rudimentary tools, the women discovered 263 bodies in what is now considered to be the largest mass grave in Mexico. The chapter analyzes the relationship between these women and cartel members and how their collaboration transforms the way many women view the humanity of criminals and state actors.

. . .

My research builds off the stories of the women I have introduced here but also draws on my long-term research in villages in northern Mexico, particularly a place I call Santa Ana and the people I have come to know there over the years. In *When I Wear My Alligator Boots*, I documented the experiences and aspirations of young men, who are drawn to the allure of narco-trafficking due to the opportunities and prestige it affords in a region subjected to extreme poverty.

One of these young men was Octavio. He was born and raised in Santa Ana, where I first met him, now almost two decades ago, when he was a young and vibrant fourteen-year-old who lit up his home village with his energy and sense of humor. I was in my early twenties and eager to begin my research but struggling to adapt to living with my host family (Octavio's aunt and cousins) and learning Spanish. I was having difficulty understanding some of the conversations of the family I was living with. Elsa, Octavio's cousin, was a particular challenge with her fast-paced and informal way of speaking, which regularly left me feeling lost.

My first clear memory of Octavio was from a day I was poring over my Spanish dictionary trying to decipher a word that Elsa kept using. Octavio walked in and asked, "What word are you looking for?" He took pride in helping me with my Spanish when he could and often volunteered himself as my unofficial and sometimes quite deliberately unreliable translator. "*Donta,*" I said. "It's not in here." "What?" he asked, confused. "*Donta,*" I repeated, "Elsa keeps saying '*Donta mi mamá?*' What does it mean?" Octavio burst into laughter. Elsa came out to find out what was so funny. "*Dónde está!*" Octavio annunciated clearly, breaking up the words that Elsa had joined together as *donta* and explaining that it was a shorthand for "where is she." "Your Spanish is not the problem this time," he said, smiling mischievously at his cousin. "Elsa's Spanish is the problem!" The misunderstanding was quickly resolved with laughter and "*donta*" became a regular part of Octavio's own vocabulary—a word he used to tease both Elsa and me equally. This was just the first of many instances that revealed Octavio's playfulness and ability to diffuse a difficult situation.

Over the years, I watched Octavio grow up, have children, get married, and become an adult. But his infectious energy and spirit remained unchanged. He dyed his hair several assorted colors and could still perform circus tricks on his bicycle, riding backwards with a pack of kids following in his dust. He never failed to make everyone around him laugh. On my yearly visits to the village, I was always grateful for the opportunity to enjoy his presence.

Yet, in an instant, everything changed. In 2022, I was at home in Vancouver following the social media accounts of activists and search collectives in Mexico, which produce a consistent stream of reports of disappearances. Each post includes the phrase *"Se busca"* (in search of) and the photo, name, and description of yet another missing person. All of a sudden, I was shaken when I recognized the face of Octavio. When his face showed up on my news feed—until then made up of faces that were strangers to me—I knew that Octavio had become one among the many thousands who disappear in Mexico every year.

The announcement of Octavio's disappearance was made by a local collective and soon reverberated through the tight-knit community of Santa Ana. In a frenzy of communication, I was hastily filled in on the scant details surrounding Octavio's disappearance. One day, Octavio had stepped out of his home to run some errands, including purchasing a suit for his role as *padrino* at a quinceañera party for the daughter of a friend. He never returned. Rumors and speculation swirled among his friends and family, with theories ranging from cartel violence to the jealous retribution of his wife for presumed infidelities. The police were notified and they took statements but did not continue with the investigation. Each family member of Octavio I communicated with seemed to have their own explanation of what had happened and who might have paid the police off not to investigate his disappearance.

On learning this news from a distance, and without more information or the presence of his family and friends to commiserate with, my first reaction was to go through all my old photos of him.

I flipped through the images, inadvertently searching the pictures for any sign of what might have happened to him. Photos from years ago would probably not reveal any information about his disappearance but they were all I had. My reaction reminded me of the responses of many I had interviewed for this book, like Leticia, who searched for their missing loved ones even in crowds far from Mexico. When someone disappears, anything, even old photos, can be a potential clue given the lack of information about their whereabouts. The news of Octavio's disappearance left me disconsolate and uncertain. The research I had been conducting about the disappeared in Mexico had become much more personal and unsettling.

In February 2023, I returned to Octavio's home village to visit and also to enquire further about what had happened to him. I knew that he had been part of the constellations of young men of working-class background all over the region who are recruited by the cartels to either move illicit drugs or sell them locally. I learned that Octavio had been associated with the drug trafficking organization that once held a strong grip over the region. As a local dealer, he had exclusive rights to sell in a settlement near his village and strategically located on the road connecting major cities in northwest Mexico, where long-haul truckers regularly stop. The main rumor circulating locally was that Octavio disappeared because he got caught in the turf war between competing factions of the Sinaloa Cartel. Relatives and friends looked for his body in the desert and tried to make the police investigate the case for over a year, to no avail.

Maribel, Octavio's aunt, told me that police officers said that he disappeared because "he was probably involved with the narcos," implying that his fate was not worthy of investigation. For Maribel and those of us who knew him, this is the type of blanket dehumanization that not only allows for the violence of the war on drugs to continue unabated but also erases that someone like Octavio was, in addition to a local dealer, a father, an animated and joyful man, and for me a dear and supportive friend. It is a dismissal that all families of the disappeared encounter to various degrees and one that profoundly shapes activism against drug violence in ways that I will describe in more detail in the next chapter.

Maribel's response to this police indifference was directly to the point of Octavio's predicament and indeed, to that of this book: "Maybe he disappeared because he was working for the mafia. Maybe not. It doesn't matter, it's still not right what happened to Octavio. They still have to investigate."

1   *"They Started Off as a Busload of Victims"*

On August 12, 2012, a bus full of people who had been personally affected by the violence of the war on drugs in Mexico crossed the border at Tijuana to start a month-long caravan across the United States. Many of them had lost loved ones. Others had fled from bloodshed or been forced out of their communities. These people said that they were bringing with them "a message of pain" to the American people. Beneath the tall, double-fenced border wall with a view of Tijuana beyond, members of the press and supporters gathered on both sides to welcome the caravan. The main instigator and public figure of the tour was the famed poet Javier Sicilia, who told the press: "We will travel across the United States to raise awareness of the unbearable pain and loss caused by the drug war, and of the enormous, shared responsibility for protecting families and communities in both our countries."

Sicilia became an activist in 2011 after his twenty-four-year-old son, Juan Francisco Sicilia, was found dead with six others in a car outside the city of Cuernavaca. As I mentioned in the introduction, this incident fortified growing public criticism of the Mexican government's discourse and of the impunity it created by constantly dismissing murders like those involving Sicilia's son as "cartel violence" involving "narco-traffickers." Javier Sicilia has since insisted that his son "had nothing to do with the cartels." His activism has drawn attention to the fact that the US and Mexican war on drugs targets not just drug dealers and cartel members but also ordinary, law-abiding, middle-class citizens.

At the border fence, I joined the other activists I had just met on the bus. They were mostly middle-class Mexicans; some identified as Indigenous. Twenty cars and another bus full of scholars and supporters followed along behind the bus carrying the core group of activists. It quickly became apparent that many of the activists were there because of their personal experiences and recent trauma and loss, rather than because of a political or ideological position regarding drugs and the war on drugs. In fact, most of them had not spent much time thinking about how the loss of their loved ones was related to decades of foreign policy around the drug trade. Rather than being actively recruited for the caravan, many participants had sought out the principal organizers and activists because they had seen them on their local television channels. The caravan offered them a community with which to mourn as much as a platform from which to protest.

This chapter follows the initial arc of politicization for many relatives of the disappeared, especially mothers, as they came to calibrate their own positions, both affectively and politically, to a community of other victims and a set of convictions about the place of Mexico in the transnational war on drugs.[1] The process of politicization was long and sometimes difficult, both emotionally and conceptually. On the Caravan for Peace, this process emerged through the emotional intensity of the relations people created with each other and with members of the media and public. Many people joined the caravan to share their personal stories, not to offer policy recommendations. But because of the nature of the events and interactions they generated with journalists and the public throughout the tour, they were often called upon to bring a "message," and at first that message was simply one of suffering and pain.

They Began with "A Message of Pain"

When the bus arrived in San Diego at the border fence and the members of the caravan stepped off, they were quickly surrounded by crowds of people, including journalists, television crews, and local NGOs and support groups. The members of the caravan later told me that they initially found that experience overwhelming, for many of them were visiting the United States for the first time and most of them spoke very little English. When journalists asked them "Why are you here in America?" and "What is your message?" most people said something about bringing a message of "pain." This was also the part of Javier Sicilia's speech that seemed to resonate most strongly with the activists (figure 1). But journalists kept asking questions such as "What can the United States do for you? What is it that you want us to know?" Many people on the bus at this point did not have well-rehearsed answers or clear talking points from which to work. While some participants had been on previous caravans through Mexico, the binational nature of this caravan shifted the grounds of the discussion as we shall soon see.

For the first few days of the caravan, it was evident that many participants were uncertain about how to engage with this platform of activism. With their losses still recent and raw, public articulation of their experiences often overwhelmed them with emotion. For others, translating the deeply personal nature of the

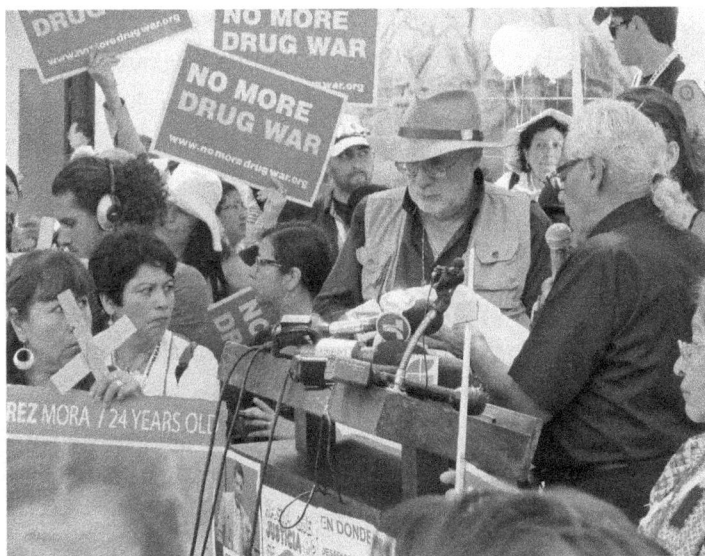

FIGURE 1. Javier Sicilia speaks at a rally Los Angeles on the Caravan of Peace, 2012. Photo by author.

violence they had suffered into a political message was challenging. Juan Carlos's story, shared during a stop in Los Angeles, was particularly striking. As he spoke of his brothers' disappearances, he made a simple yet powerful statement: "My message is that drugs are bad. They are bad for you in one way. And they are bad for us in another way. So, stop doing drugs." This statement immediately captured my attention as it echoed a familiar refrain often used to rationalize aggressive antidrug campaigns. In conversation with Juan Carlos later, he clarified his initial statement, explaining the specific harms he associated with drug use in both American and Mexican contexts.

He said that by highlighting that drugs "are bad" for Americans he meant that, as the largest consumers of drugs, Americans have experienced many negative effects of drug abuse and addiction as well as drug-related deaths. When he said that drugs are "bad" for Mexicans "in another way," he meant, he told me, that the drug trade is taking the lives of thousands of people a year in Mexico through corruption, shootouts, and violent criminal activity associated with the production, distribution, and sale of drugs. Juan Carlos's personal plea for Americans to "stop doing drugs" was born from a place of grief and hope for change, albeit different from the caravan's overarching advocacy for harm reduction and legalization as paths toward reform.

The main organizers of the caravan, in this regard, presented a fairly developed and explicit set of recommendations to officials and the media. Their primary demands included the creation of alternatives to drug prohibition such as legalization or at least decriminalization; an open discussion of drug policy reform that replaces the current criminal justice approach with a public health focus; a halt to the illegal smuggling of weapons across the American border; and concrete steps to combat money laundering, including holding powerful financial institutions accountable. They also called on the US government to immediately suspend its military and intelligence assistance to Mexican armed forces. In this way, they highlighted the neocolonial influence of US presidents in shaping Mexico's antidrug policies.

In the first several days, the academics and organizers, including Sicilia, voiced these points publicly, including the demand that the government explore the option of legalization. However, back in the privacy of the bus, many of the women I talked with expressed some discomfort with legalization. Ruth, a woman in her fifties from Veracruz whose son had gone missing in 2010, confided her reticence to me and some other women on the bus. "Really? They think that drugs should be legal?" She said she understood this on the one hand, but she added that drugs are "so bad for communities" that it made her a little uncomfortable. She said she saw a lot of people with drug problems back home in Mexico and that the thought of drugs being legal scared her. The other women we were sitting with agreed that they could not imagine that legalization could be good for their own neighborhoods either.

Ruth, along with many of the women on the tour, had been an *ama de casa* ("housewife") before her son disappeared. She had spent her days working from home, cooking, taking care of her grandchildren and family. These women were aware of the local effects of drugs in the form of criminal networks and addiction, but they had spent little time thinking about how state violence and US foreign policy were implicated in these most immediate and local experiences.[2]

Over the next few weeks, the 120-person caravan traveled fifty-seven hundred miles. It held events in twenty-six cities in the United States and generated extensive coverage in most of the major media outlets in the US and Mexico. Through media events, marches, rallies, and interviews that were planned in advance, women such as María and Ruth gradually began to close the gap between their own experiences of trauma and loss and the kinds of policy discussions that were taking place as the caravan moved along. Through conversations between these women and law enforcement officers who favored legalization, and through talks with organizations like LEAP (Law Enforcement against Prohibition), it became clearer for many how prohibition policies, not drug addiction, directly fueled the violence that robbed them of their children and that engulfed the regions from which they came.

While these activists came to place the "war on drugs" and "drug-related" violence as the central cause of disappearances in Mexico, it is important to clarify this relationship. While drugs and their trafficking play a significant role, the violence is tied to a broader range of issues. First, a significant part of the violence is driven by territorial disputes not directly related to drug trafficking, but instead to the control of areas where various illegal activities can be conducted with impunity, such as extortion, human trafficking, and oil theft, among others. Second, the violence is often symptomatic of deeper societal issues such as poverty, lack of education, and lack of opportunities, which drive individuals towards crime as a means of survival. These conditions are also the result of structural inequities and policy failures which are ostensibly legal but contribute to the environment of violence. Third, corruption is a significant contributor to the violence. When government institutions, law enforcement agencies, and judicial systems are infiltrated by organized crime, it compromises the state's ability to maintain order and enforce the law.

These complexities notwithstanding, drug prohibition and the war on drugs have been absolutely critical in creating the complex situation in Mexico today and the caravan and the leadership that it later inspired made this connection explicit. As we'll see, the association between drugs and this violence is also a critical component to the discourse on guilt and innocence that has framed the response to the crisis and the treatment of the victims' families by both the public and the state.

The way that these connections became clear to many activists was through interactions among a heterogeneous assortment of people, which allowed for meaningful and politically generative connections. The mothers on the caravan whom I describe here learned to see "drugs" in a new light from agents of the US government, for example, who knew that the "war on drugs" was not just a failure but also the main cause of violence. But as I explain below, the most decisively politicizing event was their contact with Black activists, also parents and mostly mothers, whose families had experienced drug war violence in distinct yet overlapping ways in the United States. The links that were made between these two groups of activists, and the impacts they had for how victims from Mexico understood their own traumatic experiences as part of a set of wider drug war impacts, were formative.

As political scientist Janice Gallagher, who was a key participant in the US caravan's journey, points out, the MPJD attempted a feat that they had mastered on their previous caravans within Mexico: brokering relationships between previously unconnected actors to build a larger movement.[3] This time, however, these kinds of links needed to be made across the linguistic, cultural, and political border with the United States as well as across racial divides, which created new challenges that I describe below.

Forging Transnational Affinities

While the caravan relied on grassroots mobilization, most of its initial leaders were men, such as Javier Sicilia. During subsequent fieldwork in 2013, it became clear to me that this leadership was not a general feature of mothers' activism, but there was a notable absence of leadership among the mothers on this particular caravan.[4] In part, this was because the mothers on this tour were at an early stage of politicization, many having quite recently lost loved ones. According to Sicilia, the MPJD was primarily founded by men, and it was initially just men's voices who were heard when he launched the movement in 2011.[5] However, as the MPJD's caravans began to receive more attention and media coverage throughout Mexico, women, and in particular mothers, began to play a more active role in the movement. Over the next couple of years, hundreds of women came to participate directly with the MPJD and they quickly became the face of the movement.

The funding and organizing for the caravan were generated by a notably grassroots initiative through which the MPJD partnered with a broad range of coalition groups. On the US side, the human rights organization Global Exchange ran much of the funding and logistics of the 2012 tour through crowdsourcing from individual donors and over one hundred US and Mexican organizations.[6] Food and shelter were often provided by supporting organizations in the destination cities; churches, community centers, and NGOs all played a role.

The individuals on the tour who first saw opportunities for politicization were not the victims themselves but the organizers from these different institutions as well as academics participating in the caravan. For example, in a 2013 trip to Mexico City, I interviewed Pedro, one of the main organizers of the caravan. I was interested in talking to him about the politicization I had witnessed among the activists the year before. I was curious about how he perceived this politicization as an organizer for the MPJD. Pedro put it bluntly: "When they started off on the caravan in San Diego, they were a busload of victims—they ended up a busload of activists."

Pedro described how the organizers did not plan to "educate" the participants or pressure them into aligning their public comments to the caravan's public recommendations. There were no official training sessions held for the participants. But the caravan did put them in contact with mothers in the United States who were experiencing the same policies but from a different perspective. According to Pedro, what affected the participants most was meeting mothers who had organized as Mothers against Police Brutality (MAPB). This is a national advocacy group whose mission is "to unite mothers and families nationally who have had their children suffer injustice at the hands of their local Police Department. [They] will hold law enforcement accountable. [Their] mission is to have an integral role in the changes and dialogues that will protect and save lives."[7]

Despite the impact Mothers against Police Brutality had on the mothers of the caravan, Pedro clarified that when the Mexican women first met members of this group, they did not feel an immediate sense of solidarity with them. In fact, the first encounter was awkward and uncomfortable. MAPB is a multiracial and multiethnic coalition but because of the disproportionate number of Black American men killed by police in the United States many of the mothers united by this coalition are Black. In many of the larger cities visited by the caravan, such as Chicago and New York, events and marches were planned strategically to go from predominantly Hispanic to predominantly Black neighborhoods in order to, as Pedro put it, "build links between the two communities." This is a longstanding intentional practice of political organizing meant to generate bonds of trust between diverse women.[8] "Pan-ethnic" organizing also has a specific history in cities like Chicago.[9] In this case, building links between the Mexican and Black communities was meant to fortify some of the connections that Juan Carlos had already highlighted in his own way: that the war on drugs had affected both the United States and Mexico in different ways, and that it disproportionately impacted marginalized groups in both countries.

What became clear on the caravan was that many of the Mexican activists, while being intimately aware of the violence created by the war on drugs in their own homeland, were uncomfortable not just with the idea of legalizing drugs but also with evidence of actual drug use and the more insidious forms of violence that are experienced at the "user end" of the war on drugs more generally. This became particularly obvious during a march in Chicago that I attended. The march began at the Little Village Arch, near the Catholic mission where we were staying in Little Village or La Villita—a neighborhood with a largely Mexican population. The procession continued through the neighborhood of Lawndale north of La Villita and finally to the neighborhood of Garfield Park and to our destination, the New Mount Pilgrim Missionary Baptist Church (a famous and historic church often credited with being the birthplace of gospel music). While most of us were not aware of it while setting out, this route was designed to cross from the Latino neighborhood of La Villita into the predominantly Black neighborhood of Garfield Park. Not only did the route provide a vivid glimpse of how racially segregated Chicago is but it also led us to one of the US neighborhoods hardest hit by the systematic violence caused by drug war policies, with high levels of drug-associated crime, mass incarceration, and one of the highest murder rates in the city.

We wandered into Garfield Park chanting "No More Drug War!" passing blocks of tenement housing, with families sitting on rundown porches, some of which looked like they were about to collapse. We passed groups of young men standing on corners littered with garbage, who looked over at us curiously. People on the streets were gawking at the crowds of predominantly Mexican activists some of whom were dressed in traditional clothing from their regions of Mexico, many carrying huge signs featuring their missing loved ones. "What's this about?" some people yelled. Members of the caravan would stop briefly to explain and hand out fliers, but in general the crowd of marchers was ill at ease.

On this stretch I was walking with Jorge, a man from Juarez who was on the caravan with his mother; his sister had disappeared a year before. At the time, Juarez was one of the cities in Mexico most heavily hit by drug-associated violence. His sister's disappearance, like those of so many young women in Juarez, was a heart-wrenching example of that. Yet Jorge was stunned by the sights of Garfield Park, which he described as one of the "scariest" neighborhoods he had ever seen. He kept saying, "I feel like we are in a movie."

Several blocks later, we passed an alley where a Black man sat slouched against a wall with a needle still resting in his hand. The man was frail, in fact emaciated, of indeterminate age, and had clearly just shot something into his arm. Jorge stopped abruptly and pointed excitedly, hanging back in the crowd, which was marching on. "Wait, look!" he said, still pointing. He was hesitating with his camera: "Do you think I can take a picture?" I made a little frown and shook my head to deter him as the crowd finally pushed us forward.

He seemed disappointed, and as we walked on I felt conflicted about having discouraged his photo. What right did I have to dissuade Jorge's attempted photo-documentation? I tried to lighten the mood by teasing him: "You are from Juarez! Why do you need a photo of that?" It wasn't really a relevant point as it was the iconic image of the drug user Jorge was interested in, not the dangerous aspects of the neighborhood, which it actually did have in common with Juarez in some ways. But he laughed anyway, recognizing the irony that we had just minutes before been talking about how only two years prior, in 2010, Juarez had its highest murder rate in history, with 3,111 people killed that year out of a population of 1.4 million.[10]

Over the past several days, I had heard Jorge speak on several occasions of the effects of this violence on the general living conditions of his city. He described vividly what it's like to live in a city where corpses regularly turn up on street corners and shoot-outs have become a prevalent aspect of everyday life. But again, the effects of inner-city drug use, segregation, and mass incarceration in the United States were not something Jorge had witnessed before. When I asked Jorge later why he was so interested in the man we saw in the alley he said, "Because the way people live here is so very sad. The drugs and the poverty . . . people don't seem happy. And people in America are supposed to be rich!"

"They Ended Up as a Busload of Activists"

The organizers of the caravan, including Pedro, believed that Black American communities would be "natural allies" for the movement and that the caravan could integrate many of their demands and positions. But the organizers did not anticipate the cultural obstacles that would emerge. In retrospect, Pedro regretted that they did not have an introductory or preparatory discussion early on about interracial relations in the United States, international relations, or US politics in general. Pedro admitted that a large problem was, as he put it, that "Mexican mothers could not identify with Black mothers in the United States." They saw themselves and the violence they experienced back home as fundamentally different. "For one thing, it was hard for many of the women from Mexico, whose message up until then was that their children had nothing to do with drugs, to sympathize with mothers of drug addicts." Pedro explained that it was only after engaging continuously with activists from different cities that the women and men on the tour began to think about how their own experiences overlapped. "All the Black mothers they met talked about police brutality," he said. This was a big shift in perspective for many of the women on the caravan, who were mostly, until this point, more conservative and had a more moralizing view of drugs. As Pedro explained, drawing attention to the predominantly Catholic upbringing of many Mexicans, "We are much more religious thinking, more moral about the good and the bad. 'You get in trouble because you are bad.' Therefore, the Mexican mother's sons were victims because it was unfair, because, 'My son was not bad, didn't do drugs but was taken by the bad guys and something bad happened.'"

As noted earlier, the ideological discourse that has justified the Mexican government's unwillingness to investigate most of these murders has been that the deaths simply consist of "criminals killing each other off." As John Gibler notes, "If you are found dead, chopped up, wrapped in a soiled blanket left on some desolate roadside, you are somehow to blame . . . . The very fact of your execution is the judgment against you, the determination of your guilt."[11] This de facto criminalization of the dead and disappeared has been widely documented. As Ana Villareal writes, in Mexico media and state narratives criminalize the dead (and the disappeared) because "violence, impunity, and vulnerability converge in the everyday sentencing of the dead from below."[12] Almost all the people I have met over the years who have lost a loved one in Mexico, whether disappeared or found murdered, have received the same response from the police and the government: "They must have been involved." But the reality is that officials hesitate to register the missing to avoid the negative publicity of government inaction.

The impunity associated with the widespread disappearance of people in Mexico is central to the demands of activists. Attempts at reform have stalled as both crime and impunity have become even more rampant. This is why many activists in Mexico openly criticize the Mexican government's justification for its unwillingness to investigate: that the victims must have been "involved" in drug trafficking.

As I mentioned earlier, some participants of the Caravan for Peace initially shared the assumption that those "involved" could be clearly distinguished from those "not involved" in the first place. But other victims on the caravan were made nervous by such facile distinctions. One such person was Miguel, a twenty-six-year-old taxi driver. He was from Monterrey, Nuevo León, and his sister had disappeared several years earlier. After we had talked and spent time together during the first few cities on the tour, Miguel shared something quite revealing. He said, in a confessional tone, that he ends up "driving narcos around" in his taxi all the time. "You can't help it," he said. "You don't get to choose what people you pick up. And you can't tell anyway because they could be anyone, *niños y viejitos* [children and old people], working as narcos." He said they would use his taxi to observe and monitor the movement of soldiers in the city or the location of checkpoints. He had no other option but to do as they asked. Then he added, defensively, "But I'm just a taxi driver!"

As I analyze elsewhere, it was clear from our conversation that Miguel was unsettled by the activists' definition of innocence as a lack of any contact with criminal groups or criminal behavior.[13] Miguel's discomfort revealed an awareness that his identification as a "taxi driver" was not sufficient to protect him from the charge of also being a narco. The implications of this positioning can be dire, since once you are labeled as a narco in Mexico, your life becomes expendable in official perspectives, a perspective that is tacitly reproduced when victims insist that their loved ones were "not involved." What is most problematic about this discourse though, is that it implies that if victims were drug dealers or people who used drugs, then their lives were somehow less valuable and their deaths less worthy of investigation.

After I came to know others on the tour, several more individuals confided similar misgivings about just how "uninvolved" their sons and daughters may have been. Sometimes these confessions were as simple as having once found a small personal stash of marijuana in their child's possessions. At other times it was a son's acquaintance who might have been a low-level dealer. These confessions were always painful because many of the women expressed distress that the accusation that their children were "involved" was an indictment of their poor parenting skills and their failure to be "good mothers."

But this commonsense perception about their gender and kinship roles was shaken when these women met mothers in the United States who talked openly about their children's involvement with drugs and petty trafficking. For example, after listening to one of the mothers involved in the MAPB at a rally in Chicago, Antonia, who had lost a son two years earlier in Mexico, said what surprised her the most about the woman was that "she wasn't ashamed" to admit that her son, now in prison, had been a "drug addict." At the time, I was struck by the implication in Antonia's remark that she would have expected the woman to be ashamed. This is why, when I met Antonia again during fieldwork in Mexico City in 2013, I asked her about this again. Antonia admitted that her opinions had changed since that day in Chicago. She said, "You see all these mothers that seem like you and have stories like you. But then they have this narrative that, 'My son was bad, but he was bad because the system was bad.' They say, 'I was a good mother but we received bad educations, lived in a bad economy, and my son was depressed—he didn't have any choice but this.'" Antonia said that at first, she was taken aback by these kinds of stories about drugs. But ultimately, she thought "it was good that this mother didn't blame herself."

After Antonia repeatedly encountered arguments that recognized the structural causes of peoples' suffering, she, along with other mother-activists, started to discuss among themselves the greater complexities of their individual cases. Many of them began recognizing or admitting that maybe their sons were "not as good" as they had initially described them, and that—for instance—they consumed drugs. They also became more aware that "involvement" with drugs did not make what happened to their children less of a human rights violation.

As Pedro had told me when I met him in Mexico City, in Mexico there is more pressure to *limpiar* ("clean") the cases of those who are killed or go missing by denying any connection, however circumstantial, with drugs and crime. When I asked Pedro why that was the case, he said: "In Mexico there is a strong moral perspective and conservative culture influenced by Catholicism. Mothers from Mexico say that their children's suffering isn't fair because they are not bad, because they don't do drugs. Mothers in the US say that the system is racist, so their kids do drugs and then go to jail." But, as we have seen, conversations between these groups changed the way Mexican mothers came to understand these structural factors and talk about them in their public speeches and interviews.

Andreas Schedler examines survey results conducted around this time that shed further light on why mothers felt compelled to foreground innocence. The National Survey on Organized Violence (ENVO) was a nationally representative face-to-face survey which was carried out in Mexico from October 26 through November 30, 2013 among adults. The survey revealed that more than 60 percent of respondents either showed full confidence (29.5 percent) or some confidence (33.9 percent) in their capacity to protect themselves from violence by not meddling with the criminal world. About a fifth expressed some disagreement (21.1 percent). Only one eighth (12.9 percent) plainly rejected the idea that "nothing happens" to those who are not *metidos* ("involved") in crime. Schedler argues that the idea of bounded criminal violence (effecting only the "involved") was thus clearly in the majority view.

As Miriam Ticktin has argued, "Images of innocence—and the moral imperative they engender—actually have a long history of hurting those they intend to help."[14] This history has been well documented in conflicts over rights and criminality in Latin America and helps to put the mothers' concerns within a wider context. For example, during Argentina's military dictatorship (1976–1983), the government claimed that all of the thirty thousand people who were massacred or disappeared were associated with terrorists.[15]

In Colombia in the early 2000s, friction emerged between US and Colombian activists protesting Plan Colombia, a US-backed initiative to fight drug trafficking and insurgency. The protests were motivated because the plan was perceived as harmful to Colombian citizens and damaging to the country's social and political fabric. But the presence of criminal networks and political insurgents in Colombia created suspicion among US activists, and the Colombian government's official branding of certain populations as "criminals" further eroded support for the activism. As a result, a broad social movement opposing Plan Colombia never materialized.[16] Similarly in urban Brazil, accusations that critics of police brutality prioritize the rights of criminals have undermined their efforts.[17]

While there is a long legacy, beyond Mexico, that situates these mothers' imperative to maintain the innocence of their children, it emerged as a specific challenge in the context of the movement's attempt to forge a transnational activist network during the Caravan for Peace. As I argue below, this pressure to foreground innocence was also partially generated by the constraints of an activist platform highlighting women and mothers in particular.

"They Don't Cry Anymore. Now, They Fight!"

Journalists often asked members of the MPJD why the movement so disproportionately consisted of women. And specifically, why it was the mothers and not the fathers who devoted themselves to seeking out information on victims and protesting the government's obfuscations. While, as discussed before, this was not strictly true, the representation of mothers as the movement's primary voice was evident not just in media coverage, which always highlighted the image of the grieving mother, but also in the dynamics and politics of activists' activities and events.[18]

For example, at a press conference in Mexico City I attended in 2013, a group of activists came with large photos of their missing family members. After a panel where a local celebrity, government officials, and three mothers of victims spoke about "the disappeared," the event transitioned into a more informal gathering where journalists paced the room to approach people carrying photos and ask them the stories of their children's disappearances. Of the women there, eight were accompanied by male kin (sons or fathers), five came with another woman, and one came alone. In all of the cases in which women were accompanied by men, the journalists addressed the women in the group. This was the case even when it was the men who held the photos of the missing person.

I approached the woman who came alone, Elyssa. She was hanging back from the crowds of journalists. I asked her about the man on the sign she held. She said it was her nephew and that she was there "on behalf of [her] nephew's mother," her sister. She did offer the base details of her story but repeated that she was here on her sister's behalf. Later, she explained that her sister and brother-in-law lived too far outside of the city to attend any of the events and protests organized for families of missing people. Elyssa's behavior was indicative of the norms assumed by relatives of missing people who were not mothers. When approached, such participants would usually introduce themselves by defining their relationship to the victim. But when asked "why" they were there— which was the routine follow-up question by most journalists— they would say that they were there to support their sister, mother, or wife—whatever their relationship to the mother of the disappeared or deceased person was. Mothers, in short, tended to become the center of attention.

A noteworthy and regular exception was when the mothers became "too emotional" to speak. This was the case sometimes with María Elena Herrera, whose four sons had been disappeared between 2008 and 2010; by the time of the caravan, the pain of these losses remained sharp. Her two sons accompanying her on the caravan often spoke on her behalf in those moments. But her presence as a mother grieving beside them, sometimes beginning to speak but then breaking down, was powerful in itself.

Many women I interviewed, including María, described their process of politicization as one of "hardening" or becoming more "tough" *(dura)* through the emotionally intense experience of the caravan (figure 2). By the time the caravan reached Chicago, two weeks after its beginning in San Diego, many of the women who had been more hesitant at first would take to the podium with confidence, even with anger. In fact, this affective hardening is part of the public narrative of the mother in the MPJD, clear in its slogan *"Las madres ya no lloran, ahora luchan!"* ("The mothers no longer cry, now they fight!"). Nonetheless, the women expressed emotions circumscribed by a set of deeply held cultural narratives and dispositions.

There is, of course, nothing predetermined about the way people experience grief. And while the arc of these mothers' emotional journeys was shaped by the collective nature of the movement, their experiences are not necessarily the norm. Many relatives of the disappeared experience their grief in isolation and feel a great deal of shame related to the stigma associated with the disappeared. When my friend Octavio disappeared, for example, his mother became completely withdrawn, unable to communicate

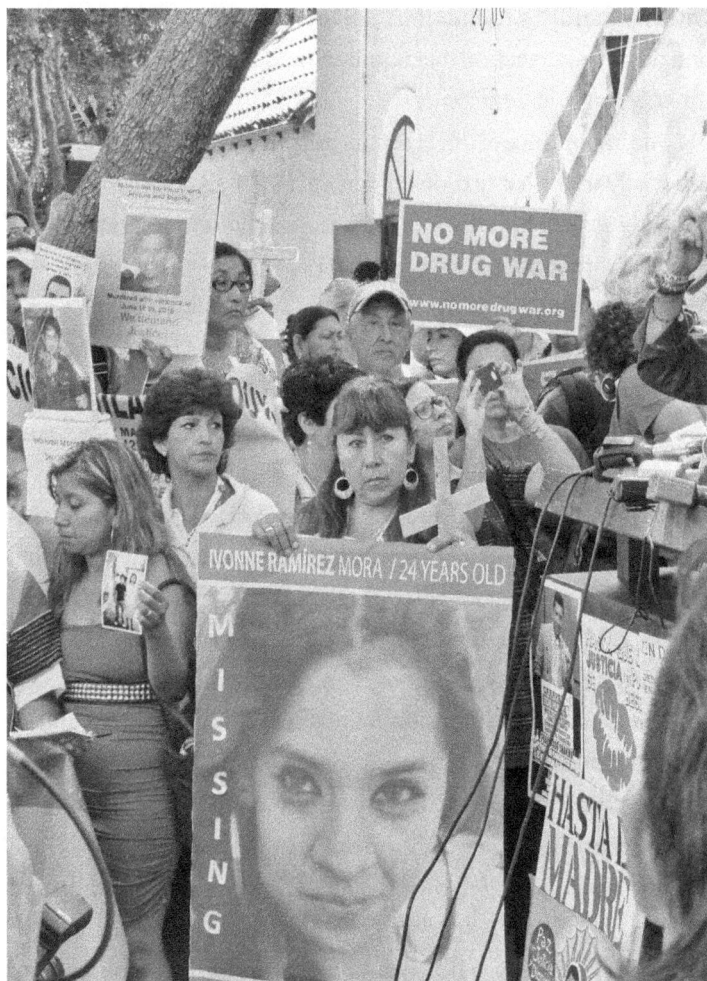

FIGURE 2. A mother stands with the image of her disappeared daughter at a rally in Los Angeles, 2012. Photo by author.

with her family or friends. She fell into a spiral of self-destruction and despair—a reaction that is understandable under such extraordinarily tragic circumstances.

The importance of affect and its influence on social movements, especially in the context of women's activism, is critical here. This is clearly seen in how the media portrays activist mothers by focusing on their emotional responses. This was most powerfully portrayed in the historical case of Mamie Till Mobley, a mother who came to prominence after her fourteen-year-old African American son, Emmett Till, was tragically murdered in 1955. Mobley's narrative in the media was often tied to emotional descriptions, and reports vividly described Mobley as sobbing and near collapse. In her analysis of the social and political turmoil that surrounded this murder, Ruth Feldstein argues that Mamie Till Mobley's feminine authenticity played out through a markedly emotionalized discourse. Feldstein argues that Mobley's emotionalism was crucial in establishing her respectability and motherhood.[19]

These affective dimensions of politics are important for understanding the experiences of the women I met, because their lives were marked and politicized by very painful and traumatizing experiences. The emotionally intense experiences I have described are narrated and articulated discursively through culturally and historically situated experiences of gender, which, in the case of Mexico, give clear prominence to the figure of the "mother." For the mothers of the caravan, the affective experience of meeting Black mothers in the United States—who framed their motherhood and their relationship with "drugs" differently—allowed for a shift in conceptualizations of motherhood and innocence, ultimately enabling these women to toughen up for *la lucha* ("the struggle") (figure 3).

FIGURE 3. A mural in Mexico City. Photo by author.

Histories of Maternal Activism

The women's protests against the "war on drugs" in Mexico are certainly part of a long legacy of mother-led movements against state terror in Latin America. As a political strategy, maternal activism is based on the belief that women are different from men in ways that explain their distinct social roles. Historically, women's association with caregiving has been used to justify their political engagement on behalf of particular issues.[20] Many scholars who have examined these struggles in Latin America have argued that when women enter the political arena they often do so as an extension of their roles in the household.[21] This is why they often become activists through their roles as "mothers," legitimizing their struggle and political activity as an outgrowth of a woman's love for her children and family.[22] In doing so, they both politicize and redefine traditional and more patriarchal notions of gender and motherhood.

Maternal activism in Latin America is perhaps most famously exemplified by the Mothers of Plaza de Mayo in Argentina. These women became some of the most visible opponents of the military regime that ruled Argentina between 1976 and 1983 when they held weekly and largely silent rallies in the Plaza de Mayo in downtown Buenos Aires demanding information on their children who had been "disappeared" by the regime.[23] Marysa Navarro's analysis of the gendered nature of this movement suggests that the image of grieving mothers was deployed strategically, as men seeking information on missing people would also "vanish" in retribution by authorities.[24] In this context, older and matronly women could more safely navigate the city, playing on the image that as mothers they were not acting on political grounds or even out of a concern for human rights violations, but rather out of the love that any good mother would feel for her children. As Navarro writes: "Their refusal to acquiesce in the loss of their children was not an act out of character, but a coherent expression of their socialization, of their acceptance of the dominant sexual division of labor and of their own subordination within it."[25]

This observation is relevant to understanding the force of dominant gender ideologies in shaping the experience of many women activists in Mexico. Like the Mothers of Plaza de Mayo, for Mexican activists their identities as "mothers" are both enabling of their political actions and constraining of their roles more generally, given that they reinscribe the gendered forms of subordination that exist in Mexican society. But the case of mothers' activism in Mexico is also distinct in the way that motherhood may morally circumscribe their roles as activists, preventing a deeper critique of gender and kinship ideologies and the war on drugs. Specifically, the stigma associated with the figures of the "drug addict" and the "drug dealer" obscures the fact that if people in Mexico die or disappear because of their "involvement" with drugs, this should neither be a rationalization of their death nor a justification for it.

Maternal activism or "maternalism" is regularly criticized for its emphasis on domesticity and caregiving and for its reification of traditional gender hierarchies.[26] Maternalism also highlights a more fundamental problem with organizing collective action around the frame of women, which is that it takes for granted that "woman" is a stable and universal category. A primary challenge to mobilizing women into collective action stems from the fact that they constitute a large and diverse group of individuals. While mothers have had the most audible voices in activism against drug war policies in Mexico, other women articulate their agency in their roles as sisters, daughters, or indeed through their experiences of violence not expressed through an affiliation with male kin. The experience of Juan Carlos and Rafael, María's sons, shows that while some men are also actively involved in protesting official policies, these gender ideologies and assumptions lead them to adopt public roles that are more supportive and from the margins.[27] This was despite the fact that Juan Carlos, for example, was logistically and practically the lead behind the scenes in the search for his four brothers.[28]

Some mothers talked openly about how the centering of maternal grief played out in their family dynamics, not just their activism. Araceli, for example, recounted how she realized suddenly and belatedly how difficult it had been for her son after her daughter, Rubí, disappeared. She said that for months after Rubí's disappearance the first thing Araceli would do upon returning home was run into her room to see if she was there or if something had moved or changed. One day she arrived home and opened the door to Rubí's room to find her son, fifteen at the time, on Rubí's bed snuggled up with one of her dolls. Her first reaction was outrage, "What are you doing in Rubí's bed with her things?" she yelled, "Get out!" Her son broke down crying and had to explain to his mom: "I miss my sister too, it's not just you who misses her." Araceli felt terrible and realized how alone she had felt in her suffering. She said, "I realized that she [Rubí] wasn't just mine, she was part of a family." But she admitted that she had not really had that in mind until that moment.

In addition to the experiences obscured by mother-led activist discourses, the political demands of Mexican mother activists are also constrained by dominant images about how "good mothers" are supposed to raise their children, such as keeping them away from drugs. As Pedro observed, and as both Ruth and Antonia suggested to me, the potency of these morally charged attitudes toward motherhood initially made alliance-building with activist women in the United States more difficult. The activism of Black women in the United States, in particular, draws from the legacy of the Civil Rights movement, which has long framed problems such as drug-related violence as a matter of social justice and institutional racism.

This is precisely the concern that intersectionality theorists aim to address. They emphasize that women's experiences with gender do not stand alone but are intertwined with other identities like race, class, disability, and sexual orientation. Intersectionality theory critiques overarching "women's action" frameworks, like maternalism, for this very reason. The focal point has now shifted to understanding how race, class, and gender intersect in women's lives, influencing and reshaping power dynamics.[29] Because ultimately, the efficacy of these movements hinges on their ability to cultivate a shared understanding while addressing concerns about the multifaceted nature of marginalization.

"Reggae, Hippies, and Freedom": Tentative Alliances in Drug War Activism

The process of politicization that occurred for women as a result of their experiences on the caravan, including what they learned from victims of the drug war in the United States, provided lasting impacts. Interestingly though, the political platform of legalization embraced on the caravan as a first step to mitigating the harms associated with the war on drugs was not easy to import back to Mexico. When the caravan returned, they, at first, made attempts to rally similar alliances with a range of initiatives in Mexico. For example, there was one particularly memorable attempt at solidarity building between the MJPD, the Students for Sensible Drug Policy in Mexico, and the Mexican cannabis legalization movement. After the caravans, these groups tried to engage some of the mothers who had been in the news and invited them to a march for marijuana legalization. Many of the mothers who were involved in the MJPD had come to see the merits of legalization in the context of drug violence in Mexico and a handful decided to accept the invitation and attend the march. Ultimately though, the event did not operate as a "march" in the sense they had imagined but more as a parade.

Ruth, one of the mothers from the caravan who attended the event, said they were all embarrassed to find themselves in a crowd of young people, dancing to reggae music and smoking pot. Ruth said she was taken off guard because the legalization advocates they had met in the United States, many of whom were police officers, were "much more serious and professional about it." In Mexico, the movement to legalize drugs, especially at that time, was much younger, left-leaning, and associated with, as Ruth put it, "reggae, hippies, and freedom." Ruth said that at one point as she was marching with the other women there was so much smoke from people smoking marijuana that "we started to cough and became very uncomfortable." They ended up lagging in the march. In retrospect, Ruth said, "It was mortifying!"

While Pedro, above, stressed the influence of Catholicism and its associated moral code as a major factor in antilegalization sentiments, Ruth's experience also suggests that it may not be the only underpinning of such views. Mexican mothers' perception of marijuana legalization as more dangerous compared to that of American mothers can be attributed to several reasons. First, historical antimarijuana narratives that emerged in Mexico continue to influence perspectives today.[30] Unlike the United States, Mexico never experienced a marijuana counterculture, hence the long-standing belief that marijuana use breeds violence, madness, and criminality persists, unchallenged by the more recent Western notion that it is a "soft" drug that for most people is generally harmless. As a result, when the caravan returned to Mexico many of the victims eventually abandoned the discourse on drug legalization that had become the cornerstone of talking points in the United States. Rather, they resumed a more locally comfortable discourse emphasizing the innocence of their children. After noticing this on subsequent fieldtrips, I returned to Pedro, one of the caravan organizers, for insight. Pedro identified this as the main "cultural challenge" that had emerged in building a transnational movement. "It's a reminder," he said, "to become more aware of the different demands of the two governments [the United States and Mexico] related to the war on drugs." Pedro explained that he thought the shift in emphasis was strategic, responding to the "different morals" involved in addressing the war on drugs.

But Pedro also clarified that while some of the victims were afraid to talk about issues such as legalization in Mexico, it was still an important part of their political awareness. He described traveling again with Ruth and a group of women who had been on the caravan in 2012 to a conference on drug policy in Denver several years later, where the same group of women resumed their talking points about drug legalization quite comfortably.

This kind of flexibility in political discourses doesn't mark an inconsistency on the part of the mothers' views, but instead indicates a willingness to build intersectional networks of affinity. This is never easy and the discomfort that Ruth and her companions experienced at the legalization march described above attests to that. But these early efforts at forging alliances on the part of victims of the war on drugs were important initial steps that created the kind of international organizing that is characteristic of some of the activism carried out today. Eventually some of these efforts would expand into much more far-ranging attempts at transnational connection, making connections with movements such as Black Lives Matter, Truth and Reconciliation in Canada, and the efforts to identify Canadian missing and murdered Indigenous women and children.

For instance, María Elena Herrera later helped form, together with her sons and other collectives convened by the MJPD, the National Search Brigade (BNB) which has increasingly sought to build community and solidarity across national lines to address contemporary disappearance across the Americas, including Central America, the United States, and more recently Canada. The BNB, which I discuss in later chapters, is also professionalized in the sense that it employs dozens of permanent personnel located in Mexico and New York City who are trained as advocates and are educated in hands-on transnational solidarity building.[31]

In the next chapter I describe how many women who returned to Mexico after the caravan largely disengaged from the MJPD. They resumed a daily existence marked by uncertainty around their loved one's cases. Without the momentum of the caravan and the daily support of a community of other victims, many turned their attention back to their individual circumstances, wrought by the violence that they had been protesting. In effect, they returned home to the immediacy of their own cases, mostly unresolved, and to rhythm of their everyday lives, which were characterized by waiting: waiting for information on the progress of the cases of their missing loved ones and waiting for help from the authorities.

2 *Until We Find Them*

It was a Monday afternoon, Ivonne's day off from the casino where she worked in Atizapán de Zaragoza in the state of Mexico. She was preparing a family dinner, a favorite: pork chops and baked potatoes with a spicy homemade salsa. The potatoes were cooked and the pork chops were on the counter still marinating. She started preparing the salsa when she realized that she was missing a crucial ingredient, the chiles. It was almost 7 p.m., which was when her husband Roberto was due home, but she decided to run out to buy the chiles. She grabbed her wallet and phone and ran out the door. She never returned. Georgina Ivonne Ramírez Mora was twenty-one years of age at the date of her disappearance on May 30, 2011.

Ivonne's family spent years searching for her and trying to understand what happened with little evidence to work from and even less support from the police and government officials. They became suspended in a web of bureaucratic indeterminacy and uncertainty as they waited both for news of their family member and for support from the state. Indeed, waiting is one of the defining features of the search for the disappeared in Mexico: waiting to speak to officials, waiting for police to follow up on tips, waiting for morgues to produce lists of unidentified bodies.

Waiting is often thought of as a passive experience and has been theorized as one that deprives people of agency. Scholars of the state and bureaucracies have analyzed the experience of waiting as "yielding to the power of others; . . . and in effect surrendering to the authority of others."[1] But waiting has also been explored as a more quintessential and pervasive human experience. Ghassan Hage argues, for example, that analytical attention to waiting can reveal important elements of social processes that go beyond hierarchical relationships of power.[2] The literature that has focused on waiting has shown that this process can be crucial to understanding a range of social phenomenon, from refugees' experiences of waiting to emigrate, to farmers' experiences of drought, to villagers' experiences of anticipating flooding.[3]

In this chapter, I examine the role of waiting in the experience of Mexican activists searching for their loved ones. I argue that while waiting is certainly a form by which activists are slowed down in their searches and therefore disempowered and "stuck," as scholars of waiting such as Hage have emphasized, waiting also has other, unexpected effects. The most important of these is that for many activists, the Kafkaesque routines of waiting for bureaucracies compel them ultimately to forego institutional avenues of investigation altogether and take up the roles associated with state agencies on their own. They become more than activists—they end their waiting and step into the shoes of forensics specialists, fundraisers, and negotiators.

But first, let's look more closely at what family members of the disappeared end up waiting for. Initially, they wait for acceptance or acknowledgment by the police or other officials that their family members are indeed "disappeared" rather than simply missing or unaccounted for. Second, they wait for a case to be opened, forms to get processed, files to be delivered, and government agencies to coordinate with each other. Finally, they wait for authorities to investigate or at least provide support for their own investigations. A closer look at the details of these periods of waiting reveals both the immense affective toll that slow bureaucratic processes take on the relatives of the disappeared and how they function as a crucial process of mobilization on the part of many of these families. Here, I juxtapose the experience of two women, Leticia and Lucía—who suffered delays in the context of two different states, Mexico and Veracruz respectively—to analyze both the commonalities and differences in the waiting created by their local governments. I show how their separate trajectories illuminate the centrality of waiting in the experience of searching for a loved one in Mexico.

Leticia's Search for Her Daughter, Ivonne

When Ivonne's husband, Roberto, came home, he found the kitchen exactly as Ivonne had left it: the tray of meat left out, the blender with a couple of tomatoes, the knife on the cutting board. He called Ivonne and she picked up the phone. She explained that she had just run out for the chiles and was on her way home on the bus. Roberto waited for hours. Ivonne didn't pick up his subsequent phone calls and when it was clear that Ivonne was not coming home, Roberto called his mother-in-law, Leticia.

Leticia remembers how this phone call changed her life forever. The day after Ivonne's disappearance, and after a sleepless night, Leticia and her family mobilized. The first thing she did was go to the police. She explained that her daughter had gone missing and detailed the suspicious circumstances surrounding her disappearance. The police officer she spoke to explained in a patronizing tone that it was much more likely that Leticia's daughter had run off with a lover than it was that she had been taken under nefarious circumstances.

Therefore, for Leticia the first stage of waiting was the time between notifying the police and the police acknowledging the prospect that her daughter had in fact been forcibly disappeared. Even though Ivonne was by all accounts happily married, many of Leticia's initial interactions with the state involved veiled insinuations that she had left with another man. In subsequent interactions with officers, they even implied that she might have been involved in something illegal through her work with the casino, implying that if she had been taken, she might have brought it on herself. But the officers insisted that regardless of what had happened to Ivonne, they couldn't do anything to help until a file had been opened and a legal claim was made. Leticia's daughter needed to be officially registered as missing.

After speaking to the police, the family went to the court, submitted a legal claim, and a file was opened on Ivonne. Then the family made copies of Ivonne's photo and distributed them in the neighborhood. The next day, they went to the Programa para la Búsqueda y Localización de Personas Abandonadas, Extraviadas o Ausentes (ODISEA), the official organization charged with searching for missing people in Mexico City, but were told they would have to wait seventy-two hours before they could do anything because, as the ODISEA staff said, "maybe she could come back." The following day, Leticia went to the municipal presidency office of Atizapán de Zaragoza, where she managed to track down the mayor, Jesus David Castañeda Delgado. She gave him the photocopied page with Ivonne's photo and details. "He dismissed me," Leticia said. She remembers that he suggested she go see his secretary.

Weeks passed as Leticia fostered the hope that there might be some progress with the case. Meanwhile, the officials at the Ministerio Público (MP), the public prosecutor/investigator's office, of Atizapán repeated that the missing persons file she had opened the day after her daughter's disappearance still had not reached them.[4] They said, "We're sorry, señora, but there's nothing we can do until we receive the file." Many more weeks passed before the file was received and the disappearance made it to the official registry. At that point, police officers were assigned to the case which, as I describe shortly, only resulted in more waiting.

These were the first of many moments after her daughter went missing that expanded, stretching out in Leticia's perception into an extended experience of time. That first night, lying awake, hoping to hear word from Roberto that Ivonne had come home after all. Then the police and the excruciating seventy-two hours before she could open the case, feeling that every minute mattered and was slipping away. The contrast between the urgency for family members and the slow, impassive mechanics of bureaucracies heightens the sense of desperation for victims' families.

The delays experienced by Leticia—in getting her case into the system so that the police would respond and take it seriously, then waiting longer for files—are characteristic of the experiences of many families of the disappeared. The immense frustration this creates echoed through many of the conversations I had. Lucía's descriptions of her own experiences in Veracruz, which I describe below, also highlight some of these dimensions of waiting.

Lucía's Search for Her Son, Luis

Lucía's son, Luis Guillermo Lagunes Díaz, went missing June 28, 2013, from the Port of Veracruz. Lucía began investigating at once. When she approached the authorities, they dismissed her concerns in much the same way that Leticia had experienced. At that time, the circumstances of the disappearance seemed obvious to Lucía. "This is a classic kidnapping case," she said. She cited the fact that the people who abducted Luis took his clothes, sound equipment, and identification, which gave the authorities the impression that Luis had left voluntarily. The officials immediately grabbed onto this interpretation to suggest to Lucía that Luis could have run away with his girlfriend. "I told them it was absurd, since they are both single and had nothing to get in their way if they decided to live together."

Overwhelmingly, family members of the disappeared report this first interaction with the state as being an experience of gaslighting. The police almost always insist that the missing person is more likely to have left voluntarily. Often authorities respond by implying, as they did with both Leticia and Lucía, that the missing family member left with a romantic connection without wanting to tell the family. Even more insulting to family members is the widespread discourse around the disappeared being "involved," or the dismissal of the disappearance by implying that the missing person had probably become active in organized crime and deserted their families.

On the night he went missing, Luis had asked an employee to stay with him due to previous threats and extortions he had faced. This employee initially lied about Luis's whereabouts, claiming to have taken him to the airport, but later admitted that men had come and taken Luis away. Despite Lucía's pointing to all the evidence of foul play, the authorities disregarded the fact that Luis's disappearance had involved a vehicle, unknown men, and extortion for which there had been several witnesses. When I asked Lucía why the investigators would ignore all of this, Lucía responded, "Their modus operandi is total neglect. They are inept in excess." She shook her head to add ". . . absolutely futile." Then Lucía listed more examples that made their ineptitude clear, providing a picture of the immense frustration she experienced.

For example, according to Lucía, the legal communications and summons about the case that the local investigation office sent to other authorities, including the state prosecutor's office, were written in an extremely vague and generic fashion, without the necessary level of detail or specification for follow-up. Therefore, most of these summonses went unanswered, and Lucía was left in limbo waiting for other agencies to respond. In contrast to Leticia's experience of the first few weeks, waiting for her missing persons file to even arrive at these agencies, Lucía's wait was caused by a lack of follow-up by the relevant offices once the files had been received.

According to Lucía, once the Investigation Agency of Veracruz (AVI) office received the summons that would start the formal investigation, they did nothing except take initial statements from Luis's employees.[5] After they took those initial statements, they simply ignored the summons they had received from the MP, the local-level investigation agency. Summonses mandating a follow-up in the investigation were issued on two occasions after that, also with no response. The fact that both agencies, the MP and the AVI, share the same building in Veracruz made the lack of authority of the MP and the complete lack of communication between the two agencies even more blatant.

Chasing Paper

Like Lucía and Leticia, many family members of the disappeared find themselves waiting for files: orders, memos, forms, letters, complaints, and records of registries. They wait to submit paperwork documenting a disappearance, and then they wait for that paperwork to make its way through the system, traveling from one hand to another, from one agency to the next. An important element of the life of files across bureaucratic systems in Mexico is the extent to which they are often paper-based rather than electronic. Therefore, family members end up waiting for documents to move through the postal system, and often they are searching for information in paper books and ledgers.

Family members will frequently wait for long periods of time to receive files, only to realize later that these files will not be useful after all. Lucía experienced this disappointment after waiting for agencies to coordinate to produce Luis's phone records. His phone was the most up-to-date model in 2013 (an iPhone 5) and it was active for at least a month and a half after Luis went missing. She asked the investigator's office to request the phone records from the phone company and waited anxiously for two full months for them to arrive. The office encouraged her in the assumption that the records would be useful and so Lucía was hopeful. But when the office did receive the records of phone calls made and received by Luis's phone, they said they could not interpret them and could not track his location. The investigators said they did not have the technology to track it, emphasizing that they simply "don't know how." At that point, they had to send them out for interpretation. "The more hands fumbling with the information," Lucía said, "the less certainty or trust one can have in its outcome." Lucía was immensely disappointed by this response, especially after the long wait for the records.

Lucía's and Leticia's cases both highlight the considerable neglect, lack of coordination, and impassivity of the authorities in handling their cases, and their stories exemplify what many others looking for missing family members have described. Such delays would be difficult under any circumstance but are profoundly unsettling when the safety and whereabouts of a loved one are unknown. In my interviews with other family members of missing people I heard variations of this slow-motion bureaucratic nightmare repeatedly. It is also clear from both Lucía's and Leticia's experiences that, even though they were located in separate states with different local dynamics, the mechanism of files and the inefficient modes by which state institutions communicate are two of the primary ways that both ended up waiting for legal processes to advance.

Lucía's and Leticia's early struggles in their searches draw attention to the fragmentation of state institutions and the tremendous difficulties this creates for navigating the system efficiently. But their recounting of these initial months of their searches also highlights what some scholars of the state have emphasized about the importance of understanding files and documents and their place in the ideological function of the state. Akhil Gupta argues, for example, that the everyday experiences of waiting for files and reports, while seemingly trivial, are rituals that need to be enacted before bureaucracies, as routinized performances that constitute state power and function.[6] But it's also important to recognize that these rituals are not just ideological instantiations of state power; they also have distinct material effects on victims' families, particularly in how they erode financial resources.

Waiting into Poverty

Waiting does not just disempower family members on a subjective or psychological level but also has concrete and devastating economic impacts on families, and as a result, on their prospects of being able to continue their searches. Most activists I met came from middle-class families. They had the resources to search for their family members and the flexibility to spend large amounts of time doing so. In many cases, however, the long, drawn-out nature of their searches leaves families in serious economic trouble. This was a point made by Annabel, an activist whom I met on the 2012 caravan that traveled with family members of the disappeared through the United States to raise awareness about these issues. Years later, in an interview in Mexico City, she reflected on how many of the families in the process of searching for their loved ones had significantly depleted their financial resources. She said, "They have become really poor."

Some families, for example, were homeless when they returned from the caravan before they could rebuild a new network of support. One woman from Michoacán, Annabel explained, returned with her family from the 2012 caravan and they did not have a place to live. "They weren't able to go back to their village because they were receiving threats due to how vocal they had been about the disappearances of their family." When they returned, Annabel said they were basically living on the streets of Mexico City.

Annabel took a critical stance on the MPJD's singular focus on sharing a particular political message, though many of the people who joined the caravan were left without any support upon their return home. "The movement is not concerned about the aftereffects," she said. And she noticed that many of the participants were in the same situation. But she also pointed out that "all of them had money at some point in their lives." This financial stability at some point prior to the caravan was a common thread among the participants.

This dynamic also played out for Leticia, although in her case most of her economic losses were incurred at the very beginning of her search. When I met Leticia in the caravan in August and September of 2012, her daughter had been missing for over a year and she had no idea what had happened to her, nor whether she was alive or dead. She had quit her job and devoted herself full time to finding her. Before Leticia's daughter disappeared, Leticia had, by her estimation, a good government job working in *capacitación*, helping young people get jobs.

Leticia took an active role in the investigation of her daughter's disappearance from the start, and this required financial investment almost immediately. Not only did she consistently bring leads to the police to motivate their search and accompany them on trips to follow up on those leads, but she also started paying for gasoline and food for the police during their time together. She wanted to make sure they were actually doing the work and realized that her oversight was the only way that was going to happen. Soon her primary contact in the police department began asking for bribes every day. He said that he needed the money to give to his boss to "show that he was working" and not just helping Leticia in her case. Leticia knew she would soon run out of resources. This was clear to the police too. In fact, they began urging her to sell her own car, saying she would need the money to fund the operation to find her daughter. "It was the car comment," she said, "that finally tipped me over the edge." She needed her car for the search, and she was fed up with the officers' treatment of her and what she characterized as their "blatant corruption." So she went over their heads and lodged a formal complaint, which, she emphasized, involved even more waiting and paperwork.

Three days after she made the complaint, she was stopped by two unknown men on the road that led to her house. It was the same road she took every day. The men blocked her vehicle and asked her to get out of her car. "Take off your jewelry," one of them ordered. Hands shaking, she finally managed to unclasp her necklace and hand over the rest of her jewelry as well. After they had removed all of the possession from her body, they motioned her aside at gunpoint. She glanced into the car, anticipating that they were going to remove her purse from the passenger seat. But to her surprise they left her purse right where it was. Instead, the two men stepped into her car, closed the doors, started it up, and drove away. "They left me with nothing," she said. "They left me standing alone on the side of the road." It was then that she realized the error she had made in complaining about the corrupt police officers. This was the series of events that left Leticia's financial resources depleted: quitting her job, incurring extra expenses given her involvement in the search, and finally losing her car—a substantial resource—after confronting the police about their misconduct.

Attending to Victims

Some of the early advocacy and activism among families of the disappeared and their allies managed to implement a series of laws and legislative changes meant to support families and respond more efficiently and humanely to their cases. The efforts of the MJPD were an example of this. After the caravan, the movement narrowed its focus to legal and administrative measures to support the rights of all victims in line with international human rights standards.[7] Within the first two years of the MPJD there were some successes. In 2013, under then-president Peña Nieto's administration, Mexico passed and implemented the General Law for Victims to support victims of violence and their families and established a juridically autonomous Commission for Attention to Victims (CEAV).[8] As Janice Gallagher argues in her book *Bootstrap Justice,* these were significant inroads within the state's legal structures that even, to a certain extent, managed to challenge the practice of blaming and criminalizing the victims.[9] Later, organizations such as the National Search Brigade (BNB) even started running training programs for police officers in "police sensitivity" to raise awareness of the damage done to victims' families when officers deploy some of the discourses around perceived culpability discussed above.

While these legislative changes were significant wins, in retrospect, some activists believe that their focus on legislative change and police behavior raised an understanding among relevant government bodies that outright dismissing victims and ignoring requests for support was not a politically sound approach to "managing" disappearances. But both the General Law for Victims and the CEAV have been criticized for being, in practice, mostly symbolic gestures of support. The problem has ultimately not been a lack of legislation, but rather a political unwillingness to implement these laws. To some activists it appeared that local governments decided that it was politically more profitable to at least appear to "attend" to victims than to openly ignore them. And when the state does attend to the victims to support families' searches, the very mechanisms used to do so often feel to families like another form of waiting and delaying.

These issues came to the surface in the spring of 2020 when COVID-19 shut down many of the families' searches, and many of the collective initiatives advocating for parents as well as the investigations into disappearances themselves significantly slowed their operations or moved to online formats. This deceleration of what victims felt was already colossally slow progress deepened frustrations. Another key issue that emerged, even prior to COVID-19, in relation to delays in investigations centered on how and when the government rotated the MP staff, replacing the main investigators in charge of families' cases with new personnel without informing the victims beforehand and without creating plans to give continuity to the investigations.

From the perspective of the families, this meant that the core investigators on their cases would suddenly be inaccessible and new investigators, who knew little about their cases, would be their only point of contact. The new investigators on the families' cases would not have all the facts for a given case nor contact information for the people who would. In such cases, the family members themselves would have to help the new investigators catch up on the investigations and in the process, they often needed to repeat the same personal accounts of the disappearance already recited many times before. For these reasons, the families made the modest request that the MP implement continuity plans for the investigations and also send these plans to the families.

While the MP initially agreed to these requests, it failed to follow up. In June of 2020, now under the presidency of Andrés Manuel López Obrador (popularly known as AMLO), the Colectivo en Búsqueda de Verdad y Justicia (Collective in Search of Truth and Justice) wrote an open letter addressed to Abel Galván Gallardo, then head of the Special Prosecutor's Office for the

Investigation of Forced Disappearance, in response to failed government follow-up with this agreement.[10] While the letter was prompted by the failure of officials to send the information they promised, it also included a brief but scathing critique of the slow progress of investigations. The letter notes that since their collective was formed in 2013, "we have seen three presidents, at least four attorneys general and dozens of prosecutors and public ministries who have heard our cases but have not made any progress."

The letter also took aim at what has become the dominant government strategy since the early 2010s in responding to activists: the creation of *mesas de trabajo,* "working groups" (sometimes translated as "participatory investigations"). *Mesa de trabajo* is the blanket term used for meetings between government officials of the various entities charged with attending to cases of the disappeared and their families. These meetings often involve opportunities for the families to voice their concerns, pool information, and be informed on the progress of government response to disappearances. But activists argue that participatory investigations have ultimately become a key mechanism to delay the search and delay action. The letter states: "We've already lost count of the minutes and agreements we have had that are only lost in pretense and managing our pain." The letter goes on to ask, "Why do you call on us? (*Para qué nos citan?*) To fill your registrations and make your reports of the number of working groups we've had? To manage our pain? To prevent us from protesting?"

The collectives' allegation that the government's interactions with the families are designed primarily to placate them and stifle political action rather than make concrete advances on their searches, is a powerful critique of the government's position in relation to victims. Ximena Antillón, a researcher in the Human

Rights and Fight against Impunity program at Fundar, Centro de Análisis e Investigación, an independent, nonpartisan civil society organization, amplified the critique, noting that the working groups have become the quintessential device for the administration, repression, and control of victims.[11] A particularly relevant aspect, in the context of our discussion of waiting, is Antillón's critique of the temporal dimensions of this bureaucratic management style. She argues that implementing endless working groups is a government strategy used to manage time as an exercise of power. "Attention devices" such as working groups, "operate through the imposition of a temporality that lengthens the wait. The time begins again for each official on duty, while for the victims, wear and tear and despair accumulate." Antillón believes that this is the cruelest feature of the way the government currently manages victims. This lengthening of their wait taps into the main fear of many families of the disappeared: they will die without having found their loved ones.

The particular "attention devices" that have been examined in this chapter—the back and forth between municipal and state prosecutor's offices, the slow travels of files, and the use of working groups—exemplify the way the Mexican state imposes waiting as a mode of control. Indeed, this element of bureaucracies has been theorized as a general feature of governmental power and is a trope present throughout Western cultural representations of bureaucracy more generally. Kafka's novels, for example, are well known for addressing the ways in which the power of bureaucracy is inseparable from the experience of waiting. In his story "Before the Law," published in 1919, a man travels from the country to the city to seek out "the Law," a term he uses to reference the law in general as a collective.[12] "The Law" is located behind an open doorway and guarded by a doorkeeper. The man asks to go inside. He is refused, so he asks if he will be able to enter later. "It's possible," says the doorkeeper, "but not now." The man cannot go in but he cannot turn away either so he sits down on a seat offered by the doorkeeper so that he can wait. Every time he attempts to enter, he is refused. He spends his whole life there waiting, growing old and finally dying without being permitted entry.

The story has become a parable for the individual's relation to the modern state. But there is a more specific element of Kafka's parable that resonates with the experiences that relatives of the disappeared have in relation to the "attention devices" singled out in the open letter. Kafka writes that the "the doorkeeper often conducts brief interrogations, inquiring about his home and many other matters, but he asks such questions indifferently, as great men do, and in the end he always tells him he still can't admit him." Why does the guard bother to ask these questions if the answers don't matter? Perhaps for the same reasons the collective identifies in accusing the government of continuously consulting with them without actually making plans or progress: to "manage their pain. To prevent them from protesting."

This interpretation of the doorman's interrogations becomes more relevant as the parable continues, and we learn of the bribes the guard takes. In Kafka's story, as the man waits by the door for years he eventually bribes the doorkeeper with everything he has on him. The doorkeeper takes the bribes but explains to the man that he is only accepting them "so that you do not think you have left anything undone."[13] In other words, interrogating the man and even accepting his bribes is a way of managing him, much as the collective accuses the Mexican government of doing with working groups, minutes, and agreements. Some family members of the disappeared in Mexico eventually feel a similar motivation to continue labyrinthian pursuits through the quagmire of Mexican bureaucracy: to know they are at least doing something, doing whatever they can, even if the path seems futile.

The collective's open letter concludes by asking: "What's the point of giving us psychological attention if you only revictimize us with your negligence"? But the question is rhetorical because their letter has already answered this. The point of the attention is to placate, to make it seem like the government is doing something, to simulate a sense of care.

Unlike Kafka's man from the country, who indeed grows old and dies while distracted by the maneuverings of the doorman, many of the women I came to know eventually learned quite clearly that official channels of support and state-sponsored investigations were merely simulations, as the collective's letter charged. In that realization, hard-won through unsettling experiences of waiting, a transformation also occurs for many activists.

The Power of Waiting

The way that families are left waiting for support for their investigations looks like a straightforward absence of state support. And this fits with the dominant narrative about neoliberalism in Latin America: that it is a top-down antistate and pro-market program implemented through policies of deregulation, financialization, and the dismantling of the welfare state. But while neoliberal economic globalization has ideologically demoted the role of the state in peoples' lives, the state nonetheless continues to be a key actor.[14] In fact, scholars of the state have emphasized that its power is often exercised precisely by its absence.[15] Javier Auyero argues, in reference to Argentina, that the way that people experience neoliberalism or globalization is ultimately in "rather shabby waiting rooms, uncomfortable lines, endless delays, and meager and random welfare benefits."[16] In Mexico, neoliberal reforms have had a similar impact in terms of shrinking the government programs that would have formerly been present in peoples' lives.

And as we have seen, waiting disempowers the families in their engagement with Mexican bureaucracies, underscoring Pierre Bourdieu's famous observation that "waiting implies submission" and is one of the foremost ways of experiencing power.[17] Ultimately, the state's technique of making its subjects wait has, as Anna J. Secor notes, the effect of "holding in suspension the promise of justice."[18]

These are precisely the reasons the very notion of "hope" has been criticized as ideological for creating what Lauren Berlant calls "cruel optimism," that is, a form of optimism that ends up reproducing the very conditions that prevent change from happening in the future. Similarly, in their book *Now*, the anarchist collective the Invisible Committee argues that the emphasis on hope is a detriment to action: "No one has ever acted out of hope. Hope is a form of waiting, with the refusal to see what is there." The problem with hope, as they see it, is that it undermines agency. They argue that to hope is "to remove oneself from the process so as to avoid any connection with its outcome. It's wanting things to be different without embracing the means for this to come about."[19]

Yet for many families, whatever flame of hope they might have had of receiving support from the government flickers into darkness during the time that they wait. By the time I met Lucía, seven months had passed since her son had disappeared, and she had been to countless public agencies and tried every possible means to find her son. "I have made uncountable trips—I do it gladly for him—but it doesn't have to be like this." Lucía said that authorities add a bureaucratic nightmare to what is already a tragedy: "We are twice the victim."

But in the absence of direct state support other subjectivities emerge. As they wait, for many families, it is not their submission that grows. Instead, Lucía, Maria, Leticia, and many others in their situations experience a reckoning, not just with how they are positioned within the state structures supposedly aiding in their searches but also in how they must carry on and move forward if they want answers, or even justice. This is why, as we shall see, Leticia and Lucía, as well as others, stopped waiting and took matters into their own hands, carried out their own investigations and formed their own collectives with local families.

Therefore, one of the most significant impacts of government indifference, negligence, and corruption is that many parents and relatives ultimately stop expecting help from state officials after waiting or being abused by them. Many families respond by developing their own expertise, forming their own networks, and proceed to carry out most of the functions of investigating cases themselves. As a result, they also become the networks to which other relatives of the missing turn. Araceli Salcedo Jimenez, whose daughter Fernanda disappeared in 2012, said, "the families have had to become investigators, forensic experts, trackers of mass graves, and even lawyers. And all of this because the government refuses to face the problem."

For many families this process of mobilizing their searches beyond the support, and in some cases beyond the boundaries, of the law is a slow one. For others, this realization and subsequent mobilization happen in a single moment. Leticia conveyed this most clearly when she described the moment her car was stolen, the moment she realized her hopes that the officers on her case would be disciplined drove off along with her car. Leticia says that it was right there, on the side of the road, with no way home but her own two feet, that she gave up on using formal channels in her search for her daughter and set off to find her on her own.

3 *"Call the Mothers, Not the Police"*

No more waiting.
No more hoping.

THE INVISIBLE COMMITTEE, *Now*

One of the most famous early cases of a mother striking out on her own to investigate the disappearance of her child was that of Miriam Rodríguez, whose fourteen-year-old daughter, Karen, was abducted and then murdered in Tamaulipas in 2012. Miriam's story was broadly reported in Mexico and internationally. The *Guardian* and the *New York Times* profiled her spectacular journey as she stalked "her daughter's killers across Mexico, one by one."[1]

Miriam's story began as many do, with her daughter not returning home one night. She received a ransom request and after weeks of meetings with members of organized crime, multiple payments, and false promises, the kidnappers stopped answering her calls. It was then that Miriam realized her daughter would never come home. So she set about meticulously searching out and tracking her daughter's kidnappers and killers—eventually finding almost every one of a network of individuals involved in her abduction and murder.

Miriam started by seizing her one and only lead: the memory of the face of the man she met while trying to negotiate a ransom for her daughter. She spent hours scouring her daughter's social media and sifting through photos of all her remote contacts until she finally found a photo of the man. He stood beside a woman wearing an ice-cream shop uniform from a business two hours from Miriam's home. Miriam stalked the woman for weeks, waiting in her car outside the ice-cream shop and watching. Finally, the man she was waiting for showed up at the store at closing and left with the woman. Miriam followed them back to what she determined was his home. This information, the location of his house, was a significant step, but she knew that to get the police involved she needed more details. She needed the man's name. So she disguised herself as a pollster, cutting and dyeing her hair so that the man would not recognize her and donning an old government uniform she had from a former job at the health ministry. She proceeded to poll the man's neighborhood until she could get his name and other basic details.

Then she began the search for a police officer who would help her. Armed with a folder of meticulous notes and documentation, she made her way through the local police department roster. No one would assist her. Undeterred, she took her files to the state police and met the same refusals. Finally, she found a federal police officer who agreed to help her. In 2020, this officer told the *New York Times* under anonymity that "when she pulled her files on to the table, I had never seen anything like it. The details and information gathered by this woman, working alone, were incredible." The arrest and interrogation of the man that Miriam had compiled information on led to the uncovering of Karen's remains in an unmarked grave on a ranch outside her hometown of San Fernando, Tamaulipas.

But discovering what happened to Karen and recovering her remains was not enough for Miriam. Over the next three years, she tracked down the remaining individuals who worked to disappear her daughter, using similar investigative methods. She painstakingly researched and built cases against these people by examining her daughter's social media accounts and tracing their connections to each other and her daughter. Often following a hunch, she would track suspects online, stake out their residences, and sometimes even interrogate those they worked with. At other times, she disguised herself and attended suspects' churches or posed as an official to gain access to the inner circle of low-level members of organized criminal groups that were involved. When she built enough proof to implicate someone in the network, she would find a way to corner them while she called the police and waited for them to arrive and take the suspect into custody.

In her mid-fifties at the time of her search, Miriam at points physically ran her daughters' abductors down. On one occasion, she tackled a florist who had been involved in her daughter's abduction, pulled a pistol from her purse, and held him there until the police arrived and arrested him. On another occasion she broke her foot while chasing down another woman who had been involved in her daughter's abduction. Eventually she took down ten people. This included almost every living person in the group that had originally abducted her daughter for ransom. They were a motley group. One was a member of Los Zetas—an ultraviolent cartel established by former Mexican special forces soldiers.[2] But others were a florist, a nanny, a recently reformed churchgoer, and a struggling neighbor the family had known for years and had helped with donations of old clothes.

In part, Miriam Rodríguez's case became so well-known because she was relatively successful in her efforts to find her daughter's remains and to uncover information implicating members of Los Zetas. Her own investigations led to the arrest and imprisonment of the principal suspect in the murder and of his accomplices. But her high-profile involvement also eventually led to Miriam's brutal murder. In May 2017, two dozen prisoners escaped from the prison in Ciudad Victoria where Karen's killers were incarcerated. Miriam was worried and asked for government protection. But despite the police purportedly sending patrols to protect her, on Mother's Day 2017, Miriam was shot twelve times on her front porch.

While the media coverage and public memory of Miriam Rodríguez's plight and accomplishments often focus on her extraordinary bravery and singular dedication as a lone mother on the hunt for her daughters' killers, she was not, in fact, alone. The power of her legacy is owed, in part, to the collective of family members she brought together in Tamaulipas who are also searching for missing loved ones. During the search for her own daughter's killers, Miriam founded a nongovernmental group of six hundred families in Tamaulipas called the Colectivo de Desaparecidos (Collective of the Disappeared) who now work together in search of missing relatives.[3]

In the previous chapter I described how women wait, sometimes for years, to see progress on their cases. For this reason, when a story like Miriam's gets media coverage it is not unusual for other family members of the disappeared to gravitate toward the woman or women at the center of the media's attention. Women like Miriam, and the others I focus on in this chapter, therefore become the focal point for wider search efforts and attract other families in similar situations.

This chapter analyzes how women not only come to take on the roles of state agencies in investigating their own cases but also end up acting as investigators, negotiators, and advocates for other families. Women such as Miriam, Leticia, and Araceli, whom I focus on here, and the collectives of families they form, therefore, fill the function of police. There are now hundreds of search collectives formed by families of the disappeared.

The strategies behind individual and collective searches are not uniform but shaped to individual circumstances, local dynamics, and informal webs of support. In general, collectives build alliances and seek out support from a wide range of diverse sources and networks. Some form alliances with particular government officials who can provide resources. Others focus on gaining access to criminal organizations in search of information on unofficial burial sites and morgues. Still others, such as the collectives of Araceli and Leticia, build their own networks, drawing on both the government and various organizations (both legal and illegal).

Families of the disappeared must adjust their strategies to their local settings. What is necessary to investigate a disappearance or negotiate a ransom in the state of Veracruz, for example, is not the same as in Mexico City, Tamaulipas, or Guerrero. Similarly, the way that search collectives emerge is also shaped by the particular forms that violence and government/crime collusion adopt in each place. Araceli Salcedo's experience, which I describe next, illustrates this dynamic.

The Rise of Search Collectives

In the days after the disappearance of her daughter Rubí from the town of Orizaba, Veracruz, in 2012, Araceli kept returning to the same places to search for her: the Red Cross, the Institute of Social Security (IMSS), and the regional hospital. When she went to the police to report the abduction, she encountered many of the same obstacles faced by other families, so she spent her time searching in every other local place she could think of. She made the same rounds to the Red Cross, the IMSS, and the hospital almost every day because these seemed like the most obvious places where Rubí might re-emerge. Eventually Araceli realized that she kept seeing the same people wandering around these places. She finally went over to a woman she recognized. She stopped her and asked, "Excuse me, are you looking for someone?" "*Sí, a mi hijo*" ("Yes, for my son"), the woman said. It turned out that her son had been kidnapped the same day as Rubí. Eventually she discovered that nine people had disappeared from Orizaba that same day.

In those first few months after Rubí's disappearance, five other mothers joined Araceli to form an informal network of support. They had all experienced similar obstructions and had all suffered from similar inaction from the police. Their first collective action was to come together in 2013 to confront the governor of Veracruz in front of the media and demand action publicly. While nothing came of that interaction with the governor, that episode received attention in the media and other mothers subsequently got in touch with them.

In a conversation I had with Araceli in Orizaba in 2022, ten years after she had begun her search, she marveled at the fact that those first few times she stood in the town center with a sign showing her daughter, she was there all by herself. She remembered passing out pamphlets with information to passersby and then being stopped by a police officer who took the pamphlets from her. "They were worried about me tainting the experience of tourists coming to Orizaba because it is a *pueblo mágico* (magic town). They didn't want the town to look bad." She felt alone then. But now looking back over the years, what she remembers is that she was only alone at first. As time passed, there were others standing with her. Today, she stands with a crowd. The collective of families of the disappeared in Orizaba-Córdoba, Veracruz, had grown to over 360 families by 2022. And this is only one of sixteen similar collectives in the state of Veracruz alone. Most of the search collectives in Veracruz are organizations run by mothers and they frame their efforts through maternal forms of activism.

Mother-led social movements for the disappeared have been prominent in Latin America since the period of state terrorism in Argentina from 1976 to 1983, the so-called "dirty war." But they also have deeper roots in Mexico where women have used issues of crime, violence, and injustice to carve out spaces of political engagement since the heyday of the Institutional Revolutionary Party (PRI). Despite the PRIs co-option of the independent spaces established by civil society during the 1940s and 1950s, women were prominent in civil organizing where they used the issues of crime and violence to push for societal change. In Mexico's highly gendered public sphere, women's discussion of conventional politics was still frowned upon but demands for protection and justice were considered acceptable.[4]

One of the first family-organized collectives that searched specifically for disappeared relatives began in 2009 in the state of Coahuila with a group that called themselves the Fuerzas Unidas por Nuestros Desaparecidos en Coahuila (United Forces for our Disappeared in Coahuila, FUUNDEC).[5] This group was initially comprised of twelve families searching for twenty-one men who had disappeared within the state. Similarly, in 2010, an organization called Ciudadanos en Apoyo a los Derechos Humano (Citizens in Support of Human Rights) began to work in the state of Nuevo León.[6] These organizations began by receiving reports from families of the disappeared and then investigating these cases in coordination with state officials in both states.

But it was not until the Movement for People with Justice and Dignity (MPJD) that family collectives became a widespread phenomenon throughout the country. By 2022, there were over 160 collectives working to register and investigate cases of the disappeared. There have been efforts to coordinate formally among these locally managed collectives. For example, at the time of writing, sixty of these organizations operated under the national banner of the Movimiento por Nuestros Desaparecidos en México (Movement for Our Disappeared in Mexico).[7] While this is the largest national-level umbrella organization, there are other smaller umbrella organizations as well.[8]

Most of these collectives are organized geographically, usually by state or municipality, and they respond to how violence unfolds in their local contexts. For example, in Araceli's case described above, she kept running into the same people in Orizaba in the days after her daughter's disappearance because disappearances in Veracruz tend to happen in waves. A local human rights worker explained to me that these waves of violence in Veracruz have historically targeted young people of very clear profiles, for instance, attractive young women presumably to be trafficked and able young men to serve in the labor reserves of criminal organizations.

Collectives in other states have formed in response to more specific events. For instance, one of the most well-known groups of parent collectives formed after forty-three students from Ayotzinapa Rural Teachers College disappeared from the town of

Iguala, Guerrero, in 2014. Furthermore, the collective Los Otros Desaparecidos de Iguala (The Other Disappeared of Iguala) was formed because many felt that the search for the Ayotzinapa students in and around Iguala had taken attention away from the broader insecurity issues affecting people in Guerrero. The "other disappeared" refers to the bodies found throughout Guerrero during the searches for the forty-three that were determined not to be the students who disappeared that day.[9] Another collective formed in the wake of an event is the Madres Unidas por Nuestros Hijos San Fernando Tamaulipas (Mothers United for Our Children San Fernando Tamaupilas) started by mothers who lost their children in the San Fernando, Tamaulipas massacre in 2010. In this incident, seventy-three migrants were traveling towards the United States when they were stopped, kidnapped, shot, and disappeared.[10] One survivor managed to pretend to be dead and then subsequently escaped to alert authorities about the massacre.[11] Events such as the San Fernando massacre also draw attention to the way migrants who transit through Mexico, whether from Central America, the interior of Mexico, or from other countries, are vulnerable to the same forms of violence as nonmigrants in Mexico and some collectives have formed specificality to support and organize among families of missing migrants.[12]

Other collectives are organized around the identity of the victims rather than a specific event. For example, some of the earliest active family-run collectives emerged out of the movement to address femicide in the 1990s, particularly around Ciudad Juarez. A distinct crime, femicide is defined as the murder of a woman because of her gender. Mexico has one of the highest rates of murders and disappearances of women, including queer and transwomen.[13] Collectives have therefore been organized to search for victims of femicides such as the Comité de Madres y Familiares con Hijas Desaparecidas (Committee of Mothers and Family Members with Disappeared Daughters), and Nuestras Hijas de Regreso a Casa (Bring Our Daughters Home) to name just a few. Collectives are also organized around the identities of those searching and their relationships to the disappeared. As mentioned above in reference to Veracruz, in the majority of cases search collectives are run by mothers and they frame their efforts through maternal forms of activism. In the case of the parents who searched for the forty-three disappeared students from Ayotzinapa, in contrast, fathers took the lead in organizing and were also the most vocal in their condemnation of the government's involvement.[14] Overall, though, it is overwhelmingly women who make up the members of such collectives in Mexico.[15]

Despite distinctions in region or organization structure, what all these collectives have in common is that they have emerged out of the lack of support by the state and because the families of the disappeared have had only each other to turn to.

Call the Mothers

"Hello . . . Romina?" A woman was crying into the phone. "Please help me. My daughter has been kidnapped and I don't know what to do." It was late, and Romina was getting ready for bed when she received this call. When her cell rang, she didn't recognize the number, but she had gotten into the habit of answering unknown numbers after her daughter disappeared. This was not the first time Romina had received a call like this. As a result of her media involvement and her leadership role in her local network of mothers, her contact information was often circulated to victims when their loved ones disappeared. After the woman on the phone paused, Romina used her most calming voice and started asking the series of questions she always did to start the process of helping a stranger on the phone.

Romina, a woman I met in 2012, often played this support role for other parents. Her son Matías disappeared in 2010. He was a twenty-six-year-old federal police officer who had left Mexico City to go on a mission with four other officers to the state of Jalisco. The officers have not been seen or heard from since. Romina receives around three calls a week from people who have had family members kidnapped or disappeared. In some cases, the people who call her say they don't want to call the police because they are afraid. In other cases, they call Romina because the authorities have done nothing despite being notified. Many women who have become vocal in protesting drug war violence also report receiving calls every week from people who have received ransom requests or are searching for their missing loved ones.

Romina thinks she gets so many calls because people saw her on television speaking about her son's disappearance and criticizing the government for dismissing all the deaths and disappearances as *"daños colaterales"* (collateral damage). The trope of "collateral damage" has persisted as a talking point by Mexican government officials for years, positioning deaths and disappearances as unfortunate yet unavoidable in a necessary war against drugs and, more specifically, against organized crime groups. For example, in April 2010, then-Secretary of Defense Guillermo Galvan referred to the deaths of civilians in Mexico as "collateral damage" in a speech.[16] This provoked anger for suggesting that Mexican civilians are expendable or that their deaths were in some sense justified. In October 2011, then-President Felipe Calderón made a similarly unapologetic argument about the unavoidability of civilian deaths in an interview with the *New York Times*, to the point that his entire failed security strategy was later referred to by activists simply as "Collateral Damage."[17]

In Romina's television appearance, she made a slightly different point about the discourse of "collateral damage," emphasizing how dehumanizing it is to both civilian and noncivilian victims. She felt that her son Matías, who was not a civilian but a police officer working for the Mexican government, was often counted as one more statistic in the "war on drugs." Romina emphasized that he was not just a number but that the dead and disappeared, whether civilian or officials, are *real* people. "They have names," she said publicly, "they have families looking for them and waiting for them." It was after making these comments that she started getting calls at all hours of the day and night from people, mostly women, whose husbands or children had been kidnapped.

Romina described how her commitment to help victims' families was also motivated by her own difficulty finding support during the early days of her search for Matías. "When my son first disappeared," she recalled, "I reached out to a mother who had been in the news." The woman she reached out to had been interviewed on a local news station, much like Romina, and in the interview she was articulate about her own son's disappearance and her difficulties getting authorities to take the case seriously. Romina found the woman's contact information and called her to ask for advice. But Romina said that "she never returned my calls." She said she felt horrible and alone during that time and felt hurt by this woman's silence. That experience makes it hard for her to refuse supporting the people who contact her. "I want to be able to help people who are in the same situation that I was then."

How does Romina help people when they contact her? Over the years she has developed a system, a set of steps she follows to make sure she is doing everything she can. First, she collects all the data that is available. Some of the people who contact her are dealing with an abduction and ransom request. In those cases, Romina collects the phone number of the abductors, the phone number of the person who has been taken, and any other potentially relevant details. Then she collects all the information that the family has that could help, such as clues to the identity of the kidnappers or information about their whereabouts. Then she coaches the family on how to talk to the abductors and how to negotiate a price down to something they can actually pay. Sometimes she will even accompany them to a predetermined location to coordinate a payment.

Romina also insists on attempting to involve the police, despite sluggishness on the police's part and resistance on the part of the family. She said that families often need convincing to get the police involved, and that she must carefully explain that she cannot help them if they do not report the kidnapping or disappearance. Romina needs the police involvement because she does not have the resources to help them herself, lacking the technology to trace the phone numbers or the protection required to accompany families to the ransom drop-off point. If the police are too slow in getting involved, Romina will start to "make noise" by going to all the government offices in Mexico City where she has contacts to complain.

Romina said, "It is much easier to help families if their loved ones are kidnapped because then there is a link," that is, a way to communicate with the abductors. In kidnapping cases, the families are contacted, requests are made, and there are steps to follow. "If their family members are disappeared, there is nothing." In other words, without those initial links to the perpetrators, it is harder to know where to start the investigation. In those cases, she helps connect the families with networks of other family members searching for the disappeared.

Regardless of the circumstance of the disappearance, Romina's strategy follows the same two parallel approaches. "I try to make the authorities uncomfortable," she said, and at the same time, "I try to keep opening doors for the victims." She does this by working through the contacts she made as a result of her son's employment as a police officer and through her own experience searching for him. Therefore, ultimately, she sees her role as speeding the process along by leveraging her experience and her networks.

Three More Stars for Ivonne

Leticia has a similar approach to Romina in supporting families of victims, though she was motivated by a different set of circumstances. After Leticia recovered her daughter's remains, as I described in the Introduction, she said she felt both deep sadness and tremendous relief. She felt relief because she knew that Ivonne had been at peace all that time that she feared she was suffering. But Leticia said that along with the flood of relief came a feeling of being unmoored. Until the moment she found her daughter's body, she had been searching for her every day and her every waking moment was consumed with the search. She had a singular purpose in her life. After finding Ivonne, Leticia realized that she had to decide whether to continue with her activism or to return to work and her more comfortable former life. She imagined both futures but ultimately found that it was simply impossible to see herself in her old life.

Leticia decided to permanently dedicate herself to activism, and this is when she started La Red de Madres Buscando a Sus Hijxs (Network of Mothers in Search of Their Children). In one conversation I had with her in 2014, she described the sense of accomplishment she had in having been able to discover and identify the remains of three bodies for families that had been searching. As Leticia put it, she thinks of these identifications as "three more stars for her daughter." Stars that shed a pinprick of light in the darkness for families of the disappeared.

When people approach Leticia about a missing person, she too has a system, like Romina. First, she carefully organizes a visit to the prosecutor's office. She says that if you go to the government with a missing person case alone, they do nothing. This was the step where Leticia's own search for her daughter stalled. She learned from that experience, and said, "You have to bring as many people with you as you can and crowd into their offices, making it impossible for them to easily dismiss you." Therefore, Leticia organizes these initial meetings with the family members and makes sure that there is sufficient pressure on the prosecutor's office with a critical mass of people so that these cases are registered rather than thrown aside.

After the missing person case has been officially registered, Leticia uses her network to distribute photos of the missing person through media channels in search of further information. Usually these posts, which during the time of this research were mostly distributed through social media sites like Facebook and Twitter, consist of an image of the missing person with a heading that says something like *"Hasta Encontrarle"* ("Until We Find Them"), *"Le has visto?"* ("Have you seen them?") or simply *"Boletín de Urgencia"* ("Urgent News").[18] The notice also includes a description of the person, where they were last seen, what they were wearing, and finally the details of who to contact or a toll-free number to call with any information. Sometimes these images will also list a reward. The circulated images are often the formal "missing persons notice" issued by the attorney general's office. At other times, they are notices designed by family members. Occasionally, and jubilantly, if a person has been found, these images are recirculated through these same social media networks with the stamp "*localizadx con vida*" ("located alive").

After fully publicizing the search through the Network of Mothers, a final step involves Leticia coordinating with the families to travel to morgues to help them through the steps of confronting and investigating the possibility that their missing loved one has been killed. This is a very sensitive and difficult phase of the investigation. At morgues, Leticia helps the families look through photos of bodies and the personal belongings recovered with them. Here, she plays an important emotional support role, as seeing the photos can be traumatic for family members regardless of whether they recognize their loved ones. But Leticia insists that it is crucial to pursue this possibility through visits to morgues, and she trusts from her own experience that even if the family finds their loved one in this way, it is preferable to the endless doubt and dread that would be in store for them if they never discovered that truth.

Leticia's role in helping families has become widely known through word of mouth and through the work of the Network of Mothers. She has become the primary contact person for people in the network in relation to their searches not just for disappearances but for uninvestigated murders and kidnappings. Leticia's reputation is so strong that often families call on her and expect her to go well beyond what she thinks she can reasonably do to help them. One of the first times she became really involved in a case serves as an example. A woman called her because her seventeen-year-old daughter, Gloria, had apparently been kidnapped.

The Case of Gloria

A few days after Gloria went missing, her cousin, with whom she was close, received a text from an unidentified number, supposedly from Gloria. The text asked that the cousin go to a specific location to talk to Gloria. It specified that she go alone. Gloria's parents thought that this was going to be the start of a bribery negotiation and felt they had to go with the cousin.

Leticia asked Gloria's mother what the police had said, and the mother admitted that they had never called them. Leticia commented to me later, "This just shows how much people distrust the police here—that they would call me rather than even talking to the police first." She told the family that they needed to report to the police before she got involved. She explained that it was important to follow the protocols to register the disappearance so that there was a record of the scope of the problem in Mexico. Later the family called Leticia back saying that they had called the police, but that the police said they could not do anything to help them. This angered Leticia, so she called the police herself. That is how she learned that the family had been lying and had claimed to have reported the incident so that Leticia would help. Leticia was frustrated by this. But, by then, she had visited the family in their home and had come to identify with the grief-stricken mother. She was also struck by the poverty the family lived in and understood that they would worry about the inevitable bribes that involving the police would solicit. After much pleading and apologizing by the mother, Leticia agreed to help.

At that point, she coordinated with the police herself, and the family was assigned an officer to accompany them to the meet-up spot. Leticia said that when they met the police officer, she took one look at his patrol car and laughed. It was an old, beat-up Dodge from the early 1980s. "It seemed like some kind of joke," she said. "The officer even looked a bit like the car: paunchy and worn-out." Leticia and the mother shared a glance at each other, and Leticia remembered the family's resistance to getting the police involved. "The whole scene just confirmed why they were so resistant," Leticia acknowledged. But they were both grateful for the bullet-proof vests and firearms that the police officer had at his disposal. "That's what the police are there for," she said. They geared up in the vests and they all piled into the car, even as Leticia wondered if the vehicle would hold up to their destination.

It was a blazing hot day and just a few miles into their drive, the car started to sputter and overheat. They pulled over to the side of the road, the officer got out, and opened up the hood to add anti-freeze to the radiator. Meanwhile, Gloria's mother was beside herself with anxiety and anticipation. As they waited for the officer to close the hood and get back into the car, Leticia tried her best to calm the mother and go over the protocol with her and the cousin for when they reached the meet-up site. They had to pull over twice more to add more antifreeze to the radiator before the trip was over.

When they arrived, they found a place to hide near the meet-up spot so they could watch and wait. At the predetermined time, Gloria arrived in a vehicle accompanied by an unknown man. Leticia and the mother watched as Gloria's cousin went out to meet with her. But as soon as Gloria emerged from the vehicle the mother suddenly sprang out of the Dodge and ran out to her daughter. When Gloria saw her, she immediately retreated and fled the scene with the man.

Despite this meeting having played out in a way that no one had anticipated, the mother and cousin had seen enough from this brief encounter to believe that the daughter had actually gone with this man willingly. Or, as Leticia suggested, "as willingly as any young woman goes when choosing to get involved with a certain type of older, criminal man." It was the way that Gloria's body angled towards the man that indicated her willingness in the mother's and cousin's opinion. They were extremely relieved to see this, and there was some resolution to the situation.

Four months later, the family was in touch with Leticia again. They wanted to let her know that Gloria had returned home. Leticia went to their house and was surprised by what she saw. While they were still living in the shack, all of the women in the family were dressed in expensive clothing and had long, manicured, fake fingernails. They did not tell her what had happened to Gloria, and Leticia didn't ask. So she never learned where Gloria had gone or why she had come back. She was struck by how dejected and depressed Gloria seemed despite her new clothes and nails. "I realized that she had gotten involved with narcos," Leticia said, "And that's how she came back with some money." With this information Leticia also gained a different perspective on the initial situation. She thought that Gloria had probably been trying to get the cousin to leave with them when she first went with the man. The meet-up was probably supposed to be Gloria's opportunity to convince her cousin to run away with them as well.

The only reason Leticia had even gone to their house on this later occasion was to convince them that Gloria needed to report to the police in order to be removed from the missing person list. But the family still did not want anything to do with the police. Leticia insisted. She said it was important for Gloria to follow the protocol to protect herself. "If she is on a missing persons registry," she said, "and if she ever needs to use her citizenship number at any time, she will be flagged by the system." Leticia feared that the officials would use this discrepancy against Gloria in all sorts of ways and, at the very least, they would most certainly use it to demand bribes from her if she went to the police on a later date. So, Leticia took Gloria to the police station herself and made sure she was removed from the registry of missing persons. She said, "I stayed with the girl the entire time it took for her to be removed from the list so that I could be sure they would not give her a hard time."

Leticia learned a lot from this incident and for that reason it stood out in her memory of all the cases she had taken. In retrospect, it was not a standard kidnapping case or a disappearance. When Gloria made contact, the purpose was to connect with her cousin, not to request something in exchange for her return. All of the details were off in ways that Leticia would not learn to recognize until later, after she had much more experience with such cases. But Leticia also learned from Gloria's case about how unpredictable the parents can be in delicate negotiation situations, and she moved on from this incident with a much greater awareness of how important the task of managing the parents is in negotiation or meet-up circumstances.

While Leticia was relieved that Gloria was alive and well and had gone "willingly" with her supposed abductor, she was frustrated because this was exactly the possible scenario that officials often used to dismiss disappearances ("she must have gotten involved with the wrong people" or "she probably ran off with her boyfriend"). Therefore, the incident with Gloria served as a warning for how complicated the issue of reporting to the police can be—and yet, as I explain below, many activists insist reporting is important.

When to Call the Police

Leticia's experience with Gloria highlights people's reticence to involve the police but it also indicates how important the police are for the efforts of collectives and women such as Leticia when they involve themselves in other families' searches. While women sometimes bypass the police and government entirely, often they use the police selectively at different points in their search. Leticia, as I described in chapter 2, had been harassed and robbed by the police officers originally assigned to her case. Despite those experiences, she still made selective use of police resources whenever she thought they could help, as was the case with the police officer who accompanied her to the meet-up for Gloria. Leticia has very little trust in the police in general, but she recognized the importance of having access to their resources such as vehicles, weapons, and the bulletproof vests they wear during ransom negotiations.

Like Leticia, many women involve the police only at strategic moments in their search. For example, they will call the police to arrest suspects but only after they have compiled all the evidence to clearly implicate them. They do this so that the police only have to come in and make the arrest, rather than waiting for the police to compile evidence or locate the suspects themselves. This was Miriam Rodríguez's strategy; as I described, on one occasion she even held a suspect at gunpoint until the police arrived to arrest him. Therefore, while family members and their search collectives do much of the heavy lifting in investigations and ransom negotiations, for the most part this is not vigilante justice. They do not punish or arrest the perpetrators themselves.

In addition to knowing how to involve the police, knowing which officers to approach is also important. Miriam in Tamaulipas, for example, had to drag her meticulous files around to many officers before she could even get someone to agree to help her. Sometimes finding the right officer is a matter of finding someone who is simply not afraid to intervene. Other times, it is a matter of finding someone who is not already implicated in some way with the suspected perpetrators. All of these dynamics are different in each individual case and are often shaped by the specific constellations of state/criminal interactions in local contexts.

Araceli Salcedo described one of the first kidnapping investigations she helped with in her role as the leader of the collective of families of the disappeared in Orizaba-Cordoba, Veracruz. One day she received a call from a woman who said "Señora, I'm calling because I know the work you do. I just saw a girl at a hotel here in Orizaba, and she is clearly not willingly with the people she's with." Araceli urged the woman to take a photo of the girl, whom the woman said looked to be fifteen years old, so that she could see her face. The woman sent the photo, and Araceli began searching to see if she could find a case file on the girl. She called the federal authorities in Mexico City and sent them the photo. They confirmed that this girl had been kidnapped, and there was a file on her. They would come as soon as they could.

She then went straight to the local police in Orizaba. The federal police would not get there until the next day at the earliest and time was essential under these circumstances. She explained to the local police that the federal authorities had identified the girl and that she needed help. "You know what they said? They told me they couldn't do anything to intervene in the situation. They said 'No, we need *el oficio de colaboración*' (a "joint investigation agreement") to work on a case being handled by federal authorities." Araceli was beside herself. "How is this possible?!" she said. "This is a child. First, we rescue her, then we deal with the paperwork." The local police refused to attend to the situation, deferring completely to the *federales,* who didn't arrive until 9 the next morning. When they arrived, they went to the hotel where the girl had been spotted, and with the photo and the help of the staff they managed to identify the room where the girl and her kidnappers were staying. Though the kidnappers escaped, they were able to rescue the child, who was safely returned to her family.

Over the course of her own search and her experience helping other families, Araceli has learned that local authorities in her municipality are not useful in assisting with searching for disappearances in her region. Orizaba is located along a trafficking route for both women and drugs and there is by now ample documentation that local police have long-standing agreements with the criminal organizations that work in these areas.[19] However, Araceli has been able to identify federal police officers who are willing to assist in certain cases, and her strategy is to find forms of support beyond corrupt local networks.

While there are differences between Romina's, Araceli's, and Leticia's support roles with victims, they all leverage the skills and knowledge they have gained through the particularities of their own searches. Romina, whose son has not yet been found, has less by way of advice to offer victims in searching themselves. But she is able to use her substantial personal connections in the police force and her familiarity with government structures to help smooth the process for families who need help. Leticia, on the other hand, has particular expertise in navigating the complicated systems of morgues and communal graves, gaining access to these sites and guiding the victims' families through the search process. Leticia has also learned in what capacities the police can be useful despite her early and traumatic experiences with the officers assigned to her own case. Finally, Araceli uses her local knowledge of alliances between police and organized crime to steer families away from dead ends and towards the forms of support she has identified at federal government levels.

Registering the Disappeared

Leticia, Araceli, and Romina are all determined that families should register their missing loved ones through official channels not only for tactical reasons (namely, to access the technology and the resources available to state agencies), but also because of the importance of the official record. Many commentators have pointed out that the estimated number of people who have disappeared in Mexico is egregiously inaccurate and underestimated. There are a number of reasons for this. Official figures are undercounts because of the negative optics for the government and the implication of government corruption, negligence, or involvement. The numbers are also inaccurate because families often hesitate even to report their missing family members for fear of reprisal from criminal elements and awareness of the complicity of the very state actors they would have to report to.

Araceli's insistence on registration was particularly striking to me because of her own experience after Rubí went missing, which exemplified many of the reasons families don't want to go to the authorities. When Araceli first went to the local police after

Rubí was abducted, they told her that she should not report the kidnapping. The officer she spoke to told her: "The best thing to do is nothing. Because if you say anything you will probably never see your daughter again." Araceli interpreted this as a threat and immediately suspected that local police were complicit with the disappearance of her daughter. So instead of filing a formal report with the local officials she drove three hours to the state capital of Xalapa, where she was bumped around to different investigative agencies all of which took her information.

But at every step of this process, officials in these agencies told her that she would have to return to Orizaba, where Rubí disappeared, to submit a complaint there. She explained, "I can't go there, because the perpetrators are there and my family is there." By then she had received several suspicious phone calls and hangups but no ransom requests and so she finally presented her case to the delegate in Córdoba, the city twenty kilometers to the east of Orizaba. But it quickly became apparent that the officials there were also involved. She could tell because she showed them the number from which she had received phone calls, hoping to trace it, and she could see that they recognized the number. The proof of this came just hours after she left the office, when she received a text from that same number telling her that she would regret having gone to the police: "Now we'll never return your daughter." This devastated her, because at first she believed that this indeed might have impeded her daughter's safe return, and as time went on she felt tremendous regret thinking that if only she had waited and kept silent maybe things would have gone differently.

Over the months and years that followed though, she met many other families in her situation and began to see that her own actions had probably made little difference. Some families told her that they had not gone to the authorities, fearing retribution from the kidnappers, but their children or spouses were not returned anyway. Others had the opportunity to pay ransoms, and their loved ones had still never been returned to them.

The collective of families in Orizaba that Araceli leads estimates that only one out of every six disappearances in Veracruz are reported to the authorities, and from Araceli's experience it is clear why families are hesitant. It is not only because they fear retribution; because of the bureaucratic obstacles described here, it is often difficult even to register an individual as missing in the first place. But as the estimates from Veracruz indicate, getting these disappearances on the record is extremely important because it is the only form of documentation that they disappeared in the first place.

Elsewhere in the world where disappearances are widespread, activists also highlight the importance of documentation. For example, Ather Zia analyzed the case of the Indian-controlled Kashmir Valley, where activists, mostly Muslim women, individually and collectively search for the more than eight thousand Kashmiri men who have been forcibly disappeared by the Indian Army.[20] Zia points out that since there are few official documents directly acknowledging that disappearances exist, this missing documentation functions ideologically to deny the existence of a problem. Technically speaking, if there are no "First Information Reports" (the report the police must receive for an investigation to begin), then there are no "disappearances" in the first place. Zia writes that by blocking these reports through bureaucratic obstruction, "it appears that the state has found a way to disappear the very disappearances themselves."[21]

In Mexico, the difficulties families encounter in even registering their family members as disappeared function as a similar double erasure. This is also reflected in the government's firm public refusal to distinguish the "disappeared" from the "missing." Thus, officials often dismiss demands by family members to open an investigation by claiming that their loved ones simply "went off somewhere." For example, in its 2015 report assessing the state of impunity in Mexico, the Inter-American Commission on Human Rights noted that the term preferred by the Mexican government is *personas no localizadas* (persons not accounted for).[22] Alejandro Anaya-Muñoz and Barbara Frey point out that this language gives the impression that the disappeared are gone for a variety of potentially innocent reasons and not necessarily because of human rights violations, which effectively shields the state from any potential blame.[23]

These are just some of the ways that the Mexican government's logic of negation refuses to acknowledge the disappeared or the plight of family members searching for them. The insistence on the registry is one way that activists, advocates, and family members of the disappeared resist the erasure of their loved ones.

The Collectives That Shouldn't Exist

Citizen-led collectives have been important grassroots efforts to counter these erasures but many activists emphasize their limits. Araceli pointed out that a major problem collectives confront is that they create fragmentary networks of support. In her state of Veracruz, there are at least sixteen different collectives and various divisions and tensions have emerged among them, mostly because they receive different and unequal forms of support from the government and international organizations. "In Veracruz we should be a movement for all of Veracruz," Araceli said. "We're not a chain of OXXOs," she added, referencing the largest franchise of convenience stores in Mexico.

In general, search collectives receive very little funding and support from the state. Historically, their lack of resources had a crippling effect on their sustainability. Sometimes women end up leaving collectives because of their lack of resources. As previously discussed, there have been many members of collectives who, in the process of searching for their loved ones, have significantly depleted their personal financial resources and savings. Collectives often rely heavily on financial and logistical support from both domestic and international NGOs and other civil society organizations. However, the lack of coordination among both civic and family run groups has also been a major obstacle to these groups' actions. Recently, there have been increasing efforts among civil society groups to offer more coordinated support.[24] But as the stories I've outlined here indicate, there's no one-size-fits-all approach to local search strategies, which is why collectives shape their efforts to local circumstances. This underscores some of the challenges that national and international organizing faces in trying to implement more coordinated responses (figure 4).

Many activists see the formation of search collectives themselves as, at best, institutionalizing the deprofessionalization of what should be the bedrock of any democratic society: basic law enforcement and the protection of the human right to life. As Araceli remarked: "The thing about collectives is that they should not exist at all." She explained that they should at least not play the role that they are forced to: conducting investigations that should be run by professionals and funded and organized by the state. Therefore, while the work of collectives is remarkable, laudable, and necessary, the way that their feats and those of individual women like Miriam

FIGURE 4. A collective of family members in Veracruz prepares for a search, 2019. Photo by Daniel M.G.

Rodríguez are heralded as heroic—and even naturalized as emerging from a mother's instinctual responsibilities—can distract from the fact that such extraordinary initiative on the part of individuals and collectives reveals the failure of the Mexican state to protect its citizens.

The question that must be asked then is: How has it become normalized that when someone disappears in Mexico the large majority of their relatives, if they dare to act at all, decide to call people like Leticia, Araceli, or Romina, rather than the police? In this chapter, I have explained why individuals make that decision to bypass the police and turn to other families instead. But this offloading of state responsibility onto the shoulders of mothers and families is not simply a negation on the part of the state, but is inseparable from the neoliberal turn in Mexico. In the last chapter we saw how waiting is one of the ways that family members of the disappeared experience the state's apparent retreat as a result of neoliberalization. The emergence of search collectives is another effect of the withdrawal of the state. This is not an isolated case of citizens taking on roles that seem very much traditionally reserved to the state but rather is part of a much larger trend.

The historically high homicide rate in Mexico coupled with a "weak" state have meant that justice has often been delivered through informal channels.[25] Neoliberalism has accentuated this dynamic as it encompasses not only economic restructuring, such as privatization and free trade, but also new practices of governance that encourage the transfer of state responsibility for mediating social conflict to civil society and forms of "self-regulation" for both individuals and groups.[26]

In Mexico, this has resulted in an offloading of traditionally held state responsibilities, like environmental regulation, onto nongovernmental organizations.[27] The rise of *grupos de autodefensas,* or community defense groups, in Mexico is another instance of this offloading. For example, after the eruption of violence that resulted from former President Calderón's joint police and military initiative, known as Operation Michoacán, there was a marked increase in the vulnerability of civilian populations in the state. Residents responded by organizing vigilante groups to defend themselves against both military and cartel incursions. Antonio Fuentes Díaz documents the rise of community defense groups in Michoacán and shows how these groups exemplify the construction of organizations that replace or challenge state functions, establishing alternative forms of security and justice.[28] Yet, as this chapter and the next show, in the context of disappearances in Mexico it is especially women who take on roles traditionally reserved by the state in even the most neoliberal of advanced democracies: specifically, the work of police officers, investigators, grave diggers, and ransom negotiators.

4 A Rage So Fierce She Didn't Notice Her Feet

Fernanda Rubí Salcedo Jiménez disappeared in Orizaba, Veracruz, in September 2012 when she was twenty-one years old. I met her mother, Araceli, at a press conference in Mexico City in February 2014. The room teemed with journalists, television crews, politicians, and activists. At the front stood two dozen family members of the disappeared, including Araceli. They were holding banners with images of their missing relatives and Araceli was holding a photo of her daughter. Activists took to the podium to emphasize the scale of the crisis of disappearances in Mexico. After the speakers were finished, the media encircled the family members, interviewing and recording them. While the media was eager to document the event, the relatives were equally determined to have their stories heard. In fact, as the conference ended and many of the crews and journalists left the room, the family members began to rotate around the thinning crowds themselves, reversing the flow of attention in the room. They approached the remaining journalists to make sure their stories were shared. At this point, as I held my camera documenting the event, Araceli approached me together with two of her companions. She asked if I would like to take a photo of them with the images of their children. They

FIGURE 5. Family members stand with images of their disappeared loved ones at a press conference in 2014. Photo by author.

got into position to display their poster boards for my camera (figure 5).

Then they told me the stories of their sons and daughter whose images looked out from the signs. They said that they were there in Mexico City hoping they could get more traction with government officials than they had in Veracruz, where all their respective investigations had stalled. In Mexico City, too, it is very slow, they said. Araceli added: "Even when they pay attention to our cases, what they do is open an investigation and after that officials make no progress with cases. Then they just close them seven months later." But in Veracruz, they hadn't made any progress at all. "All the government officials are Zetas," Araceli said, "They say they can't help but the reason they can't help is that they are involved, and they are

afraid." They all agreed on this point, speaking quickly and sometimes over each other into my audio recorder to describe the corruption they had encountered. The conversation became intense
as they finally all converged on descriptions of their shared experiences with one politician in particular, Javier Duarte, the governor
of the state of Veracruz at the time who, they said, was complicit
with the criminal forces that had led to the disappearances of their
children.

I turned my audio recorder off as soon as they mentioned
Governor Duarte by name, which was my protocol when people
made allegations about specific individuals. My concern was that
if such claims had yet to be corroborated, and convictions were not
in place, it would put my research participants and myself at risk to
implicate officials publicly or even have a record somewhere of
them doing so. The act of turning off the recorder was necessary
but also sometimes seemed hollow. On this occasion, for example,
journalists and news crews circled with their own cameras and
recording devices and sometimes stopped to hear the stories of relatives of the disappeared, whose names were identified on the
signs they carried and the shirts they wore. Their accounts, in other
words, were being recorded by others—even if they might not
make it to the public record. In fact, two of the women from the
town of Orizaba had made a banner with their missing daughters'
photos and the words in big letters: "Duarte is corrupt. Authorities
Protecting Criminals. Orizaba in the hands of organized crime."

It was also common in my conversations with family members
of the disappeared that they would delve into an account of the
intricate acts of corruption that had occurred during their interactions with government officials. Most families searching for the
disappeared have interacted with an official or a politician whom

they thought was complicit, or at least negligent, in their family member's disappearance. Activists are often eager to talk about this, as such experiences are sometimes a pivotal moment in their politicization. These experiences are characterized by slow movement through a complex bureaucracy, trying to find answers, in a process in which they hope they can trust a relevant official, only to feel ultimately betrayed. While I heard numerous stories of corruption and negligence, most were ultimately left out of these pages because of the concerns I just mentioned.

At other times, victims' accounts of officials' involvement in organized crime were eventually validated publicly, as was the case with the former Governor Duarte. Duarte's impacts on the searches of several families came back to me at various points during my research before he was finally convicted in 2017. The most memorable time Duarte's name came to my attention was in 2015, when I next saw Araceli—this time in a video that had gone viral online. The video shows Araceli approaching Governor Duarte and his wife as they arrive at the state building in Orizaba. As she sidles up to him, she holds up her poster featuring her daughter, Rubí, and follows him up the steps as he ascends a long walkway towards the building's entrance. He sees her and doesn't even slow down. He knows who she is. She yells out, "This is not fair! You are here with your family. But my daughter—where is she?!" Duarte ignores her, averting his gaze and continuing as if she is not there. He tries to brush her off by saying he'll talk to her later. "You'll see me, when?" she asks, and he tries to push past her, but she gets in front of him. "Please, sir, come on, stop." He says, "Make an appointment with my prosecutor." He moves past her as she responds: "Your prosecutor is good for nothing!" But Araceli pursues him shouting: "Here is your 'magic town'—where they kidnap our children."

Behind them, the beautiful town of Orizaba is visible: lush green mountains in the distance and colonial architecture in the foreground, all of which earned the town the label of a *"pueblo mágico"* (magic town) as Araceli had pointed out sardonically.[1]

Finally, Araceli comes around Duarte and positions herself directly in front of him, showing him the picture of her daughter. He tries to walk past her, but she blocks him. His discomfort grows and then settles on his face in an uneasy yet smug grin. This grin provokes Araceli further, and she yells at him: "You act as if it's nothing! Stop laughing at me, and get that smile off your face, Mr. Governor. Wipe that smile off your face! I have not really lived since that day." They both continue up the stairs with Duarte picking up his pace. Araceli is relentless, emboldened by his indifference. Her dark hair is immaculate, pulled back from her face and her features are set in determination. Her red turtleneck matches the hue of the governor's red vest, creating an unexpected aesthetic balance to the scene. As Araceli shouts at Duarte, he evades her, giving man-hugs and shaking hands with the people he passes as he continues walking. He says: "We'll talk later." Araceli says "When? When will you meet with us?" Again, he says "Talk to my fiscal agent." She responds, "Oh, please your fiscal agent is the same as all of you, *pura corrupción* [pure corruption]." He laughs and keeps going, pulling his wife in closer to him. She laughs too, continuing up the steps. "Laugh! Laugh! And hope it doesn't happen to your family! Because when it happens to you, in your magic town, then you'll know what it means to suffer. When you haven't seen your daughter for three years and two months, sir. Congratulations on your magic town."

This video quickly circulated on social media. There was something cathartic in seeing Araceli unleash her frustration on a powerful figure who had emerged as a clear example of corruption and

FIGURE 6. Mural with faces of the disappeared in Orizaba, Veracruz. Photo by author.

indifference in the face of missing peoples' cases. Duarte's smug indifference was displayed clearly on the screen. It was alarming not just because of his own behavior but also because of how the people he was shaking hands with willingly facilitated his evasion of Araceli, apparently undisturbed by her situation and pleas.

While Araceli's allegations were highly publicized, she was not alone in making allegations against then-Governor Duarte. Many others suspected that Duarte participated in disappearances, or at the very least, deliberately overlooked them. During his time in office as governor (2010–2016), Veracruz experienced unprecedented levels of violence and disappearances. Duarte alleged that this violence was caused by criminal organizations who were fighting for territory, but his governorship was riddled with accusations of violence by state officials, including the administration's alleged involvement in the murder of seventeen journalists in Veracruz during his six years in office (figure 6). There were also at least thirty-six hundred forced disappearances in Veracruz during the same period.[2]

Two years after Araceli's confrontation with Duarte, the accusations that she and her companions made about the governor when I first met them were corroborated by a state investigation. After mounting allegations of corruption, Duarte abruptly resigned from office in October 2016 and fled the country. The same month, a judge issued an apprehension order against him after the Veracruz attorney general determined that he had siphoned off around $35 million in state funding through shell companies during his governorship.[3] Other incidents emerged as well. For example, during his governorship, a Veracruz state official was detained after being found carrying $1.9 million in a backpack at the Toluca airport in the state of Mexico.[4] Duarte was arrested six months after his resignation in Guatemala in a joint operation between Interpol and the Guatemalan police.[5] He has been convicted for those crimes and, more importantly, he also now faces additional charges concerning his participation in the forced disappearance of thirteen people.[6]

Governor Duarte loomed large in the struggles of several women I met from Veracruz. However, these women's experience of obstruction from high-level government officials and their suspicions of corruption is not atypical nor unfounded in other regions of the country as well. In fact, by 2018, at least twenty former state governors were either incarcerated or under investigation for corruption-related charges in Mexico, most but not all of them members of the PRI.[7] While Duarte is by now one of the most famous of these cases, another high-profile case was that of Tomás Yarrington

Ruvalcaba, the PRI governor of Tamaulipas. He was arrested in 2017 and extradited to the United States in 2018 on charges of "drug trafficking, money laundering, and racketeering" for his alleged ties to the Gulf Cartel.[8] Even more recently, there has been another wave of arrests against governors. In July 2020, Governor César Duarte (PRI) of Chihuahua was arrested in Florida on charges of embezzling public funds while he was in office. In June 2021, former Nayarit governor Roberto Sandoval Castaneda (PRI) was arrested for taking bribes from the Jalisco New Generation Cartel (CJNG) and the Beltrán Leyva Organization Cartel after more than eight months on the run.[9]

Drug-related collusion has by now been documented at all levels of government in Mexico, something I explore more below. But scholars have shown the specific role historically played by governors in mediating between government and organized crime. Since the early years of prohibition in Mexico in the 1920s, governors, especially in northern states where illicit crops were grown and trafficked, have had a direct role in controlling and profiting from drug trafficking.[10] From the beginning of the drug trade, producers and traffickers depended on political protection, and governors were the first to control local protection rackets. Eventually, the military and the police became institutional mediators between traffickers and politicians and the networks and power balances among these actors, and the levels of violence they have generated, has shifted significantly over time.

A Brief History of Collusion in Mexico

There are three overlapping political and historical processes that have been foundational in generating drug-associated violence in

Mexico over the past few decades, of which disappearances are a significant component. Neoliberal reforms have facilitated both illegal and legal trade, strengthening the drug trade and weakening the government bodies that would have been charged with dealing with the violence associated with it. Prohibition policies have provided the rationale for funding the militarization of the country, creating increased impunity and human rights violations. Finally, these processes, which are part of global structural changes, have touched down in Mexico during times of significant shifts in the political parties holding power.

Entanglements between criminal organizations and all levels of government have been longstanding in Mexico. For decades, these alliances were secure under the Institutional Revolutionary Party (PRI), when there was relative stability in the networks of criminal groups and the government forces colluding with them. In fact, throughout the twentieth century, drug trafficking in Mexico was comparatively free of violence while under the purview of the PRI.[11] Networks of symbiosis between cartels and government officials allowed most actors involved to benefit: officials took bribes, drug traffickers maintained low profiles, and criminal groups kept violence in check so as not to provoke undue attention.[12]

These relations of complicity remained mainly out of the public gaze during the PRI's seventy-one-year rule. Early on, there were allegations of politicians working with drug traffickers, but these were never fully adjudicated. It was not until the 1980s that officials were publicly exposed as being closely involved in drug trafficking and illicit activity more broadly. A catalyzing incident occurred in 1985 when US Drug Enforcement Administration (DEA) agent Kiki Camarena was abducted and murdered in Mexico. The first accounts of the murder pointed to the Guadalajara

Cartel as the culprit. However, it was later confirmed that Mexico's own intelligence service, the Federal Directorate of Security (DFS), was involved in the death of Camarena. The DFS was later disbanded, but public officials' roles in drug trafficking and corruption continued.[13]

In 2000, the PRI lost the presidency for the first time and this led to some significant shifts in power. Vicente Fox, the Partido de Acción Nacional (PAN) candidate who won the 2000 elections, was in part successful by running an anticorruption campaign that highlighted the previous PRI president's inability to thwart corruption allegations of personal enrichment at all levels of the party.[14] As part of the anticorruption efforts on which he had campaigned, President Fox selected Genaro García Luna to head up Mexico's Office of the Public Security Secretary (SSP) and anticorruption efforts.[15]

Instead of reducing drug trafficking activities, these political shifts resulted in a sharp increase in violence throughout the 2000s. Scholars of the period explain that the ascent to power of Mexico's opposition parties diminished the ability of the Mexican government to control crime.[16] During the PRI's reign, criminals could traffic drugs into the United States if they fulfilled the conditions of not being visibly violent and not selling drugs within Mexico. New politicians from the PAN lacked the experience, networking, discretionary powers, and established protection rackets to maintain the conventional pact. With the growth of a multiparty government after the PRI began losing elections at all levels of government, trafficking organizations could no longer rely on the state for protection of their smuggling routes. Instead, they outsourced this role to private armies of their own creation.[17]

These developments came to a head in 2006, when newly elected President Felipe Calderón, who had won Mexico's second

PAN presidency, made a strategic security decision that would have lasting implications.[18] With financial and logistical support from the United States, President Calderón officially announced the "war on drugs" in Mexico and proceeded to deploy federal military forces to fight organized criminal groups on Mexican soil.[19] The first troops Calderón deployed were to the states of Michoacán and Baja California, but over the course of his administration he sent tens of thousands of military personnel throughout the country. In doing so, he captured many of the high-level targets established by the United States and Mexico. But rather than stifling drug trafficking activities, this "kingpin" strategy created instability among criminal groups caused by temporary power vacuums. Rivalries between organizations emerged, which resulted in skyrocketing levels of violence and disappearances.[20]

These moves were bolstered and precipitated by the Merida Initiative, the US-Mexico joint strategy to combat organized crime and drug trafficking. The Merida Initiative was formally established in 2007 and has served as one of the primary frameworks for US-Mexico security collaboration since.[21] It was designed as a way for the United States to provide security assistance to Mexico, with a particular emphasis on military involvement. Scholars have noted that the objectives went beyond security in the strict sense of antiterrorism and antitrafficking because they highlighted economic safety and the strengthening of the neoliberal state, allowing trade to flourish and protecting corporate interests.[22] In fact, the militarization of Mexico under the drug war has its roots not in a sudden surge of drug cartel activity, but in the North American Free Trade Agreement (NAFTA) and the US strategy of "pushing out its borders" to encompass its North American partners in an economic and security region.[23] That said, there were direct security outcomes of the Merida Initiative as well, which included prison reform, the militarization of law enforcement, and the rapid expansion of maximum-security prison facilities in Mexico.[24] While both presidents, Fox and Calderón, took part in these negotiations, then-SSP Secretary Genero García Luna was by now largely responsible for spearheading the Mexican side of the Merida Initiative. And as the secretary of SSP, he was also, in many ways, considered to be the principal figure behind the war on drugs.

As early as 2007, García Luna was suspected of having connections with two drug trafficking organizations, the Sinaloa Federation and the Beltrán Leyva Organization, but Mexico's Attorney General's Office (PGR) denied those claims.[25] It was not until December 2019 that García Luna was finally arrested in the United States on charges including conspiracy to traffic cocaine. It was later revealed that García Luna took millions in bribes from the Sinaloa Federation during his time as a public official.[26] Ironically, it was precisely during the time he was taking these bribes that he was also responsible for implementing the militarization of Calderón's war on drugs strategy. In fact, the historian Benjamin Smith has suggested that he likely used some of the money from the cartel to fund the massive increase in federal police in Mexico, whose numbers rose from six thousand to about thirty-seven thousand in a six-year period.[27]

The use of the military within Mexican borders for internal "public safety" issues remained legally dubious even after Calderón authorized this action. Mexico's Constitution, like most in the world, prohibits the use of armed forces in domestic security except under specific conditions, such as a state of emergency. But when Enrique Peña Nieto from the PRI was elected to the presidency in 2012, he continued this militarized security strategy (while also creating the National Security Commission [CNS]) and moved the federal police under the Secretary of the Interior (SEGOB). In order to legitimize the continued use of military operations for the war on drugs, in November 2017, Congress and President Peña Nieto signed the Ley de Seguridad Interior (Law of Internal Security) which aimed to legalize the use of the military within Mexico's boundaries.[28] The law was roundly criticized because it granted the president near-unrestricted powers to deploy the military for internal security situations at his discretion while increasing impunity for human rights violations committed by military forces.[29] Beyond increasing the repressive power of the state, militarization is problematic for other reasons as well. Military personnel are not trained to investigate crimes or even make arrests. Moreover, not only does the military supplant police forces in some key functions, but police forces themselves have also become militarized, receiving army-style equipment as part of the war on drugs and often being commanded by military or ex-military personnel.[30]

By 2018, Peña Nieto's administration was over, and Andrés Manuel López Obrador, from the center-left Morena Party, was elected to serve as the first Morena coalition president in Mexico. President López Obrador, like Calderón and Peña Nieto, also ran on an anticorruption platform but his position was distinct from his predecessors as his stated political ideology was more progressive. For example, one of López Obrador's central commitments was to demilitarize Mexico and in November 2018, the Supreme Court struck down the Law of Interior Security passed by Peña Nieto's government precisely because it "[normalized] the use of the armed forces in public security issues."[31] Instead, López Obrador's security policy centered on the creation of the National Guard (GN). Ultimately, however, many of the National Guard's forces come from the Army and Navy and in September 2022, Mexico's Senate voted to put the National Guard fully under military control, in a policy reversal that sparked outrage among human rights groups.[32] In the end, instead of decreasing the violence associated with a militarized "war on drugs," López Obrador's approach has only increased it. By 2022, the security situation in López Obrador's fourth year was remarkably worse. Twenty-two of Mexico's thirty-two states had higher incidences of homicides than they did six years prior, with ten states showing an increase in homicides of more than 100 percent.[33]

Despite its questionable legality under the Mexican Constitution, the militarization of the war on drugs has also been encouraged by the US government through the Mérida Initiative. Later, the US government, and particularly the Pentagon, instituted a policy to favor the Mexican Navy as more trustworthy than the Mexican Army.[34] But in the last decade documentation has also mounted exponentially connecting the Mexican Marines to disappearances.

Dawn Paley has chronicled several high-profile cases of disappearances at the hands of the Marines between 2011 and 2018.[35] What further incriminates the Mexican state regarding these allegations is that in all these cases, the Attorney General's Office failed to investigate them. Paley quotes Raymundo Ramos, the president of the nongovernmental Human Rights Committee of Nuevo Laredo, stating this bluntly: "They open investigations, and first they investigate and criminalize the victims, then their family members—but they never, ever touch the Marines."[36] The fact that even these high-profile disappearances, which received significant media coverage, were not investigated indicates the scope of impunity shrouding disappearances in Mexico. This was highlighted by the UN Committee against Enforced Disappearances, which in a

2022 report stated that impunity for acts of disappearances is near "absolute," with a conviction rate of between 2 and 6 percent and with only thirty-six cases of enforced disappearance ever prosecuted at the national level.[37]

But one incident involving a state actor's involvement in human rights violations in Mexico did garner international attention. In October 2020, former Mexican defense minister under President Peña Nieto, General Salvador Cienfuegos Zepeda, was arrested in the United States.[38] He was to face charges of drug trafficking and money laundering from his activities during his time as defense minister. This made him the highest-ranking Mexican military member to be arrested by US authorities. But in November 2020, President López Obrador pressured the US government to drop all charges against Cienfuegos and return him to Mexico, where he promised to bring down on him the full weight of the law. However, in a jarring reversal, after Cienfuegos's return to Mexico in January 2021, Mexican prosecutors cleared him of all charges, citing lack of evidence. In fact, López Obrador claimed that the United States had fabricated the charges against him.[39] With this ultimate failure to prosecute, the incident brought international attention to the rampant impunity of state forces in Mexico, this time under a self-identified progressive president who claimed to have broken from state impunity under Peña Nieto's presidency.

Untouchables and Political Accusation

A ProPublica investigation into Cienfuego's arrest and the subsequent fallout underscored the event's significance. The report indicated that while Cienfuego's arrest was widely portrayed by officials in the United States as "part of a broader U.S. effort to take on high-level drug corruption in Mexico," US prosecutors were in part reacting to testimonies from the trial of Joaquín "El Chapo" Guzmán Loera, the notorious former leader of the Sinaloa Cartel. El Chapo became emblematic of the far-reaching tentacles of drug trafficking and corruption in Mexico but his trial in the United States, which concluded in a guilty conviction in 2019, also highlighted the massive bribes paid to top Mexican officials—some of whom had close working relationships with the United States.[40] The irony of the US government attempting to position itself outside the forces of corruption shaping the war on drugs in Mexico, while also trying to cover its own implication in this corruption, goes beyond the failed attempt of US authorities to indict Cienfuegos. Often, the human rights crisis in Mexico is oversimplified by international observers as a consequence of "national character" or a "culture of violence," unfairly attributing sole responsibility to Mexico. The stance that countries like the United States and Canada have taken in support of the war on drugs but in contempt of Mexico's presumed role in the violence is deeply hypocritical, for there is nothing inherently "Mexican" about the violence the country has experienced over the last few decades. This violence, as I have argued here and as many authors have shown, is a result of a series of political decisions and historical circumstances also shaped by US and Canadian funding, training, and influence.

Nicholas Jon Crane and Oliver Gabriel Hernández Lara have pointed out that an offhand reduction of violent events to a matter of "national character" is common in the portrayal of some historical events, particularly by non-Mexican commentators. At times, femicide has also been characterized as a phenomenon that is geographically bound to Mexican territory. Another telling example is how the Ayotzinapa killings in 2014 have sometimes been framed as merely an echo of Mexican violence from the 1968 Tlatelolco massacre, when the Mexican Army assassinated hundreds of unarmed civilians who were protesting Mexico City's hosting of the 1968 Olympics that year.[41] These interpretations ignore the contingencies of the international political and historical processes that have come to bear on current forms of violence in Mexico, including the impact of militarization, neoliberal restructuring, and drug prohibition policies that have been shaped by international actors, most importantly the United States.

The common narrative that seeks to establish Mexico as the source of drug war violence relies on a further naturalization of "Mexican corruption" that is both broadly conceptualized and uniquely historicized as part of the story of Mexico's past and present in a way that upholds the naturalizing views of violence in this country. Political scientist Peter Lupsha has even suggested that it is difficult to historicize corruption in Mexico because it is "as eternal as the Aztec sun."[42] But while corruption runs historically deep in Mexico, as I have emphasized in this book, it does not spring eternal but is instead produced by a series of historical contingencies.

In fact, scholars of corruption have noted that changing notions of legitimacy shape what is perceived as corruption in the first place.[43] In most contexts, corruption is understood as the illegal and dishonest behavior of those in power who use their influence for personal gain. For example, the quintessential act of corruption is the bribe—demanding money for a service or favor. But corruption is a broad discourse of political accusation as much as it is a political fact. And the focus on corruption in Mexico distorts the picture of who is responsible and who is benefiting from the violence of the war on drugs in multiple ways.[44]

Foremost, the exclusive focus on corruption in Mexico distracts from the ways people in power in the United States and elsewhere internationally profit from illegality in perfectly "legal" ways. The United States, along with other wealthy nations including Canada and the United Kingdom, has benefited in multiple ways from the war on drugs but by different means than actors in Mexico and through mechanisms either deemed legal or punished so minimally they may as well be legal. A significant portion of the profits of the drug trade go to the United States, and not just to the criminal organizations and corrupt officials there, but also to major financial institutions and their shareholders. Banks are one of the main actors that profit from the drug trade, laundering billions of dollars for the cartels while not being considered "corrupt" by the general public.

US exports of firearms, ammunition, and explosives to Mexico have increased significantly since the launch of the Merida Initiative in 2007 and now average more than $40 million annually.[45] In her book *Exit Wounds,* Ieva Jusionyte shows how firearms legally imported from the United States have been used in some of the worst human rights violations in Mexico in recent years.[46] Other key legal sectors that profit from current antidrug policies as well as from illegal trafficking are the military-industrial complex, which benefits from inflated antidrug budgets, and construction enterprises, which create the infrastructures for smuggling, such as roads, tunnels, and even buildings.[47] The private-prison complex in the United States also profits from the high number of racialized drug-related incarcerations, as do governments and corporations. US law enforcement and border patrol agencies receive generous budgets to combat trafficking organizations and can also directly seize illegal assets through US drug forfeiture laws.[48] There is certainly a record of clear-cut corruption in relation to the drug trade in the United States as well.[49]

Recognizing the role of the United States in providing demand for drugs while also participating in mechanisms of "corruption" that some see as embedded within Mexican "culture" shows how important a regional perspective is, one that acknowledges these transnational connections. The ideological effect of acknowledging Mexico's autonomy, and even suggesting that there is a culture of corruption and violence there, allows the United States to claim that Mexico is responsible for its own problems, rather than recognizing that its own economic policies contribute to poverty and violence in Mexico.[50]

And just as people can benefit from illegality in legal ways, people in power can also use money obtained from illegal sources for the public good. In his book *The Dope,* historian Benjamin Smith has argued that historically government officials in Mexico would procure money through "corrupt" channels and use it for public goods and services, not simply for individual gain.[51] He makes this point by documenting the history of protection rackets, which up until the 1970s were the dominant form of political control, whereby state governments charged traffickers in exchange for not imposing the law. Though many officials controlling protection rackets got very rich, others sought to distribute at least some of these funds through official state programs, such as building schools and roads. They did so while, at the same time, keeping the violent disputes associated with the trade at bay.[52] Smith notes that now such arrangements would be seen as straight corruption, which in a strict sense they are, but that in the early twentieth century many in Mexico saw them as a solution to the potential violence generated by the drug trade, a trade that emerged as a response to US demand.

The historical lens through which Smith views corruption reveals its complex character and the variable moral judgments attached to it over time. Such a perspective underscores that practices deemed corrupt were once considered necessary evils in service of social stability and public welfare, despite their illicit origins. These examples show how amorphous and historically situated "corrupt" practices have been throughout Mexican history, how in the past so-called corrupt acts by officials were not intrinsically linked to violence, and how in the twenty-first century these practices involve myriad powerful actors who are based outside Mexico. Today, corruption has evolved and become much more entangled with violence and the suffering of ordinary citizens, altering the social fabric and challenging the very notion of public good.

Against this backdrop, the accounts of impunity and collusion, epitomized by the involvement of figures such as former Governor Duarte in Veracruz, cast light on the formidable obstacles faced by families in their search for the missing. How do these family members navigate the intricate and pervasive connections between the state and organized crime? How do these collusive actions between the state and criminal groups impact their efforts to search for their loved ones? I began this chapter with the example of Araceli's confrontation with Governor Duarte in Orizaba. While some, like Araceli, have taken an explicitly confrontational approach, animating a strain of activism which I will describe later, this is not the most common response. Most family members of the disappeared work within the dense system of connectivity between the state and organized crime to find answers about their loved ones. They do so by strategically engaging officials and criminal organizations in ways that do not threaten the interests of either, by selectively making use of the state resources that are available to them, and sometimes even by bypassing officials and engaging criminal organizations directly in search of answers.

"We're Not Looking for Justice"

The major practical issue that those looking for the disappeared confront is how to best solicit support for their investigations from government officials and police when they may well be embedded in the networks of organized crime responsible for disappearances. One way that search collectives manage this problem is through public assurances that they are not looking for those responsible nor seeking out justice but that they are singularly interested in finding out what happened to their loved ones. The Brigada Nacional de Búsqueda (the National Search Brigade or BNB), makes this argument explicitly. The BNB organizes an annual event which brings together more than 140 search collectives from across Mexico. Together they conduct a large-scale search for their relatives and host a series of community-based public awareness events through schools and churches. The BNB coordinates with authorities, journalists, anthropologists, and other allies and raises funds across North America.

Because the BNB coordinates across such an array of contexts and regional situations they need to be particularly careful about navigating local dynamics. In their press releases and mission statement, they specify that the BNB "does not look for the guilty." Their aim is "to find our disappeared loved ones without criminalizing and stigmatizing people. . . . Far from punitive justice, we seek tranquility and peace in the lives of relatives, loved ones and families of the disappeared."[53] In other words, they are not seeking out the people who are responsible for the disappearances but just want to know what happened to their relatives. BNB organizers call this a "humanitarian approach," which takes as its only aim finding the disappeared.

On the one hand, this approach foregrounds the top priority of many families. As one member of BNB said to me in a 2017 interview: "We just want to know what happened. The truth is more important than justice." But the stance is also an explicit tactical decision that recognizes both the failure of the existing legal frameworks to advance justice and the fact that officials are more likely to support an investigation if they will not be implicated and if there is assurance that relatives will not do anything to threaten or anger the cartels.

For some, this is purely a strategic stance which does not reflect a deeper disposition to indeed give up seeking justice. Several members of the BNB are strikingly blunt about this in private. For example, when I asked one man who was searching for his sister why they would not be looking for justice, he said: "Of course, we want justice and want to make them [the perpetrators] pay. But what's more important right now is that we find out what happened and to keep ourselves safe while we search."

In Carolina Robledo Silvestre's ethnographic coverage of a group of families searching for the disappeared in Sinaloa, she documents how these families have a clear understanding that "not seeking the guilty" is the only way for them to ensure any kind of collaboration with the state government with respect of the technical aspects of locating and identifying the disappeared.[54] Robledo Silvestre quotes the leader of this collective saying: "If I told the government that I was looking for those responsible, they wouldn't even lend me their dog, never mind their forensic experts. It's impossible for the government to return the disappeared. Their motto is, if there are no bodies, there are no dead, and therefore no disappeared. The government will never deliver the disappeared because it's not in their interest."[55]

As this person made clear, "not seeking the guilty" is a way of facilitating access to government resources. This was apparent, as I described in chapter 3, in the approaches of both Leticia and Miriam, who made selective use of the police for resources and at strategic moments in their searches. The strategy to "not seek out the guilty" is a signal of how thoroughly disenfranchised victims of violence have become and how hegemonic the impunity is. That those searching for the disappeared must promise not to hold anyone accountable in exchange for being able to investigate is an ominous indictment of how normalized human rights violations have become.

The search collectives' public proclamations that they are not looking for justice are sometimes directed more at criminal actors than at officials. In those cases, this purported disinterest in justice is meant to dissuade potential threats from organized crime, for some collectives have faced significant repercussions from cartels. Since 2010, at least twelve searchers have been murdered, and in each of these cases the victim's activism and search-related work appears to be the reason behind their homicides.[56] Search collectives have received anonymous threats warning them to desist in their investigations. In response, one woman from a group of mothers in Sonora posted a video in January 2022 directed at the cartels where she said: "We aren't looking for the guilty, we're not looking for justice. We just want to bring them home, we have the need to bring them home because good or bad, guilty or innocent, for us they are our life."[57]

Public pleas such as this also solicit safe passage and access to territory from which the public and the police are generally restricted. In some cases, these requests have also involved ad hoc collaborations between collectives and members of criminal groups. For example, during the third BNB gathering, a perpetrator gave information on the location of the grave and identity of one of his victims, asking in return that the BNB organizers search for his own disappeared brother.[58]

These kinds of temporary alliances are complex and varied. After experiencing the frustration of trying to acquire official support for their investigations, some activists go another route entirely: instead of embedding themselves in family-led networks they decide to concentrate their efforts on making connections with drug trafficking organizations. The first example that I came across of such an approach was particularly instructive about how some people have opted out of cooperating with the government in exchange for more promising connections to organized crime.

This was the case with Sofía, who I met in 2012, after she had spent two years pursuing what she called "clean" channels of investigation to find her missing son. When I met with her again in 2014 in Mexico City, she told me, "I'm done with begging for help from the authorities." She decided she would focus her efforts on making connections with local members of organized crime because she felt that these were "honest criminals" whose positions were straightforwardly self-interested, unlike the government officials she had interacted with. In her town in northern Mexico, it was clear to her how to establish these connections. She dressed up, went to the "right bars"—by which she meant the bars associated with criminal networks—and, as she put it, "I started by making friends." For an attractive and charming woman in her late thirties like Sofía, this happened easily. "I got lots of useful information just by chatting with people in these places."

One of the most useful things she learned was that the official morgues she had spent months visiting, sometimes repeatedly, were not the only "legal" morgues in her state. Through conversations with her new acquaintances, she learned of hidden morgues managed by the government, as well as "false morgues," that is, morgues whose names had been changed to make them harder to find. When she learned this, she became adamant that she would do whatever necessary to gain access to these places, even if this meant violating laws or putting herself in danger. But while her efforts at making friends in lower levels of criminal networks had helped her realize that her search had initially been too restricted to officially accessible locations, this strategy didn't help her gain access to the undocumented burial locations she was learning about. To do this, Sofía had to make connections with more influential members of local criminal networks. Sofía said that even arranging these meetings involved bribery and then more bribery to get into the morgues she had initially missed. I did not ask Sofía for details about how she got the money to follow through on this line of bribery, because she made it clear that this was not the important part of her story. But she mentioned more than once that she did "all sorts of dirty jobs." She was also honest about not having any second thoughts about her determination to do "whatever she had to." What is important about her story is that eventually, in 2015, Sofía was able to find the remains of her son, in one of the unofficial morgues to which her efforts finally led her.

"I Did It without Looking Down"

Araceli and I kept in touch after our first meeting in 2014 in Mexico City but I did not see her in person again for eight more years. I had always planned to follow up with her but in the meantime most of my research focused on other parts of Mexico, in places that I imagined to be safer than Veracruz because I had denser social networks that helped me better navigate local dynamics. But in 2022 I decided to visit her in Veracruz because a colleague and friend from neighboring Puebla offered to accompany me.

I was nervous about spending time in Veracruz because this state has one of the highest rates of disappearances in Mexico and in 2017 had in fact been dubbed "Mexico's State of Terror" by the International Crisis Group.[59] Just reaching the state from Mexico City meant traveling over a toll road where my Pueblan colleague said we wouldn't be able to stop if I had to go to the bathroom. "It's too dangerous," she said. "On this road if people break down and they need to call for help for a flat tire, no one will come." She explained that this stretch of road is known for a high rate of highway robberies. The road also crosses the "red triangle," which is where many collection points of *huachicol* (stolen fuel) are connected by pipelines that cross that area. Therefore, in those municipalities organized crime exerts strong territorial control. For these same reasons, Araceli had been checking in with me regularly by text as we drove to Orizaba, making sure I was safe, which further rattled my nerves. While I had been conducting research on drug-related violence in Mexico for a long time, by then my own sense of safety was shaped by a tension between an awareness of how much violence ordinary people in Mexico suffer and the relative security my position of privilege as a white academic based in Canada had afforded me up until that moment.

All of this was on my mind after my friend dropped me off in Orizaba and I finally stood alone waiting for Araceli in the gorgeous town center in front of a beautiful church, listening to the traditional Mexican folk music drift from a café across the road and enjoying the sunshine warming the *zócalo*. I was still a little tense from the journey when Araceli at last appeared from around the corner. She saw me and even behind her mask I could see her beautiful smile light up her face. But then two huge men came around the corner just on her heels. They approached quickly, towering over her from behind. I flinched, seized momentarily with fear. Araceli then turned and motioned to them. "These are my *compañeros*," she said. It took a few minutes for my heart to stop racing as I realized these men were her bodyguards.[60]

We all went to a nearby café and the bodyguards sat amicably at the next table. I bought them sodas and they settled in as Araceli and I began a long, intense conversation, reminiscing about how much things had changed, and hadn't, since we last saw each other in person in 2014. I told her about seeing the video that sprang up on my news feed of her confronting former Governor Duarte in October 2015. I asked her about that day and if she had planned to confront him. "I just wanted to talk to him," she said. On the morning of the Governor's visit to Orizaba Araceli's friend had called and told her that he would be there as part of the promotion of Orizaba as a "magical town." At that point, it had been three years of Duarte evading her and canceling meetings that she had scheduled. She had approached him in public in the state capital of Xalapa on several occasions and he had always brushed her off, saying the same thing, "I'll make an appointment with the fiscal . . ." She saw that moment in Orizaba in October 2015 as, hopefully, just another opportunity to get Governor Duarte's attention. She went to the town hall in Orizaba that day with the sign of her daughter, planning to implore him again to help with her case.

Araceli said when she arrived at the town hall, her two body-guards were nervous. "Because they thought you were in danger from Duarte?" I asked. "No, it was more like they were worried about what I had planned. They kept saying, 'Araceli, what are you going to do?'" I looked over to them as she said this. They nodded, confirming her account. The bigger guy shrugged and smiled, widening his eyes as if to imply that he had been worried things would get out of hand. I asked if she had been surprised that the confrontation unfolded the way it did—with Duarte refusing to stop for her and her following him so far up the stairs. Araceli said that, looking back, what surprised her the most when she watched the video was not that she followed him so far but that she managed to do so in such high heels. "I did it without looking down once," she said. "How could I have moved up those stairs so quickly in those heels without tripping and without even looking down at where I was stepping?" I hadn't noticed that myself, as you can't really see Araceli's shoes in the video. She said, "I realized that I was so over-come with rage in that moment that I didn't even notice my feet."

But when she arrived home later that day, after confronting the governor, she collapsed on the couch, spent from the interaction and feeling humiliated and defeated. She remembers sitting on her couch feeling angry and crying. Twenty minutes after she arrived, her seventeen-year-old son called on the phone. "Mom are you okay?" he asked. "Yes, of course, *hijo* . . . *Por qué?*" "I saw you on the internet." Araceli said she hadn't really been aware they were being filmed. There were of course cameramen there but she had had public exchanges with Duarte before. This was just the first time that someone took video of it and posted it on social media. In the brief time since the confrontation, the video had gone viral. Her son had seen the whole interaction.

In the days that followed, the video reached over a million views and the thousands of comments it generated on social media and local news were equal part applause and criticism. Some people admonished Araceli for being naïve enough to assume the governor would know what had happened to her daughter, implying that Rubí was clearly up to no good. But most reacted with disgust and outrage at the behavior of Duarte and his wife. The Orizaba newspaper *El Mundo* also filmed the interaction and then widely publicized it. Only two days later, another Orizaba newspaper ran a front-page story with the headline "Rubí Linked to Los Zetas" claiming that it was Araceli's daughter who was linked to the then-dominant cartel in the state. The article's author went on to claim that the mother's demands were "ordered by political opponents" of Governor Duarte.[61] The blunt accusation was a transparent attempt to defame and dismiss Araceli's potent and highly publicized criticism of the governor and to imply that Rubí had disappeared because she was involved in crime and that, therefore, her disappearance was not worthy of official attention.

.   .   .

In this chapter, I have described the structural factors and patterns of corruption that have undermined the searches for the disappeared in Mexico as well as the many ways in which activists have confronted this collusion. In the process, I have argued against portrayals of the violence in Mexico that view it as emerging from an unchanging cultural disposition. As many anthropologists have explored, this is one of the ways the notion of culture has been manipulated not only to essentialize and exoticize what are contingent political and historical phenomena, but also to blame the victim of much wider neoliberal forms of domination, of which the war on drugs is a primary example today.[62]

Through the stories of individual mothers navigating state/crime alliances I have shown that while corruption is systematic in nature and persists beyond the acts of specific individuals, this does not diminish the reality and validity of family members' frustrations with individual politicians and officials, such as former Governor Duarte. This is how women like Araceli, Sofía, and so many other relatives of the disappeared experience the war on drugs and its violence and impunity: through individual acts of negligence, corruption, and contempt by particular officials.

Sofía's decision to seek information from criminal actors as well as the efforts by search collectives to assure both the state and local cartels that they are not looking for the guilty are different strategies to navigate the fraught and opaque interconnections between the government and organized crime. Araceli's bold attempts to publicly shame Governor Duarte were her way of confronting his complicity and more broadly the corruption plaguing different levels of government and undermining grassroots efforts to find the disappeared.

5   *"Without a Body There Is No Crime"*

Every Mother's Day, which in Mexico is celebrated on May 10, mothers gather all over the country to protest and raise awareness about their missing children. In May 2016, Lucía met with other members of the Solecito search collective in the center of Xalapa, Veracruz, to prepare for their annual march for Mother's Day. They were wearing shirts with photos of their children and many of them also had banners with photos and details of their children's disappearance. The women assembled and were discussing their route when suddenly a black pickup truck tore into the square. Two men jumped out of the back. They ran through the crowd, distributed pamphlets, and then jumped back on their truck and drove away.

Later, over a cup of coffee in Mexico City, Lucía told me what happened next. "I took one of the pamphlets," she said. Many of the women did, thinking it was related to the march. But when Lucía unfolded the pamphlet, she immediately understood what it was.

When I asked her what the pamphlet said, she showed me a picture on her phone. The pamphlet had a handwritten note, stating, "This is where all of Veracruz's disappeared are, with help from MP and Governor Duarte. From Quinto of the CJNG." It was a map with coordinates for a location outside Xalapa, marked with 'x's' labeled "bodies." Lucía recognized the place, known as Colinas de Santa Fe. Her group had considered it as one of four possible locations to search for graves.

Though Lucía understood the significance of the map, she didn't immediately share it with the others. "There was so much going on in my mind," she said. She quietly collected all the pamphlets she could find and stashed them in her pockets.

The mothers continued their march (figure 7), and it was not until later that day that Lucía raised the topic of the pamphlets again. When they finally got a chance to examine the pamphlets together and understand the importance of the information, they reached out to the police for support. They were met with silence. After several weeks of inaction on the part of the police, they finally decided to start searching the site on their own. This was not a decision they took lightly. It was dangerous to go to this place on their own. And they knew they lacked the expertise to properly investigate and assess the site. But it was clear that they would not receive support from the local government, and the wait to follow up on this tip had already been too long. At that point, Lucía contacted Roxana Enríquez Farias, a forensic anthropologist who had founded a nonprofit organization called the Mexican Forensic Anthropology Team (EMAF), based in Mexico City. She came to Veracruz and led a workshop with Solecito to help them prepare themselves for what they might find and to make sure they knew how to properly handle any evidence.[1]

Then the mothers began to dig at the place specified on the map. The methods they used were rudimentary. They walked and looked for places where the ground had a different texture or where there were irregularities in the color of the soil. They noticed where

FIGURE 7. Women march to protest disappearances in Veracruz, 2019. Photo by Daniel M. G.

there was less foliage and where shrubs may have been removed. When they found a spot that looked suspicious, they inserted a two-meter metal rod into the ground, removed the rod, and smelled the tip. If they smelled any hint of rot or decay, they would dig in that spot.

On their first dig, they found fifty bones, including a torso with a head. The remains that Lucía and her companions found that day in Colinas de Santa Fe, Veracruz, were part of what would be identified as the largest mass grave at the time in Mexico. The search continued until 2019. With the eventual assistance of other state and nonstate actors, 156 graves with 298 skulls were eventually found in this place.[2]

The discovery of this mass grave, and the events that followed, raise a number of issues that are important for understanding the nature of violence in contemporary Mexico. The phenomenon of undocumented mass graves in this country is widespread yet their existence is obscured in multiple ways. These graves are secret by nature—hidden by the murderers who sought to bury the evidence of their crimes.[3] The experiences of the women of Solecito show that the existence of these graves is obscured by the government as well, given that the police initially refused to follow up on the tip the mothers had received.

And yet, despite these efforts at obfuscation, elements of criminal groups sometimes deliberately reveal the locations of mass graves. In this chapter, I draw a counterpoint between this case in Veracruz and another example of the way violence is showcased by factions of organized crime in northern Mexico to analyze how such patterns of visibility can depend on how criminal organizations are aligned with other groups and the state at a given moment. Finally, I'll suggest that these various forms of negation, concealment, and revelation of mass graves and other evidence of violence help us understand how families and activists experience the disappearances associated with the war on drugs in Mexico today.

"All of Mexico Is a Grave"

The phenomenon of "the disappeared" has been variously characterized as defined by absence, invisibility, lack of representation, and the impossibility of categorization.[4] The act of making a person disappear negates the evidence of the crime as well as the individual's body, its location and identity. Those labeled "disappeared" are, by definition, nowhere. It cannot be proven that they were murdered or even that they are dead.

States responsible for human rights violations have long denied that the disappeared existed in the first place, something that has been apparent in the Latin American dictatorships supported by the United States.[5] This was famously articulated by the Argentinian dictator Jorge Videla, who when asked at a press conference about the disappeared responded: "If they are not here, they do not exist. And as they do not exist, they are not here. They are neither alive nor dead. They are disappeared." Thousands of Argentinians disappeared under the 1976–1983 military dictatorship under this discourse of denial.

The Mexican government has employed a similar strategy of denialism. A recent example from Sinaloa illustrates this. Although official figures show that homicides have decreased in Sinaloa in recent years, the number of disappeared has increased. From January to August 2021, there were 1.79 homicides and 3.03 disappearances per day in the state, which means there were 69 percent more disappearances than homicides.[6]

The irony is that many officials boast about a reduction in homicides while they continue making disappearances invisible. Since disappearances are not included in the number of homicides, the deaths are not counted and the crimes are not prosecuted. Journalist Abraham Sanz reports that from September 2020 to August 2021, only 1.88 percent of disappearances in Sinaloa were prosecuted.[7] And yet, in 2022 Deputy Attorney General Manuel Carrasco commented on the decrease in homicides: "I think we closed the year on a good note. There was a considerable decrease in comparison to 2020. We will continue to apply the strategies that worked regarding the investigation and prosecution of crimes."[8]

The government refuses to acknowledge the full extent of these homicides and disappearances because it would highlight its failure to maintain law and order, protect its citizens, and effectively combat organized crime. Furthermore, officials fear that acknowledging the scale of the disappearances in Mexico could deter foreign investment, harm the economy, affect diplomatic relations with other countries regarding human rights, and undermine its international image as a tourist destination.

It is precisely because of this refusal to acknowledge the existence of the disappeared that the discovery of an unmarked grave is powerfully destabilizing of government narratives. And for the family members desperate to find out what happened to their relatives, such a discovery can generate a profound, if conflicted, sense of hope.

A *fosa clandestina* (clandestine grave) is an unmarked place where the bodies of one or more people have been buried with the intent of hiding the remains; it is "any site that has the purpose of hiding or destroying evidence"; it is a space that "at the very least, derives from a series of illicit acts."[9] Illegal burials became standard practice of criminal organizations and state actors during the administrations of Felipe Calderón and Enrique Peña Nieto and persist in the current administration of President López Obrador. Such graves are hallmarks of modes of governance where people are too afraid to report crimes to the police: impunity is rampant, and murderers simply hide the bodies to conceal the crime.

While the largest at the time, the grave discovered by the women of Solecito in Colinas de Santa Fe was certainly not the only such site found in Mexico. Whereas in 2006 only two undocumented mass graves had been officially discovered in Mexico, since then hundreds have been discovered every year. In 2016, a group of journalists produced an investigatory report called *"A dónde van los desaparecidos"* ("Where the disappeared go") that documented significantly more clandestine graves than those the Mexican government acknowledges. In fact, they indicated that from 2006 to 2016 almost two thousand unmarked graves have been discovered.[10] The rate of discovery seems to have increased dramatically as well. In August 2019, Deputy Secretary of the Interior Alejandro Encinas confirmed that at least 3,024 clandestine graves had been found between 2016 and August 14, 2019.[11]

One of the first widely publicized discoveries took place in 2010. Juan Viveros and Nabor Baena, the two caretakers of the abandoned "Dolores" mine, located on the outskirts of the city of Taxco in Guerrero, started hearing noises of trucks coming and going from the mine late at night. Soon they began to smell putrid odors emerging from that place. It was at that point that they discovered that an entrance to the mine that had previously been sealed had been reopened. Police and workers used ventilation equipment to descend deep underground and found bodies that had been, over time, thrown down the mine shaft.[12] Just how many bodies were discovered was never entirely clear from reports. News outlets reported 55 bodies. The Attorney General's Office reported 41. Local officials reported 64. Families who went to the morgue estimated there could be around 120.[13] As we will see, inconsistencies such as these are a feature of how clandestine graves have been documented in both official and unofficial records. While the Dolores mine was one of the first mass graves to become widely known through media coverage, since then such uncoverings have become increasingly commonplace.

In August 2010, just two months after the discovery of the Dolores mine, the Mexican Navy located the bodies of seventy-two migrants from Honduras, El Salvador, Guatemala, and Brazil who had been executed and buried in a mass grave in San Fernando, Tamaulipas. The migrants had been traveling north toward the US border when they were stopped, kidnapped, and killed.[14] This grave, which was quickly identified by the Mexican Marines thanks to the testimony of the sole survivor, held the remains of the sons and daughters of the collective Mothers United for Our Children San Fernando Tamaulipas, described in chapter 3.

Tamaulipas was in the news again in March 2011 for events that also later led to the discovery of additional clandestine graves. That month, buses arrived in Reynosa, Tamaulipas, with missing passengers. Suitcases sat abandoned on the luggage carousel, which prompted concern from employees in the bus station.[15] Soon, it became clear that at least 193 individuals had been taken off buses at checkpoints at the hands of Los Zetas and disappeared; this time the victims appeared to be primarily Mexican nationals. The remains of these people were eventually discovered in forty clandestine graves in the area.[16]

These Tamaulipas massacres were two of the largest early incidents connected to the discovery of mass graves in Mexico, and as is generally the case the reasons for these massacres remain largely unknown. Some suspect the victims were originally taken to be held for ransom or to work for the cartel. Other reports indicate that the rivalry between Los Zetas and the Gulf Cartel at the time resulted in orders from Los Zetas to investigate and kill potential infiltrators.

In general, these kinds of conflicts between criminal organizations have been the prevailing interpretation of how such graves come to exist. In fact, in looking at the geography of clandestine graves in areas of Mexico where enduring conflicts among criminal groups and armed forces have been waged, a pattern emerges to suggest that those places contained layers of accumulated graves. The Fifth Element, an organization in Mexico dedicated to investigative journalism, reports that many of these locations are also along the borders with the United States (including Ciudad Juárez in Chihuahua and San Fernando in Tamaulipas) and in the port cities of Acapulco in Guerrero and Veracruz in Veracruz.[17] These are also places that have been heavily militarized and where *autodefensas,* or citizen-led defense groups, have emerged to protect local people from both drug cartels and the military and police.[18]

But many disappearances do not fit into the narrative of drug traffickers in territorial conflict. Natalia Mendoza describes a case in Caborca, Sonora, where the local collective of relatives excavated the body of a man who had disappeared shortly after suing the mining company for having cut his health insurance before he could undergo surgery related to a work accident. By teasing out the connections between the local criminal organizations and the mining company, Mendoza suggests that the dozens of disappearances in this area may have as much to do with protecting the mine as they do with drug trafficking or with control of smuggling routes.[19]

Regardless of the individual circumstances that lead to the creation of these graves, they have been found all over Mexico (see map 1).[20] This is why many activists use the phrase "all of Mexico is a mass grave" to describe the omnipresence of clandestine graves all over the country. This is also the phrase that Padre Alejandro Solalinde, an outspoken human rights defender, used in 2014 in the wake of the Ayotzinapa disappearances, which involved forty-three students from the town of Iguala and had a particularly powerful impact nationally.

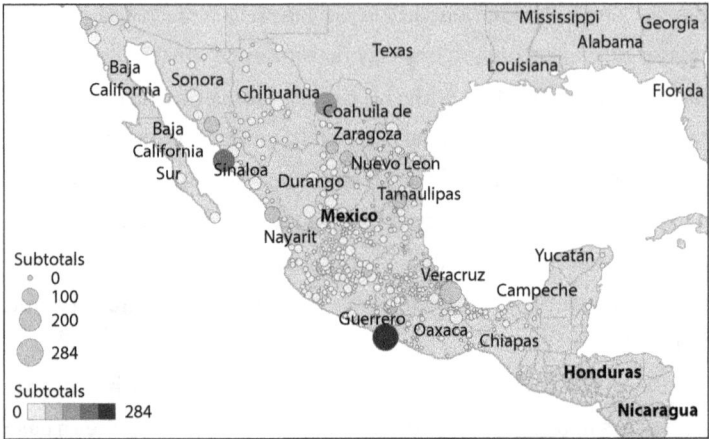

MAP 1. Discoveries of unmarked graves in Mexico, 2006–2023. Map by Caitlyn Yates.

Not the Graves They Were Looking For

The Ayotzinapa disappearances involved forty-three left-wing activist students from a rural teachers' college in Ayotzinapa, Guerrero, who were on their way to a protest to commemorate the massacre of students in Mexico City in 1968. As was the tradition, they commandeered several buses for their trip. In the town of Iguala, police officers who were part of the military wing of cartelized sections of the Mexican state kidnapped and eventually killed them. After the students disappeared, the Mexican government, police, and military first attempted to blame the disappearances on "the narcos." But in the following weeks and years, it became clear that these disappearances and assassinations were ordered by government officials and implemented by armed men who were *both* narcos and state agents.

Ayotzinapa remains one of the most symbolic and well-known cases of enforced disappearance in Mexico because it made clear, perhaps for the first time to international onlookers, that state agents are fully embedded in the fabric of drug trafficking organizations, and that extreme violence and disappearances, contrary to what official and media narratives say, are often generated by the state rather than by "narcos."

In this case, the parents of the students organized immediately to demand action even though there was little evidence of what had happened. Unlike many collectives that often take time to form as family members find each other, the mothers and fathers of the forty-three students already knew each other and mobilized quickly. It was in part because of this that they were able to build a powerful public movement in support of their case.[21] Within just a few days of the disappearances, the parents organized parties to search surrounding hills for the bodies of their children. They soon discovered a mass grave with the remains of more than two hundred people. But the grave did not contain any of the disappeared students. They kept searching the countryside and, in the following days and weeks, family members together with investigators found a new series of mass graves just miles outside of Iguala.[22] These graves did not include the missing students either. Because of the publicity surrounding the Ayotzinapa case, the finding of these graves received media coverage both nationally and internationally. That they had found a mass grave of such proportions and it was not even the one they were looking for served as a startling indication of the pervasiveness of disappearances and mass graves in Mexico. Those bodies of those victims had been killed in separate incidents without connection to each other and their disappearances had been unreported. These remains came to be known as "the other disappeared" and the families of these victims eventually organized on their own, buoyed by the discovery of each other and the attention received by the case of the forty-three.

When I visited Lucía in Mexico City in 2016, she explained that Solecito also started seriously considering searching for graves on their own only after the Ayotzinapa case in 2014. As was the case for the mothers and fathers of the forty-three students, the discovery of the mass grave in Colinas de Santa Fe failed to bring Lucía closure, as she did not ultimately find evidence that the remains of her son were there. Their efforts instead opened up an impressive grassroots mobilization that set forth searches in the surrounding countryside. The efforts of Solecito were also widely publicized and inspired other groups in Veracruz to begin searching in their own areas.

"They Took Them Alive, We Want Them Alive!"

The unearthing of mass graves and the forensic work to try to identify the disappeared have been important for bringing disappearances to public attention. The literature on this subject underscores the healing and restorative effects that exhuming unmarked graves can have on family members, providing them with some closure when they find the bodies of loved ones. Many see the practice of exhuming graves and potentially identifying bodies as an act of resistance against the erasure of memory and the denial of the disappeared.[23] And especially in deeply Catholic areas of Mexico, it is also culturally significant for the physical body to be present in the mourning process.[24]

However, the excavation of graves is also a contentious issue among activists and relatives of the disappeared. Some activist groups adhere to a principle that the search be conducted "under the presumption of life," that is, with the expectation that their loved ones are alive. This is partly a practical consideration as searchers look for information in jails, in hospitals, among the homeless, within sex trafficking circuits, and in mental health institutions. Prioritizing the living helps guide search priorities, making locating someone in the above situations more urgent than if they were deceased.

The presumption of life also advances an ethical and political commitment. As María Elena Herrera stated, "We always speak in the present tense about the disappeared. That's how we honor their existence."[25] Many people echo this sentiment, aligning politically with the popular slogan, *"Vivxs los llevaron, vivxs los queremos!"* ("They took them alive, we want them alive!"). This phrase became widely recognized in Mexico following the forced disappearance of the forty-three students from Ayotzinapa (figure 8). And it was also central among the mothers of the disappeared during the military dictatorships of the 1970s and 1980s, particularly in countries like Argentina and Chile.

The political significance of the presumption of life lies in the understanding that, in the context of disappearances, a person is deemed alive until proven otherwise. This presumption not only puts the onus on authorities to investigate and ascertain the fate of the missing person, but also ensures that their rights and welfare are safeguarded until their status is confirmed.

Melissa Wright analyzes the historical emergence of this perspective, arguing that the presumption of life is a response to the government's denial of these disappearances. The slogan, "They took them alive, we want them alive!" confronts this denial, asserting their existence and demanding accountability from the state. It

FIGURE 8. *"Vivos los llevaron, vivos los queremos"* ("They took them alive, we want them alive"). Graffiti in San Cristobal de las Casas, Chiapas. Photo by author.

embodies the activists' resolution to challenge the prevalent denial of disappearance and demand justice.[26]

The presumption of life does not inherently prevent the search for the bodies of the disappeared in graves, but some activists and relatives committed to it oppose the practice. This creates tensions among some search collectives seeking to unearth hidden burial sites, sometimes without legal or forensic assistance. Opposition to exhumation is multifaceted, ranging from concerns about preserving the dignity of the victims and ensuring a clear chain of custody for the remains, to concerns about the lack of resources for identification and the inability to contribute to legal proceedings. As a result, some groups advocate for justice through established institutional channels, endorsing excavations only when done lawfully and using proper scientific methods.

These controversies are not exclusive to Mexico. The Mothers of Plaza de Mayo in Argentina notably split into two factions during the 1980s due to disagreements on how to approach unmarked burials. Both factions, the Mothers of Plaza de Mayo Founding Line and the Mothers of Plaza de Mayo Association, aimed to uncover the truth and seek justice for their disappeared children, but their methodologies and political ideologies differed. The faction led by Hebe de Bonafini within the Mothers of Plaza de Mayo Association resisted exhumations as well as the payment of compensation by the government. They believed that the traumas of disappearance needed to remain in public consciousness to prevent national amnesia and argued that mourning could weaken activist solidarity, leading to a reconciliatory stance towards the state. Hebe de Bonafini encapsulated this stance by stating, "What are you going to protest when you accept the exhumations and the indemnification? In no way whatsoever, I don't want a dead body. What I want is the murderer!"[27]

Kamari Clarke's observations in Colombia echo this sentiment, where public mobilizations against violence and disappearances challenge a social order that lacks accountability.[28] Clarke notes that these forms of "unforgiveness" are affective displays, manifesting in widespread memorializations aimed to counter the state's inaction, refusing to transition to "business as usual" without the return of the disappeared. The demand "They took them alive, we want them alive!" aligns with De Bonafini's position and Clarke's findings, underscoring an irreconcilable stance and a rejection of conventional justice systems that do not fully acknowledge the victims' suffering, thereby demanding a re-narration of their experiences beyond the state's formal mechanisms.

In contrast, as discussed in the previous chapter, some Mexican collectives have stated their intention not to pursue the murderers but to seek answers enabling them to locate their loved ones' remains. Among the myriad issues arising from the exhumation of mass graves, the primary concern for groups like Solecito has been the proper management of the remains. Confronted with a severe lack of resources for identification, they grapple with whether to use their findings to bring closure to families or to leverage them in the pursuit of justice.

Even with a Body, "There Is No Crime . . ."

As in the case of the families of the forty-three and many other search collectives, for Lucía and her companions finding the mass grave in Colinas de Santa Fe was not the end of their searches but just the beginning of a new phase of struggle. By 2022, Solecito had helped exhume 374 bodies in Colinas de Santa Fe and another site nearby called Arbolillo in Alvarado. But only thirty-five of these remains have been identified.

In most cases where unmarked graves are discovered, families struggle to have the bodies identified. Search collectives estimate that only 1 percent of the remains found in clandestine graves have been identified. There are a variety of reasons for this. First, the state agencies that are responsible for processing and identifying bodies are severely underfunded. In Veracruz, for example, until only recently the chief of the forensic laboratory had to handwrite the names of the thousands of individuals who have turned in their own DNA trying to match remains in their repository. The records have not been digitalized, and as a result, the DNA samples cannot be searched and matched.[29]

It is also technically challenging to make accurate identifications when remains are compromised or mistakes are made during
their unearthing that result in damage to the samples. This has
been a problem at several sites in Veracruz. In one site, 18,680 bone
fragments were found but only two people have been identified.[30]
In yet other cases, remains have not been identified because the
state agencies in charge have not been able to process the identification requests. This problem goes beyond Veracruz. In other
states, family members have reported that district attorney's
offices are even losing track of the bodies under their own custody.[31] Therefore, whereas lack of resources and infrastructure certainly contribute to undermine the identification efforts by officials, activists also emphasize that these impediments are not
always unintended but express a lack of political will to process
identifications.

Even after graves have been discovered and officially registered, the information about them is often then obscured by state
agents. For example, not all of the states in Mexico even admit to
having mass graves. The governments of seven states claim there
are no graves in their territories even though these claims are
refuted by the federal Attorney's General Office. Furthermore,
each state consistently underreports the number of found graves.[32]

In investigating these graves, journalists also come up against
an elaborate quagmire of vocabulary that each district attorney's
office uses to designate places where bodies have been discovered
and removed. For example, Veracruz's district attorney's office
refers to a hole with charred bone remains as a "burial pit." They
also call it a "body destruction center." In contrast, the state of
Coahuila's DA office refers to sites where metal drums are used
to burn people and where remains were found as "clandestine

inhumation sites."[33] Because of this inconsistency and the use of euphemisms, it is difficult to accurately innumerate the scope of identified clandestine graves. And yet these are only some of the threads of secrecy woven around these graves. Their locations and even the fact that they exist at all is obscured by bureaucratic processes.

One of the most blatant and shocking instances of state obstruction came to media attention in 2016 when it was discovered that in the states of Guerrero and neighboring Morelos, state officials literally *reburied* remains found in clandestine graves in new secret graves under state orders. These reburials took place before most of the remains could be identified or their cases investigated.[34]

Public Secrets

Despite the layers of secrecy and obfuscation I have just described, local people often know of the existence of hidden graves nearby. In fact, it is usually this local knowledge that brings these graves to light.

For example, while clandestine graves are assumed to be hidden in solitary and remote places, the *"A dónde van los desaparecidos"* report has shown that this is not always the case. Graves are often uncovered in busy areas and sometimes in central urban locations. In the spring of 2011, for instance, a couple who lived in the city center of Durango, the capital of the state of Durango, was woken up by noises made by soldiers entering the property. The soldiers excavated the patio and found twelve bodies directly beneath their home. They had apparently been buried there before the couple moved in.[35]

While in this case the couple living on the property allegedly had no idea of what was hidden beneath them, in other cases the locations of graves are locally known, or at least suspected. Tips from local people are often the sources by which clandestine graves are found. These tips are often received by collectives of family members and ordinary citizens rather than the police. In one of our conversations, Araceli described the first tip she received in her role as the leader of the Orizaba search collective. It was a phone call from a local farmer. The farmer had noticed a strange indentation in one of his fields and suspected something was underneath, especially after he saw Araceli and other mothers protesting the disappearance of young people in the main square of Orizaba. Suspecting there might be bodies buried in his field, he decided to call Araceli. His suspicion was correct and the tip led to the discovery of a grave.

In many cases, the tips come from anonymous sources. For example, a collective of families in the Sinaloan city of Los Mochis estimates that a third of their search efforts are in response to tips from unknown sources, many of which lead to discoveries. Other collectives report similar numbers of anonymous tips, many of which lead to discoveries.[36]

The crucial role of anonymous sources as a tool used by collectives in their searches underscores the importance of informal networks as conduits of sensitive information. The extent to which this information emanates from drug trafficking organizations or networks associated with them is generally unknown or at least unverifiable. In the case of Solecito, the map and additional information given to the mothers was signed by the Jalisco New Generation Cartel (CJNG). Lucía described the look of the pickup truck and of the men that distributed the fliers as consistent with the cartel's aesthetics. Certainly, the kind of information conveyed in these tips—such as the exact coordinates of a mass grave—indicates a level of insider knowledge.

The dissemination of this information also demonstrates that these graves are not as secret as they may seem. Even local residents without any specific insider knowledge can observe unusual vehicular activity during the night. Such activities become particularly conspicuous when they take place in areas with no clear purpose as a destination. Common indicators of such sites can include frequent appearances of expensive vehicles or noticeable disturbances in the soil. In numerous instances, graves associated with illegal activities have been discovered in areas that locals have suspected could harbor graves for years.

As we have seen, the drug economy is dependent on the complicity and often direct involvement of those very actors from whom this knowledge is meant to be kept secret: the police, government officials, and the military. And the involvement of these state actors is also supposed to be secret to the public. But this knowledge constitutes what anthropologist Michael Taussig calls "public secrets"—that is, secrets that include a public awareness of some of their elements and that therefore are not secret in the strict sense.[37]

This contradictory oscillation between revealing and concealing communal graves reflects a larger dynamic whereby elements of organized crime fluctuate between flaunting their violence—demonstrated by the gruesome display of victims in public places—and concealing it by hiding the evidence of their murders. According to Angelica Durán-Martínez, this behavior varies depending on the interactions between the government and factions of organized crime. Durán-Martínez argues that violence becomes visible and frequent when trafficking organizations compete for territory and the state security apparatus is fragmented. By contrast, violence becomes less visible and less frequent when the criminal market is monopolized and the state security apparatus is cohesive, either at the federal or state level.[38]

For instance, consider again the events that unfolded in Veracruz on Mother's Day 2016. Solecito received the tip about the location of the Colinas de Santa Fe mass grave from the CJNG, possibly driven by their ongoing territorial dispute at the time with their rival cartel, Los Zetas. Solecito has asserted that the government of Veracruz was closely aligned with Los Zetas. This means it is plausible that the CJNG's decision to disclose the mass grave's location was an attempt to undermine a government aligned with their competitor.

Recent violence near Santa Ana, one of the villages in northern Mexico where I have done long-term fieldwork and where my friend Octavio disappeared from, also illustrates the dynamics of visibility and invisibility that operate when trafficking organizations compete for territory. And the events that have transpired there over the last year provide a useful comparison for understanding why some acts of violence are sometimes made more visible than others.

"Safer to Stay Disappeared"

As I mentioned in the introduction, the area in northern Mexico that I have visited over many years has become a battleground between rival factions of the Sinaloa Cartel. The sons of Joaquín "El Chapo" Guzmán, collectively known as Los Chapitos or La Chapiza, have been fighting their father's former ally Ismael "El Mayo" Zambada García, who is affiliated with Los Rusos.[39]

The effect of this turf war has been devastating. Friends described local stores shuttered at 3 p.m. and roads shut down with confiscations of weapons, drugs, and vehicles, as well as *levantones* ("disappearances") and shootings occurring daily in the area. Amid this violence, individuals working for Los Rusos were either murdered, disappeared, or given the option to switch alliances under amnesty.

Because of the competition between these factions and the lack of state intervention there was little effort among either party to hide evidence of their murders. In the fall of 2022, an incident in a *colonia* about twenty minutes from Santa Ana became, for many locals, emblematic of the stakes of the territorial conflict. A man drove through town playing a song called "Soy el Ratón," a famous *narco-corrido* celebrating Ovidio Gúzman, one of El Chapo's sons. Before the schism between the factions, this would not have been an uncommon occurrence. After all, there are hundreds of *narco-corridos* about El Chapo himself as he is considered to have been one of the most powerful drug traffickers in the world. But knowingly or not, the man in the car was declaring a dangerous allegiance in an area now under threat of takeover by El Chapo's sons. And indeed, when the car came to a stop at the central intersection in the *colonia,* a young man emerged from the adjacent OXXO parking lot and shot the driver in the head. By all accounts, the killer was a foot soldier of Los Rusos reasserting territorial control against the musical invasion by Los Chapitos. But there was no attempt at carrying out this assassination under cover, or at hiding the body. To the contrary, the gunman clearly meant for his disciplinary act to be seen as a public warning. This tragedy did indeed serve as a warning, as the news circulated quickly through local communities.[40]

This was the overall context in which my friend Octavio disappeared. But no one knew exactly what happened to him. With Octavio's disappearance weighing on me, I returned to Santa Ana in February 2023 when it seemed safe enough to visit. While Octavio had been gone for many months by then, it was my first time back to the area and seeing his family in person since his disappearance. Upon my arrival, I learned that another local man, Rico, had also disappeared. No one had said anything about this to me before. And the first few people who mentioned it to me did so uncertainly and were hesitant to provide details.

While Rico was not a close friend, he was a fixture in the community. That's why I was puzzled that I was hearing about this for the first time. There had been no online announcements or media campaigns as when Octavio disappeared. However, the absence of a public campaign wasn't entirely unusual. As I've mentioned before, many families opt not to report disappearances, sometimes due to fear of retribution, other times because the associated stigma leads families to closely guard the disappearance as a secret. But I was particularly confused by Rico's disappearance because I was sure I had interacted with him in the last few months on social media—I made a mental note to go back over our communications.

Eventually, people opened up about what had happened the day that Rico was taken. I heard variations from a dozen different people but it was Elsa, my closest confidant, who supplied the most detailed version of events. Rico's troubles had started when his brother, Enrique, broke the rules: he was dealing drugs without seeking permission from Los Rusos or making the requisite payments. "When you start dealing, you have to ask permission, pay a plaza fee, and distribute their drugs," she explained. Enrique didn't do any of that and had been selling on his own. In short, he'd disrespected Los Rusos' territory.

And so it was not entirely a surprise to anyone, at least in retrospect, when the convoy of trucks arrived in Santa Ana looking for Enrique. However, he was not there, as he had fled after receiving a tip-off from a friend. When the men discovered that Enrique had escaped, they began looking for his family members. Enrique's mother, a respected woman in her sixties, was their first target. They seized her by her hair, parading her out onto the dirt road. A group of children aged between three to six followed her, sobbing, clutching at her clothes, and hugging her knees. From inside their own house right across the road, Isaac and Elsa could hear the screams and cries. In an effort to protect her own children and family, Elsa shepherded everyone under the bed in her room. Only Elsa and Isaac remained out in the open, anticipating their home might be next, but thankfully, they were not targeted at that time.

Because of the crying children, the men eventually released Enrique's mother (a decision to which I'll return to say more). Instead, they took Enrique's brother, Rico. He was dragged into the desert and subjected to brutal torture as the men tried to extract information about Enrique's whereabouts. Rico didn't know where his brother was, but they beat him mercilessly, pulled out his teeth, and left him for dead in the desert. Miraculously, he survived. Hours later, Rico staggered back into the village, naked and battered, having managed to squirm out of his restraints.

There were still questions around Rico's survival. Did they mean to kill him? Or just scare everyone in the village? They didn't try to bury him or get rid of the evidence. They just dumped him out in the desert. For all these reasons, and a general sense of uncertainty, Rico left Santa Ana. Would they bother coming back for him if they found out he'd survived? Probably not, but reportedly Rico thought it wasn't worth finding out. The uncertainty of whether they had meant to kill him led Rico to flee and "disappear" just in case they might come back for him. He seemed less invested in maintaining this story to me at least. When I texted him later with a hopeful hello, he responded warmly in his usual fashion, sending blessings to my family. He has, since then, quietly returned to Santa Ana.

Rico's simulated disappearance reminded me of stories and rumors I'd heard in other parts of Mexico. Friends and relatives of the disappeared would sometimes report seeing glimpses of their absent loved ones in cars, or flashes of them in crowds or on buses. One man told me he was sure he'd seen his disappeared cousin in a crowd but when he called his name, the man had looked at him with no recognition in his eyes, only to turn and disappear again into the masses. That man's theory was that his cousin had been forced into labor for a drug trafficking organization. And these kinds of accounts seem to reflect a more general, uncanny sense that the disappeared could be out there living another life, not of their own choosing, a suspicion held by many family members. It is, in fact, fears about these alternate lives of potential abuse or suffering that make the recovery and identification of remains a comfort for some families.

Rico's ordeal and the recent conflicts in Santa Ana underscore that the visibility of violence goes beyond a simple dichotomy of displaying and concealing it. Elsa described Los Rusos's latest methods as "lazy," discarding bodies that hold no value to them without any particular intent to display the victims. In her perspective, their treatment of victims not only reflected the impunity they enjoyed in the area but also a general sense of indifference. This indifference also highlights that despite well over a decade of truly staggering revelations and discoveries of mass graves all over the country, not much progress has been made with either identifications or prosecutions. This is something that Lucia's group, Solecito, discovered firsthand. Members of the group at times resorted to panhandling for money on the street to help fund their identification requests. Similarly, of the forty-three students disappeared in Iguala in 2014 only three remains have been identified.[41] "Without a body," the saying goes, "there is no crime." But in Mexico, as we have seen, even when a body is found, the state often does not acknowledge the crime.

.   .   .

In this chapter, I have explored how the discovery of clandestine graves has been a crucial dimension of human rights activism in Mexico. While harrowing, these indications of widespread violence and impunity also potentially allow long-awaited closure for many families.

The uncovering of these graves also encapsulates a central tension in the processes that variably make violence visible in Mexico. When collectives and activists reveal hidden burial grounds, they make visible evidence of crimes that have been deliberately concealed by state and criminal organizations, even if as we have seen, these unearthings create controversies and debates. Furthermore, sometimes making violence visible on the part of the cartels, through the revelations of graves or the display of the bodies of victims in public spaces, is as much about asserting territorial control and spreading fear as it is about helping victims' families find justice or answers. For many there are risks involved in revealing evidence of disappearances; as we saw in the case of Rico, there are also sometimes reasons to hide evidence of a *reappearance,* times when making one's presence and survival known could re-endanger oneself or one's family.

The uncovering of mass graves is historic and powerful because of the ways that these revelations provide families with evidence of disappearances with which to push back against the state ideology of negation and its practice of obfuscation. But as I have emphasized in this chapter, the state's reactions to these discoveries have shown that clandestine graves are not just buried underground. The identities of the victims are obscured by the refusal of officials to help find these graves in the first place and also to process the evidence when it is found. Human remains are made doubly secret in that they are first hidden by the murderers and subsequently, when they are discovered, hidden by the government. Despite these multiple efforts at burying the disappeared, the efforts of the search collectives have overcome these recursive acts of negation. In this way, the discovery of mass graves by search collectives unravels the very concept of the disappeared because at least some of the missing reappear—even if not in the living form that their loved ones had hoped for.

Conclusions

Desert Colors

In February 2023, I walked through part of the Sonoran Desert in
northern Mexico in the company of some of Octavio's relatives. We
were led by the intuition of Octavio's cousin, Elsa, who had a suspicion that his remains might lie there. The region is among the
most barren of the Sonoran expanse, with only sparse shrubs
twisted down by the wind and relentless sun. In February the
desert stretches out in the same brownish hue. Elsa scoured the
horizon with her gaze and looked for flashes of blue, the color of
the shirt Octavio wore the day he disappeared.

I had walked stretches of this desert many times as a graduate
student when I first lived in Santa Ana almost two decades earlier.
In fact, I remember tracing these steps with Octavio's grandmother, now deceased. We would scan the horizon looking for yellow, the color of the *biznaga* edible flower she would use for its
sweet pulp. I was glad Octavio's grandmother wasn't with us now,
looking for the blue of his shirt instead of the yellow of flowers.

Only in recent months had Elsa grown more suspicious that
Octavio's body might be in this part of the desert. The troubling
events surrounding Rico's failed disappearance and the pursuit of
his brother Enrique had altered Elsa's perspective on what might

have happened to Octavio. Up to that point, Elsa and Octavio's aunt had focused their search on potential communal graves closer to Mexicali, where a collective of families had unearthed other remains. They had also devoted significant time to investigating an area about fifteen miles away, following an anonymous tip that Octavio's body had been discarded there, which proved to be a false lead.

It was the indifference with which Rico had been abandoned in the desert after he was tortured and left for dead that led Elsa to contemplate searching closer to home. "You don't need to dig in the ground to find evidence of their crimes around these villages," she said. Armed with this insight, in late 2022, Elsa and her children began regularly combing the vast expanse of desert closer to their home. They moved methodically, much as we did that day, searching for traces of Octavio in and around the area where Rico had been left.

On that gray February day, we aimed for that same area, stretching far into the desert's expanse. Elsa carried a walking stick, which she used to part the shrubs and examine anything that seemed out of place. Elsa explained that she wouldn't dig in the ground herself, a practice that some worried would potentially damage evidence. She didn't think it would be necessary if she found Octavio, because she didn't think they would have buried him. But she also specified this because she was a little defensive about searching the desert ground at all.

Her defensiveness was rooted in disagreements in the family over the search for Octavio's remains, which mirrored the broader divisions and tensions I discussed earlier among collectives. For example, Octavio's mother supported searching for him alive, but she opposed seeking potential graves. Her reluctance wasn't political but emotional; she couldn't bear the thought of Octavio's death. In fact, a few months after his disappearance, a body has been discovered near Mexicali. However, Octavio's mother refused to provide the DNA that would allow the police to confirm its identity. Eventually, Elsa and Octavio's aunts persuaded Octavio's estranged father to provide a sample for DNA testing. The test came back negative; the body wasn't Octavio's. Other family members objected to searching the ground for different reasons. As Octavio's uncle warned: "The most likely outcome is that they will find some other family's relative and end up losing those remains to the abyss of the forensic bureaucracy." He was referring to the stories of recovered remains getting lost or rehidden by the state in other parts of Mexico. However, Elsa's method of traversing the desert didn't involve the tools usually used to penetrate the earth, such as shovels or rods. She was convinced that Octavio would have been discarded there with the same disregard as Rico and the other bodies found in this region.

We had a specific destination in mind that day: the spot where Rico had been abandoned by the men from Los Rusos in the vast, arid expanse near Santa Ana. As we walked, I was distracted by the realization that this place was disturbingly close to the mostly deserted former *campo* where I had stayed during my more recent visits to Santa Ana—and was staying now.[1] I liked this place because of its proximity to Santa Ana via the desert stretch that had grown familiar to me during my visits and because it was removed from the constant social pressures of the village. My acquaintance with the caretaker also made me feel safe there, despite the remoteness of the location. The spot Elsa led us to, a tree beside a rock, was equidistant from the village and the camp. "Why didn't you tell me all this was going on right here, before I rented again in the *campo*?"

I asked. She waved away my worry with her hand. "That was months ago," she said. "Things have calmed down now." With Enrique gone and Octavio absent, she didn't believe anyone in the village would dare to "break the rules" again and provoke the cartel factions fighting for control of territory in the region.

To clarify her point, she began explaining the logic behind the targets chosen by the cartel factions. She recounted how Enrique had been caught after he replaced a transmitter up in the mountains, one which Los Rusos had set up to monitor the military's communications, for another transmitter for its rival faction, Los Chapitos. When Los Rusos discovered this, they began looking for him. However, they didn't target him merely for the transmitter switch. They wanted him dead for serving two organizations at the same time. "And you know how much they paid him for that task? One hundred dollars. That's how much money he made to risk his life and that of his family," Elsa told me. And while Elsa didn't know the specific circumstances under which Octavio was taken, she suspected something similar had happened to him because Octavio had confided in her that he was considering a counteroffer from Los Chapitos. Elsa was fairly certain that he decided to take it and keep working for Los Rusos as well.

"So you understand, they are *niños pendejos* ["foolish children"] who don't know that *no puedes comer sopa donde lo scupas* ["you don't shit where you eat"]. If you do," she said, "they are going to screw you because in this *valle* everyone finds out about everything that you do and this is what happened to Enrique and Octavio and they didn't see the consequences coming." She concluded her commentary by referring to my concern that the place where I was staying was nearby: "So it doesn't matter where you stay, they're not interested in you." Her dismissal of my safety concerns was a reassurance I'd heard repeatedly when visiting this place: that as a *gringa,* the cartels were not interested in me.

While I understood the point Elsa was making, I felt uneasy with the familiar logic that seemed to suggest that the disappeared had somehow brought it upon themselves. To be fair, Elsa wasn't saying that they "got what they deserved." She was only stating that the disappearances of Octavio and Enrique (if not Rico) resulted from specific sets of circumstances that, at least in these instances, might have been avoidable. However, after meeting people elsewhere in Mexico whose loved ones had vanished under various conditions, and witnessing how their tragedies had been dismissed by this very logic, I found it difficult to accept a rationale that even subtly assigned fault to those directly impacted.

Elsa herself had nearly been *levantada* ("picked up") during the worst of the violence in the region when she was mistaken for someone else at an OXXO in a nearby *colonia.* She was shoved into a car and, according to her, was released only because of the great fortuity that she knew one of the people in the car, who recognized her. They had worked together in a fishing collective many years ago before going their separate ways, and the man had started working for Los Rusos while she got a government job in a human resources department. After taking her phone and reviewing all her communications to verify that she was not, in fact, who they were looking for, they gave her the benefit of the doubt and released her with apologies. Elsa had told me this story a few days prior. I reminded her now that even she, a respectable middle-aged mom with a good government job could get swept up in the violence, and that she had been saved only by that unlikely and incidental personal connection.

But it was clear by this point in our conversation that Elsa was not really interested in questions of blame. Her comment about the rationale that cartels use to choose their targets was mostly an attempt to make me feel safe. To Elsa, the issue of "guilt" or "innocence" was a concern only for politicians, academics, and those seeking resources from defensive government agents. With her walking stick, her family, and her jugs of water, out here in the desert, it wasn't particularly relevant whom Octavio had been working for when he disappeared.

As we took a moment to rest near where Rico had been beat up and abandoned, having arrived at our destination with no sign of Octavio, I thought back over everything my friends in Santa Ana had experienced over the time since my last visit. What struck me most was Elsa's recounting of moments where human compassion was evident amid the turmoil: when her would-be abductors apologized for their mistake; or when the men who had dragged Enrique's mother into the road let her go, moved by the tears of the children. These glimpses of empathy among the "narcos" were not unique to Elsa's experience. I heard similar stories elsewhere in Mexico. This recurring theme, which contrasted so starkly with portrayals of state actors as cold and indifferent to people's suffering, hinted at a complexity that requires more consideration.

"Narcos Have Mothers Too"

When Elsa initially described how Enrique's mother was freed by the men who had seized her, attributing this mercy to the sight of the children weeping and clamoring at her feet, it seemed far-fetched to me. These same men had proceeded to strip Rico of his clothes and brutally extract his teeth one by one. They then left him to die in the desert. This was all the more striking because Rico is an extraordinarily gentle man. He's calm, rotund, and perpetually maintains a kind expression. While his demeanor may not evoke the same level of sympathy as a cluster of crying toddlers, the notion that those brutal men were capable of being swayed by their empathy for the children seemed implausible. And yet over and over again as people recounted the events of that day, they would supply this detail to explain how it was that Enrique's mother had been released by the same men.

This narrative reminded me of some collectives' attempts to form alliances with or solicit help from drug trafficking organizations, believing that these organizations might, despite their involvement in disappearances, feel some empathy for the victims' families. It also made me think of the conversation I had had with Lucía in 2016 when the Solecito collective discovered the grave in Colinas de Santa Fe with the tip from the CJNG. Lucía had pointed out that in giving them the tip that led them to their only breakthrough, "the cartel provided more help than the government." At the time, this had raised the question, in my mind at least, of why the cartels would want the family members to find mass graves. As I mentioned before, my own assumption had been that the CJNG wanted to undermine the government of Veracruz because it had alliances with their rival cartel. Lucía had a different but not incompatible interpretation. When I asked her why she thought the CJNG wanted the mothers to find the grave, she began by telling a story about one of the other mothers in Solecito. This woman's son had disappeared and a few months afterwards, a young man came to her and delivered the news that her missing son was indeed dead, as she had feared. He knew, he confessed, because he had been assigned the task of burying him. He told the mother that they had both been working for the cartel and had become friends. But the people he was working for killed her son when he discovered information that he was not supposed to know. The man said, "'Look, they're gonna kill me too and I want you to know . . . I want you to find your son." He described the road and the tree under which he had buried the body. He said, "They made me do it because I was his friend." Lucía paused and then suggested: "In this case, you have a friend of the victim who was interested in people, especially the mother, finding out what happened." The story also indicated how hierarchies within the cartel shaped different levels of involvement in murders. This woman's son and the man who buried him were both "narcos," according to the woman, but it was clear they had a low status in the cartel. The fact that drug bosses made the young man bury his friend, perhaps as a warning or perhaps as a lesson, also indicates the everyday tactics of discipline and terror and perhaps even victimization that low-level narcos are subjected to. More notably, in concluding her story, Lucía said, "They have mothers too. Even the narcos have mothers."

This observation is perhaps self-evident in outlining that narco-traffickers are humans beings after all, but it also makes a powerful political statement about the insensibility of police officers and government officials who, in their disregard for the fate of the disappeared and of the anguish of their parents, seem not to have mothers after all. Since the message in the media and state narratives has always been that it is drug trafficking organizations that are responsible for the deaths and disappearances in Mexico, because of their intrinsic brutality, it was striking for Lucía to basically make a case for the inherent humanity of "narcos" in the midst of her own search for her missing son, who was himself likely taken by members of a cartel. Her story about the young man helping her friend find the remains of her son was as much about the government's disregard as it was about drug trafficking organizations. Further, it underscores how negative, frustrating, and disappointing the interactions of Lucía and other members of Solecito with government officials have been. The implication was that while those working for the cartels may be responsible for violent and destructive actions, at least they will actually help family members on occasion to find the remains of their loved ones and therefore find answers and some sense of closure.

I tried to clarify this interpretation with Lucía by commenting that "government officials have mothers too." She conceded, "They do have mothers." But then she came to the point: "Why does a criminal act more humanely than the authorities? The authorities don't see us as worth their time or effort. We are just votes walking around. And that's all they want from us, our vote. And after the voting is over, that's it, you're on your own."

How is it possible that a grieving mother who has lost her son, by all accounts, to "drug related" violence would see government officials as less sympathetic to them than known drug traffickers? While it should be clear by now that there is a good deal of complicity between criminal organizations and the state, the fact that, as a whole, Lucía perceived officials as acting less humanely than the direct perpetrators of disappearances warrants further reflection.

It may seem, on the surface, that Lucía's relative empathy for "criminals" aligns with a long history of the romanticization of drug trafficking in Mexico. This is aptly attested to in expressions of narco popular culture such as *narco-corridos,* which celebrate the lives of drug traffickers, or the *telenovelas* and niche fashion trends that imitate the style of famous *capos* (cartel leaders). Scholars have argued that this "narco culture" draws from a long legacy of "charismatic criminality" in Mexico, linked to the heroes of the Mexican Revolution.[2] *Narco-corridos,* such as the song "Soy el Ratón" I mentioned before, are a good example of this because traditional *corridos* documented and celebrated the lives of heroes of the revolution. In northern Mexico, Robin Hood tales celebrating cartel elites are a standard feature of local oral histories. Stories of churches built with donations from generous narco-benefactors or of drinking water infrastructure created or improved through narco funds are commonplace. Drug traffickers, in short, are often perceived as being "of the people" and even as protectors of the poor.[3]

Scholars of narco-culture have pointed out that the respect and admiration people express for narco-culture is often correlated to social class, with working-class people as the primary consumers and admirers of narco-culture. Lucía is a highly educated, economically mobile woman in her fifties who neither fits the profile nor generally espouses the view that drug traffickers are modern Robin Hoods. But like other families of the disappeared Lucía held the view that they would more likely receive support from "narcos" than officials.

This is why some families have increasingly sought help from criminal groups to find their missing loved ones. In 2018, after two police officers were kidnapped in Culiacán, Sinaloa, their families addressed a letter to the Sinaloa Cartel, pleading for information and for their return. Similarly, in May 2020, a mother publicly appealed to the CJNG's leader, El Mencho, for information about her four sons who disappeared in Ocotlán, Jalisco, in December 2019. Many of these pleas contain positive portrayals of the cartels, with phrases such as "we appeal to your great hearts" and "I know that you are good," accentuating their humanity and reflecting a belief that drug traffickers might assist them.

In June 2023, in one of the highest-profile appeals of this sort, Delia Quiroga, a spokesperson for the Colectivo 10 de Marzo and member of the Madres Buscadoras de Sonora, publicly called for a "pact for peace" with the leaders of Mexico's top ten criminal groups to reduce violence. The proposal asks for three basic commitments: respect for dignified burial; respect for the life and freedom of movement of victims' mothers, relatives, and collectives during the search for their loved ones; and a ceasefire in armed conflicts unless in legitimate self-defense. President López Obrador expressed his support for the initiative, which brought the issue of negotiating with criminals to reduce violence into public discussion.

But as we have seen, for Lucía and others, this tactical and affective opening toward members of the cartels is a product of their antipathy towards government officials. Much of Lucia's individual experience as well as that of Araceli in Orizaba was shaped by her interactions with one official in particular, the former governor of Veracruz, Duarte, who has left a lasting impact on the way they perceive the state.

"It Wasn't the Narcos, It Was the State"

By pure coincidence, or "God's will" as she saw it, Araceli went to Guatemala just days after the then former-Governor Javier Duarte was captured there. She had been invited, along with other women from collectives in Mexico, to participate in a forensic workshop about the search for the disappeared as part of the Third International Forum for the Application of Forensic Sciences. When Araceli learned of Duarte's arrest and imprisonment, she felt that the timing was meant to be. "We ask God a lot, 'Why me? Why did this happen to my child?' But this showed me that sometimes *los tiempos de Dios son perfectos* ["God's timing is perfect"]. I went to protest at the jail with another mother." Araceli said, "When I heard that he was in jail I said, *'Lo que es la vida'* ['Life gives you surprises']." As if talking to Duarte, she said: "You laughed at me once but today I can be here once again demanding to know what happened to our children. And now you can't make fun of me, because you are in jail and I'm on the outside raising my voice for my daughter."

Following his arrest in Guatemala and extradition to Mexico regarding the investigation into his embezzlement of millions of US dollars in public money in 2018, Duarte pleaded guilty to criminal association and money laundering. He was sentenced to nine years in prison.[4] While Lucía, Araceli, and other women and collectives from across Veracruz were relieved and somewhat vindicated by Duarte's initial arrest, the charges and the sentence did not match the crimes they knew him to be responsible for. Lucía and her collective Solecito in Xalapa, Veracruz, decided they would not stop until Duarte's involvement in the disappearances of their family members was investigated. They prepared a criminal complaint demanding investigation into his involvement in the thousands of disappearances that took place in Veracruz during his governorship.[5] Finally an investigation was opened after Duarte's successor, PAN candidate Miguel Angel Yunes Linares, won the governorship on a campaign promise to establish a truth commission to investigate the forced disappearances during the Duarte administration as well as the prosecution of public officials responsible for criminal acts.[6]

In February 2018, Veracruz State Attorney General Jorge Winckler Ortíz opened an official investigation into 202 forced disappearances committed by state-level security officials during Duarte's administration.[7] This resulted in nineteen apprehension orders for former public security officials for their alleged participation in fifteen forced disappearance incidents, totaling 202 victims, that occurred in 2013.[8] The investigation was aided significantly by evidence provided by Lucía and her collective. As the investigation continued, State Attorney General Winckler Ortíz began to uncover information that incriminated not only public security officials but also former-Governor Duarte himself, including recordings of him during his administration discussing the "problem" of nineteen bodies dumped in front of a police station in El Lencero, Veracruz.[9] On June 6, 2018, the Attorney's General Office of Veracruz filed a new set of charges arguing that Duarte had "some degree of responsibility in various disappearances that occurred in the state."[10] In November 2022, Duarte was charged with forced disappearance, though that case has not moved forward given ongoing stays *(amparos)* submitted by his legal team.

Despite these steps forward, Lucía continuously expressed frustration with the State Attorney General's progress on the case, and with his slow and uneven response to evidence and tips presented by the collective. Lucía and other members of the collective felt that his team was deliberately obstructing the investigations and specifically excluding some cases that they were requesting be investigated. For example, in 2017 the collective had uncovered the charred remains of several bodies in one site. But Winckler Ortíz repeatedly denied their existence as well as the existence of a property in Tihuatlán, a municipality in the north of the state, which had been discovered to have been used as a clandestine cemetery since 2011. At one point, Lucía said, "He is doing everything in his power to be an obstacle for us." What became clear to her was that while Attorney General Winckler Ortíz's willingness to go after corrupt officials was historic, he was interested in pursuing only his political enemies.[11]

Therefore, Lucía was not surprised when in September 2019 President López Obrador announced that two warrants of arrest had been issued for Winckler Ortíz on charges of kidnapping and forced disappearance.[12] The Veracruz attorney general was accused of the kidnapping and torture of Francisco Zárate Aviña, a former collaborator of his political rival Luis Ángel Bravo, also a state prosecutor during the Duarte government. Winckler Ortíz fled and was a fugitive for three years before he was caught and arrested in July 2022. He has filed a number of stays, which has slowed any potential trial that may emerge. As of December 2023, he was being held at the Almoloya de Juárez maximum security prison in Mexico State in pretrial detention.[13]

Governor Duarte's imprisonment and Winckler Ortíz's arrest were moments of reckoning for Veracruz despite receiving little international attention. But several other incidents involving state actors' involvement in human rights violations in Mexico have recently made international headlines, notably General Cienfuegos Zepeda's arrest and release in 2020 and 2021 as discussed in chapter 4. A powerful and long-awaited admission of state involvement in disappearances transpired in September 2022, when the Mexican government announced that an official inquiry had found the 2014 disappearance of the forty-three students from the town of Ayotzinapa to be a "crime of the state" involving every layer of government.[14] As we've seen, the families of the disappeared students, as well as civil society groups and local media outlets, had long accused the Mexican army of playing a significant role in their disappearance. But it was not until August 2022 that the country's former attorney general, Jesús Murillo Karam, who had been accused of covering up the probable massacre of the forty-three students, was charged with forced disappearance, torture, and obstruction of justice. Murillo Karam was the first high-level official to be detained in connection to the Ayotzinapa case. Then, in September 2022, General José Rodríguez Pérez, who was a colonel based in Iguala the night the students were abducted in 2014, was also arrested, along with two other members of the military, for their direct involvement in the torture and murder of six of the students.[15]

As we have seen, the Ayotzinapa case became a powerful rallying cry in Mexico because it soon became clear that these disappearances and assassinations had been ordered by sitting officials and implemented by armed men who were working for both organized crime and state agencies. This made apparent, perhaps for the first time to international onlookers, that state agents are fully embedded with drug trafficking organizations, and that the extreme violence and disappearances of the war of drugs are often generated by the state rather than by nebulous and supposedly nonstate "narco" actors. The recognition of the state's culpability is embodied in what has become an extremely popular rallying cry in Mexico after the incident in Ayotzinapa, *"No fueron los narcos, fue el estado"* ("It wasn't the narcos, it was the state"). This slogan openly challenges the government's recurrent explanation that violence is the result of internal conflict among the cartels and shows how the overuse of the label "narco" misnames and disguises the state-run forces also responsible for the violence.

This marked a notable radicalization relative to the discourse that had been embraced only a couple of years earlier by some members of the 2012 Caravan for Peace, who as we have seen insisted that their missing or dead relatives were not "narcos" and therefore were "innocent." This position, as noted earlier, is premised on the idea that the deaths and disappearances of people who engage in criminal activity are somehow less worthy of public attention and of efforts to search for them. In contrast, the more recent activism refuses to discuss the alleged identity or positionality of the victims and chooses, instead, to name the perpetrators. In other words, this more contemporary political stance problematizes the way government discourses and action take "innocence" as the crucial criterion that disappearances and deaths must meet in order to register them as "grievable" in the public sphere.[16] The slogan *"No fueron los narcos, fue el estado,"* captures the uncanny atmospheres that define Mexico by hailing the state through the same discourse that it has for decades used to dismiss the deaths and disappearances of hundreds and thousands of its citizens.

But while the involvement of the state in violence in Mexico is increasingly recognized, the ramifications of this recognition for those searching for the disappeared remain unclear. This is in part because activists like Lucía and Araceli, for example, have to navigate the involvement of individual politicians and officials, not "the state" as some abstract entity. But what has confirmed the structural, rather than purely individual, character of the state involvement is that when complicit officials are arrested, such as former Governor Duarte, the officials who replace them are often eventually revealed as themselves implicated. Indeed, Jorge Winckler Ortíz had once been quoted saying "Veracruz is an enormous grave," echoing a statement made by activists elsewhere and across Mexico. But in hindsight, his use of the phrase had a different valence as he knew better than most the truth of these words.

Focusing on individual officials is in many ways as frustrating and ineffective as the "kingpin" strategy promoted by the United States DEA, which focused on going after the main *capos*. This strategy destabilized cartel power structures but subsequently generated more violence as the leaders' arrests resulted in temporary power vacuums and criminal groups' splintering as new "kingpins" fought for control of territory and the organizations themselves. Similarly, the strategy of imprisoning high-powered officials charged with corruption, trafficking, or disappearances has also often resulted in those officials being replaced by others who are eventually implicated in similar crimes themselves.

The limitation of both the kingpin and individual state actor strategies reveals, again, a deeply entrenched criminal-political system. In Mexico, as we've seen, the relationships between government actors and criminal organizations have a deep history. This is clear in the history of the PRI's historic arrangements with drug trafficking organizations but also in the ways that many of these arrangements have persisted through the transition of power to subsequent governments under different political parties, such as the PAN (for example in the role of governors as mentioned before).[17] It has been increasingly important for activists in Mexico to focus on government corruption to combat the state's discourse that consistently seeks to shift blame onto the victims. But it is also important to keep in mind that the abuses of power we have seen by the state do not emerge in a vacuum nor is this corruption the outcome of some inherent property of Mexico alone. While this book has focused on how Mexican civilians have confronted the violent legacies of state corruption in their own country, as discussed in chapter 4, it is crucial to emphasize the wider economic processes that have produced this corruption and duly implicate powerful actors outside of Mexico, particularly in the United States.

The violence that Mexicans experience as a result of the war on drugs is part of the same crisis that manifests in different ways in the rich drug-"consuming" countries as well. As I write these conclusions from Canada, I am acutely aware of the impact of these same drug policies here, where currently an average of twenty deaths a day result from people ingesting toxic drugs that are illegal and thus unregulated.[18] The lack of access to a safe supply of drugs combined with punitive drug prohibition policies results in thousands of families left mourning avoidable deaths. I also think of the Mothers against Police Brutality in the United States, whose own grown children are gone under a different set of circumstances—killed by the police or incarcerated for drug related crimes, one of the primary ways that the war on drugs plays out in the United States. Their situations are different from the families in Mexico described in this book, but their losses are generated by the same unwieldy and destructive policies that manifest in different ways across different geographies. And their missing loved ones—either dead, disappeared, or in jail—are just as worthy of justice, regardless of the circumstances or reasons they are gone. Highlighting these commonalities is important for the possibility of solidarity among the victims of the war on drugs through transnational movements and trajectories of resistance.

"Hasta La Madre!"

What does it take to mobilize political opposition when lives are lost to violence? Certainly, one of the central ethical and political problems that relatives of the disappeared originally face is how to have their disappearances and deaths register as injustices in the public sphere in a context where appeals to the police are often dismissed as a result of the missing person's presumed "involvement" in illicit activities.[19] In this book, I have argued that this prerequisite of presumed innocence places significant limitations on activism.

This pressure to foreground the "innocence" of the victims is further constrained by some activists' roles as mothers. Further, the book has shown how a major challenge for the families of the disappeared is how to garner support from the government when officials may well be directly or indirectly responsible. Therefore, the problem on a practical level isn't whether their loved ones are innocent but rather whether the officials are.

In this book, I have focused on case studies and activists from various parts of the country, each with distinct levels of organization and engagement in public forms of activism. Some are well-known and experienced activists whose searches led them through the intricate labyrinths of police and court bureaucracies, forcing them to wait for years for progress on their cases, usually to no avail. Many emerged from the quagmire of state bureaucracies as more politicized activists, choosing to stop waiting for officials to act and taking matters into their own hands. They often undertook the work that detectives and publicly funded forensics experts were supposed to do. These are stories of women who instead of feeling defeated by the endless bureaucracies and the indifference of officials often organized with mothers in similar situations, creating a remarkable outcome: the emergence of a constellation of collectives of *madres buscadoras* ("searching mothers") all over the country (figure 9).

The determination of these collectives to find their loved ones and the ingenuity of their strategies have inspired and empowered the rise of women's activism in the country. While often interconnected, these collectives display diverse tactics and methods, and some prioritize finding their loved ones' remains over pursuing justice against those responsible. Moving away from earlier narratives about the innocence and noninvolvement of their missing

FIGURE 9. *Glorieta de las mujeres que luchan* ("Roundabout of the women who fight"). Anti-monument at the site of a former monument to Columbus, Mexico City. Photo by author.

relatives, many activists and collectives have radicalized their goals, openly naming the state and drug policies as responsible for the horrific levels of violence and disappearances that have plagued Mexico since the declaration of "the war on drugs" in 2006. One of the most remarkable, yet unsettling, outcomes of the collectives' searches has been the discovery of thousands of mass graves across Mexico. While the vast majority of the bodies found in these graves remain unidentified, those activists who did find their loved ones have achieved some closure, as when Leticia emotionally told me, "I found my daughter!" However, the discovery of thousands of remains, accelerating in recent years, has not been accompanied by a significant increase in judicial investigations. This has meant that, despite the overwhelming number of bodies, relatively few court cases have been opened to identify those responsible. In other words, the legal system in Mexico has lagged behind, revealing a troubling mismatch between the discovery of evidence of horrendous crimes and the delivery of justice.

In parallel to the work of collectives, and at the other end of the spectrum, we find those who have also mobilized to find their disappeared loved ones but do so in a more localized and improvised manner, like the people whom I have known for close to two decades in the Sonora desert in the north of Mexico. Without forming collectives, they still search for those who disappeared with the resources they have, often also looking for traces of their loved ones' bodies. And these were also victims, as in the case of my friend Octavio, who may indeed have been "involved" in criminal networks and whose disappearance is no less devastating and unsettling to their friends and families.

In tracing these interconnected stories, this book seeks to contribute to efforts to show how violence in Mexico is experienced by people in their everyday lives and to counter powerful misconceptions about violence in this country. The public narrative has maintained that is "drugs" and "drug trafficking" that are causing the violence in Mexico and there is a general assumption that this violence is endemic there. But it's important to recognize that the drug trade has become so violent in Mexico, and elsewhere, not because of illegal drugs but precisely because drugs are illegal and this creates a very lucrative market fought over by cartels.

It is the illegality of drugs that makes them so profitable and it's the absence of a legal mechanism for managing their distribution that creates so much violence. The "war on drugs" has only escalated this violence while targeting mostly marginalized, racialized, and gendered populations. Of course, this is something that scholars, politicians, and even some law enforcement officers have been saying for years. The failure of the "war on drugs" has led to the rise of antiprohibition sentiments globally, as is clear in the decriminalization or even legalization of at least some drugs in countries like Portugal, Uruguay, Canada, and many parts of the United States.

So how have these drug war policies been sustained despite their obvious failure and the suffering they produce? In this book I have traced some of the complexities of the answer to this question in the context of Mexico. On the one hand, it is because drug-associated violence is as much about neoliberalization and a history of government collusion as it is about drug trafficking per se. As the stories in this book demonstrate, disappearances in Mexico are also due to drug trafficking organizations diversifying into various forms of organized crime, not just drug-related activities. Therefore in Mexico the effects of drug prohibition and the war on drugs have ricocheted over time and space into an increasingly complex and confounding human rights crisis.

But a crucial reason why drug war policies have persisted is because their victims have been dehumanized. This is the dehumanization that leaves so many families hesitant and unwilling to report a disappeared loved one as a result of being shamed by association and frightened by potential retribution. But this network of activists, relatives, and allies has challenged this dehumanization and are *hasta la madre,* as they say, "fed up" with the war on drugs and its associated violence and impunity. The expression *hasta la madre* is a colloquialism used in Mexico not just to refer to being fed-up but more generally to indicate when limits have been surpassed or transgressed. Among activists it has become one of the central rallying cries at drug war protests. Javier Sicilia first used the term in the open letter he wrote after his son's death, and it quickly took on a life of its own. The expression has a very religious connotation in Mexico. The archetype of the mother is potent everywhere but particularly so in Mexican Catholicism, where the image of the mother, like the Virgin of Guadalupe, Mexico's national religious symbol, is revered. To say you're *"hasta la madre,"* in fact, implies that the mother herself has been insulted.

While the phrase invokes frustration, it also harnesses a power. As I have shown here, the social movement emerging to challenge contemporary violence in Mexico, while still fragmented, creates notable forms of empowerment for ordinary people and contributes to changing the debates about the war on drugs and about the Mexican state in general. These efforts also tap into a wave of social organization across the world that is challenging and demanding changes to drug prohibition policies.

People like Araceli and Lucía and other family members of the disappeared have devoted their lives to not just tracking down information on their own children, but also taking to the streets in protest against drug war policies and government collusion. What the experiences of these relatives of the disappeared and other activists show us is that drug-related violence creates more than simply death, disappearances, and grief. Their stories highlight that these experiences generate new perceptions about drug war policies and new affective dispositions: confusion and sometimes shame, yes, but also an emotional hardening that results in anger and resolve. This is the resolve that carried Araceli up the statehouse steps, barely noticing her feet. It is the resolve that led Leticia all over the United States and Mexico in her search and that prompted Lucía's collective to uncover the historic mass grave in Colinas de Santa Fe. It is the righteous anger that makes many of these women say that they decided to organize, to take over their own searches, even to scour the land for clues about their children because they are *hasta la madre* with the impunity and the violence produced by the state: that is, "We aren't going to take it anymore."

Acknowledgments

The process of writing this book was a long and intense journey, and I owe a debt of gratitude to many individuals and institutions who supported me along the way, many of whom I cannot name here. First, I express my immense gratitude to the families and women who shared their deeply personal stories. Their resilience and strength have been the driving force behind this book.

I would like to offer my thanks to colleagues near and far for their encouragement and support. I'm grateful to Josiah Heyman, Matthew Guttman, Les Field, and Alexander Dawson for providing essential guidance and assistance at different stages of this project. My colleagues at the University of British Columbia created an environment conducive to research and reflection: they include Carole Blackburn, Nicky Levell, Patrick Moore, Brett Finlay, Dan Small, Amin Ghaziani, Mark Turin, Sara Shneiderman, and Lesley Robertson. I'm also thankful to colleagues further afield—Kirsten Bell, Terra Edwards, Marco Jacquemet, Ieva Jusyonyte, Kevin Lewis O'Neill, Jack Sidnell, and Zoe Wool—who consistently inspire me through their work, conversation, and wit. I'm especially grateful to Benjamin T. Smith and Elizabeth Ferry, the reviewers for the press, for their immensely generous and insightful feedback on the manuscript and their very useful suggestions for revision.

My graduate students at the University of British Columbia, especially Hilary Agro, Michelle Hak Hepburn, Kendra Jewell, and Sydney Dawson, have been a consistent source of inspiration. I owe a particular debt of gratitude to Caitlyn Yates for her meticulous research assistance in various stages of this project, for her encouragement, and for the many hours she spent compiling the data for and creating the map in chapter 5.

Over the past decade, numerous friends have offered support in countless ways, from long walks to in-depth phone calls. Special mentions to Judith Pyke, Ruth Douthwright, Kiley Hamlin, Max Ascrizzi, and Jake Fleming. I'm also grateful to Jana McQuilkin, Anna Kramer, Dawn Allen, Ellen Wiebe, Anthony Pare, and Cory Silverberg.

My friends and family in Mexico were foundational to this work. I thank Ruth Berenice Gonzalez and Antonia Torres Gonzalez for their support, humor, and hospitality. I'm especially grateful to Amaranta Cornejo Hernández, my *cuñada*, friend, and colleague, who traveled with my brother and me on parts of this research and offered detailed and insightful feedback on a first draft of the manuscript. With a full and heavy heart, I also thank Raquel Tambo Portillo, who provided the missing piece for this project. While she is no longer with us, I hope this book will pay a modest tribute to her legacy.

I extend my thanks to the production team and my editors at the University of California Press as well as the funding organizations that made this work possible, including the Social Sciences and Humanities Research Council, the Peter Wall Institute for Advanced Studies, and the John Simon Guggenheim Fellowship.

Many activists in Mexico and the United States offered their knowledge encouragement and inspiration. In addition to the activists I profile in this book I especially thank Víctor Hugo Guzmán, Javier Sicilia, and Marco Antonio Castillo. I'm grateful to Daniel M.G. for sharing his family's story and for providing some of his photography for this book. I also thank the many collectives in Mexico for their fearless and tireless work and particularly the Brigada Nacional de Búsqueda de Personas Desaparecidas, Solecito, La Red de Madres Buscando a Sus Hijxs, and the Colectivo Familiares de Desaparecidos Orizaba-Córdoba.

I want to acknowledge the journalists and scholars who risk their lives daily shedding light on the human rights crisis in Mexico. Their work and efforts provided crucial context for this book. I especially want to thank the Quinto Elemento Lab for their meticulous reporting, which helped me make sense of the ethnographic material I analyze in chapter 5.

My family has been a foundational support in the research and writing that led to this book. My sister, Rachel, brother, Scott, and parents, Robert and Patricia, have been steadfast in their support. A heartfelt thank you to my son, stepson, and godsons—Rafael, Joaquín, Arón, and Ramiro—for the constant reminder of why this project is so important. Finally, my deepest thanks to my partner, Gastón Gordillo, without whose uncompromising intellectual companionship, love, and enthusiasm I would never have been able to complete this work.

I dedicate this book to the families searching—*las madres buscadoras*—and especially to Leticia, Araceli, and Lucía for their tireless work toward envisioning a future where no mother, and indeed no one, ever has to embark on such a search again.

Notes

Introduction

1. "Mexico's Long War: Drugs, Crime, and the Cartels," Council on Foreign Relations, September 7, 2022, https://www.cfr.org/backgrounder/mexicos-long-war-drugs-crime-and-cartels.

2. "Versión pública RNPDNO," Comisión Nacional de Búsqueda, accessed February 6, 2023, https://versionpublicarnpdno.segob.gob.mx/Dashboard/Index.

3. Homero Campa, "Con Peña Nieto, 13 desaparecidos al día," *Proceso*, February 7, 2015, https://www.proceso.com.mx/reportajes/2015/2/7/con-pena-nieto-13-desaparecidos-al-dia-143107.html.

4. Nik Steinberg, "Mexico's Disappeared: The Enduring Cost of a Crisis Ignored," Human Rights Watch, February 20, 2013, https://www.hrw.org/report/2013/02/20/mexicos-disappeared/enduring-cost-crisis-ignored.

5. César Martínez, "Desaparece una persona cada hora en sexenio de AMLO," *A dónde van los desaparecidos*, June 1, 2023, https://adondevanlosdesaparecidos.org/2023/06/01/desaparece-una-persona-cada-hora-en-sexenio-de-amlo/.

6. In the United States, well-funded interventions and programs ostensibly aimed at impeding the distribution and consumption of illicit drugs have profoundly shaped systems of governance. This has included the rise of mass incarceration as well as the expansion of legal systems, health and social welfare programs, and border security enforcement. See Michelle Alexander, *The New Jim Crow: Mass Incarceration in the Age of Colorblindness* (New York: The

New Press, 2010); Eva Bertram, Morris Blachman, Kenneth Sharpe, and Peter Andreas, *Drug War Politics: The Price of Denial* (Berkeley: University of California Press, 1996); Ieva Jusionyte, *Threshold: Emergency Responders on the US-Mexico Border* (Berkeley: University of California Press, 2018); Michael Massing, *The Fix* (Berkeley: University of California Press, 2000); Winifred Tate, *Drugs, Thugs, and Diplomats: US Policymaking in Colombia* (Stanford, CA: Stanford University Press, 2015).

7. Wil G. Pansters, Benjamin T. Smith, and Peter Watt, *Beyond the Drug War in Mexico: Human Rights, the Public Sphere and Justice* (London: Routledge, 2017). They trace how prohibitionist views on drugs in Mexico go back further than US interventions to the criminalization of indigenous healing practices, especially targeting marijuana during the late nineteenth and early twentieth centuries. They also link these views to the anti-Chinese campaigns of the early postrevolutionary decades, which employed accusations of opium addiction and opium trafficking to persecute Chinese minorities.

8. I use the term "drug-related" violence to refer to the kinds of violence often associated with or blamed on drug trafficking organizations, but often indistinguishable from violence produced by the state and corporations.

9. Alexander Curry and Leonie Ansems de Vries, "Violent Governance, Identity and the Production of Legitimacy: Autodefensas in Latin America," *Journal of International Relations and Development* 23, no. 2 (2020): 262–84: Romain Le Cour Grandmaison, "Becoming a Violent Broker: Cartels, Autodefensas, and the State in Michoacán, Mexico," *European Review of Latin American and Caribbean Studies* 112, no. 2 (2021): 137–58.

10. Throughout this manuscript I use the term "criminal" gingerly and always with implied scare quotes. In the context of the war on drugs in Mexico it is a problematic term due to its oversimplification of complex socioeconomic issues, often ignoring the conditions of poverty, lack of opportunities, or coercion that drive many into the drug trade. The term risks dehumanizing individuals, reducing them to their illegal actions rather than acknowledging their humanity and complexity. The stigma associated with being labeled a "criminal" or a "narco" can persist even after individuals have left the drug trade or served their time, hindering their reintegration into society. Moreover, the term can be used to justify violence or extrajudicial actions in the name of the war on drugs and implies guilt, potentially undermining the principle of "inno-

cent until proven guilty." Finally, focusing on individuals as "criminals" diverts attention from the state's role in creating and perpetuating conditions conducive to the drug trade.

11. Comité contra la Desaparición Forzada, "Informe del Comité contra la Desaparición Forzada sobre su visita a México en virtud del artículo 33 de la Convención," April 12, 2022, https://hchr.org.mx/wp/wp-content/uploads/2022/04/Informe-de-visita-a-MX-del-Comite-contra-la-Desaparicion-Forzada-abril-2022.pdf.

12. Cynthia L. Bejarano, "Las Super Madres de Latino America: Transforming Motherhood by Challenging Violence in Mexico, Argentina, and El Salvador," *Frontiers: A Journal of Women Studies* 23, no. 1 (2002): 126–50, https://doi.org/10.1353/fro.2002.0002.

13. Melissa Wright, "Epistemological Ignorances and Fighting for the Disappeared: Lessons from Mexico," *Antipode* 49, no. 1 (2017): 249–69.

14. Gladys McCormick, "The Act of Disappearing in Mexico," Wilson Center, March 5, 2018, https://www.wilsoncenter.org/article/the-act-disappearing-mexico.

15. Alejandro Anaya-Muñoz and Barbara Frey, *Mexico's Human Rights Crisis* (Philadelphia: University of Pennsylvania Press, 2019), 7.

16. See Steinberg, "Mexico's Disappeared." By January 2019, the Attorney General's Office had opened 975 investigations into allegations of enforced disappearances and had pressed charges in only 12 cases. And by September 2019, the office's specialized unit on kidnappings reported having only one open investigation into disappearances committed by nonstate agents. See "Mexico: Events of 2019," Human Rights Watch, December 9, 2019, https://www.hrw.org/world-report/2020/country-chapters/mexico.

17. The percentages presented are as reported by the study and have been rounded to two decimal places. As such, the cumulative total does not amount to an exact 100 percent (but 99.99 percent). Leigh Payne, Karina Ansolabehere, and Barbara Frey, "Observatorio sobre desaparición e impunidad: Informe sobre desapariciones en el estado de Nuevo León con datos de CADHAC," FLACSO México, Human Rights Program University of Minnesota, University of Oxford, 2017, 7, available at https://ora.ox.ac.uk/objects/uuid:06889a97-ed1c-46c1-bd8b-e8de149d2ce3/download_file?file_format=application%2Fpdf&safe_filename=170616_resumen_informe_nl_vf.pdf&type_of_work=Report.

18. Silvana Mandolessi, "Introduction: Disappearances in Mexico," in *Disappearances in Mexico: From the "Dirty War" to the "War on Drugs"* ed. Silvana Mandolessi and Katia Olalde Rico (London: Routledge, 2022), 9.

19. This diversity of victims reflects the range of motives for disappearances, which can include human trafficking, forced labor, kidnapping, extortion, the settling of disputes between criminal organizations, political dissent or opposition to megaprojects, or the more random outcomes of widespread generalized violence and state and cartel brutality. See Mandolessi, "Introduction," 9.

20. In the period between 2000 and 2010 there was a reduction of about 0.6 year in male life expectancy. Homicides in Mexico reversed life expectancy gains for men and slowed them for women. See José Manuel Aburto, Hiram Beltrán-Sánchez, Víctor Manuel García-Guerrero, and Vladimir Canudas-Romo, "Homicides in Mexico Reversed Life Expectancy Gains for Men and Slowed Them for Women, 2000–10," *Health Affairs* 35, no. 1 (2016), 88.

21. On the military industrial complex, see Tate, *Drugs, Thugs, and Diplomats*. On corporate profit related to the war on drugs see Dawn Paley, *Drug War Capitalism* (Oakland, CA: AK Press, 2014).

22. On racial hierarchy, see Alexander, *The New Jim Crow*; on corporate profits from drug policy and violence, see Luis Alejandro Astorga, *El siglo de las drogas: El narcotráfico, del Porfiriato al nuevo milenio* (Ciudad de México: Plaza Y Janés, 2005); Juanita Diaz-Cotto, "Latinas and the War on Drugs in the United States, Latin America, and Europe," in *Global Lockdown: Race, Gender, and the Prison-Industrial Complex*, ed. J. Sudbury (London: Routledge, 2005), 137–53.

23. Claudio Lomnitz, "Desaparecer es contagioso," *La Jornada*, September 30, 2020, https://www.jornada.com.mx/2020/09/30/opinion/017a1pol.

24. Shaylih Muehlmann, *When I Wear My Alligator Boots: Narco-Culture in the US Mexico Borderlands*, California Series in Public Anthropology, 33 (Berkeley: University of California Press, 2013).

25. José Luis Medina, "Movimiento por la Paz con Justicia y Dignidad, qué pasó a 9 años," *Milenio*, August 5, 2020, https://www.milenio.com/politica/movimiento-paz-justicia-dignidad-paso-9-anos.

26. Tim Padgett, "Person of the Year 2011: Why I Protest: Javier Sicilia of Mexico," *Time*, December 14, 2011, https://content.time.com/time/specials/packages/article/0,28804,2101745_2102138_2102238,00.html.

27. Medina, "Movimiento por la Paz con Justicia y Dignidad."

28. Estrella Pedroza, "'El movimiento por la paz es una referencia moral':
Sicilia," *Pie de Página*, January 21, 2020, https://piedepagina.mx/el-movimiento-
por-la-paz-es-una-referencia-moral-sicilia/.

29. Salvador Camerena, "Javier Sicilia anuncia una 'Caravana por la
Paz' hacia Estados Unidos," *El País*, August 10, 2012, https://elpais.com
/internacional/2012/08/10/actualidad/1344621187_278415.html.

30. Elena Azaola, "El Movimiento por la Paz con Justicia y Dignidad,"
Desacatos 40 (2012): 159-70.

31. Most names in this book are pseudonyms. At times, the kind of information conveyed in my interviews incriminates powerful actors and potentially
endangers both my research participants and myself. This means that on occasion I hid the identities of participants or changed place names or dates, cal-
ibrating my approach both to the wishes of my research participants and the
extent to which their accounts could potentially endanger them. In other cases,
I have retained original names, as for example, for activists who themselves
have become nationally and even internationally known. These include María
Elena Herrera, who, as I described above, was one of the first activists I met and
who, in November 2022, was featured in the *New York Times* Saturday Profile. I
also left the decision of anonymity up to my research participants because while
it is a common practice in anthropology to maintain the anonymity of research
informants, this has not been the practice in the context of work on the dead
and the disappeared in Mexico. Scholars working on the *feminicidio* in Juárez as
well as forced disappearance have argued that not to name the victims of violence and to anonymize their deaths is a dehumanizing gesture that normalizes
violence. See Miranda Dahlin, "To Wait amongst Shadows: Violence, Forced
Migration, and the Spectral Geography of the Juárez-El Paso Borderlands"
(PhD diss., McGill University, 2019); Alice Driver, *More or Less Dead: Feminicide,
Haunting, and the Ethics of Representation in Mexico* (Tucson: University of Arizona Press, 2015); Rosa-Linda Fregoso and Cynthia Bejarano, *Terrorizing
Women* (Durham, NC: Duke University Press, 2009); Julia Estela Monárrez Fra-
goso, *Trama de una injusticia feminicidio sexual sistémico en Ciudad Juárez*,
(Tijuana: Colegio de la Frontera Norte, 2009); Patricia Ravelo Blancas and
Héctor Domínguez Rubalcaba, "Ciudad Juárez: Asedios a la ciudadanía y
cancelación de la vida urbana," *El Cotidiano*, no. 164 (November–December
2010), 7.

32. The book of testimonies is Celia Del Palacio, *"Porque la lucha por un hijo no termina . . . ": Testimonios de las madres del Colectivo Familias de Desaparecidos Orizaba-Córdoba* (Xalapa: Universidad Veracruzana, 2020).

33. Carolina Robledo Silvestre, *Drama social y política del duelo: Las desapariciones de la guerra contra las drogas en Tijuana,* (Ciudad de México: El Colegio de Mexico, 2017); Dawn Paley, *Guerra neoliberal: Desaparición y búsqueda en el Norte de México* (San Juan, Puerto Rico: Libertad Bajo Palabra, 2020).

Chapter 1

This chapter incorporates material previously published in a different form in my article "'Hasta la Madre!': Mexican Mothers against 'the War on Drugs,'" which appeared in *The Social History of Alcohol and Drugs* 31, no. 1 (2017): 85–106.

1. One of the most important contributions of the MPJD has been its role in establishing "victims of violence" as a salient political identity referring both to the murdered and disappeared and also their loved ones. The people on the caravan who had lost family members to drug-related violence referred to themselves as "victims" or sometimes "survivors." Both of these terms are also potentially problematic but because this is how they referred to themselves at the time and in order to distinguish this group of activists from those who were on the tour in support roles or as organizers, academics, or activists more generally, I retain these terms throughout this chapter.

2. The way the issue of disappearances has pushed often apolitical women into politics is similar to the emergence of women's political consciousness in the early twentieth century in Barcelona around issues such as working conditions, access to education, and healthcare. Temma Kaplan, "Female Consciousness and Collective Action: The Case of Barcelona, 1910–1918," *Signs: Journal of Women in Culture and Society* 7, no. 3 (April 1982): 545–66.

3. Janice K. Gallagher, "The Last Mile Problem: Activists, Advocates, and the Struggle for Justice in Domestic Courts," *Comparative Political Studies* 50, no. 12 (2017): 1666–98.

4. During my follow-up field work it became apparent that many of the actions in Mexico are organized by mothers. La Red de las Madres (the Mothers' Network), which provides practical and logistical support for mothers seeking information on missing children, is a prime example. A discussion of some of the many other collectives that now exist is included in chapter 3.

5. Estrella Pedroza, "'El movimiento por la paz es una referencia moral': Sicilia," *Pie de Página*, January 21, 2020, https://piedepagina.mx/el-movimiento-por-la-paz-es-una-referencia-moral-sicilia/.

6. Some of the many collaborating initiatives were with the Atlanta ACLU, Atlanta Friends Service, Georgia Peace and Justice Coalition, Georgia WAND, Latin American Association, Southern Center for Human Rights, National Alliance of Latin American and Caribbean Communities (NALACC), National Association for the Advancement of Colored People (NAACP), Labor Council for Latin American Advancement (LCLAA), National Latino Congress, Drug Policy Alliance (DPA), Law Enforcement against Prohibition (LEAP), Latin America Working Group (LAWG), Border Angels / Angeles de la Frontera, and CIP-Americas Program.

7. Collette Flanagan, "Mothers against Police Brutality: Our Quest for Justice," interview, *Revolution*, May 5, 2014, http://revcom.us/a/338/interview-with-collette-flanagan-en.html.

8. Raquel Gutiérrez Aguilar, "Porque vivas nos queremos, juntas estamos trastocándolo todo: Notas para pensar, una vez más, los caminos de la transformación social," *Theomai*, no. 37 (2018): 46.

9. Jonathan Rosa, *Looking like a Language, Sounding like a Race*, Oxford Studies in Anthropology of Language (Oxford: Oxford University Press, 2019), 279.

10. "Ciudad Juarez Registers Record Murder Rate," *InSight Crime*, January 5, 2011, https://insightcrime.org/news/analysis/ciudad-juarez-records-record-murders/.

11. John Gibler, *Mexico Unconquered: Chronicles of Power and Revolt* (San Francisco: City Lights Publishers, 2009), 41.

12. Ana Villarreal, "Domesticating Danger: Coping Codes and Symbolic Security amid Violent Organized Crime in Mexico," *Sociological Theory* 39, no. 4 (2021): 238.

13. Shaylih Muehlmann, "The Narco Uncanny," *Public Culture* 32, no. 2 (2020): 328.

14. Miriam Ticktin, "What's Wrong with Innocence," *Society for Cultural Anthropology*, June 28, 2016, https://culanth.org/fieldsights/whats-wrong-with-innocence.

15. Diana Taylor, *Disappearing Acts: Spectacles of Gender and Nationalism in Argentina's "Dirty War"* (Durham, NC: Duke University Press, 1997), 76–85.

16. Winifred Tate, *Drugs, Thugs, and Diplomats: US Policymaking in Colombia* (Stanford, CA: Stanford University Press, 2015).

17. Teresa P. R. Caldeira and James Holston, "Comparative Studies in Society and History Democracy and Violence in Brazil," *Comparative Studies in Society and History* 41, no. 4 (1999): 716.

18. The subsequent leadership among collectives in Mexico has been led predominantly by women. In some ways this is strategic and doesn't necessarily reflect those involved. For example, Juan took the lead in a lot of the investigation of his brothers while Doña Maria has been the public-facing image of the campaign (and subsequent collectives which the sons named after her).

19. Ruth Feldstein, "I Wanted the Whole World to See: Race, Gender, and Constructions of Motherhood in the Death of Emmet Till," in *Not June Cleaver: Women and Gender in Postwar America, 1945-1960*, ed. June Meyerowitz (Philadelphia: Temple University Press, 1994), 273.

20. Seth Koven and Sonya Michel, eds., *Mothers of a New World: Maternalist Politics and the Origins of Welfare States* (London: Routledge, 2013).

21. Rosemary Brana-Shute and Gary Brana-Shute, *Crime and Punishment in the Caribbean* (Gainesville: Center for Latin American Studies, University of Florida, 1980); María L. Cruz-Torres, *Pink Gold: Women, Shrimp, and Work in Mexico* (University of Texas Press, 2023); Joann Martin, "Motherhood and Power: The Production of a Women's Culture of Politics in a Mexican Community," *American Ethnologist* 17, no. 3 (1990): 470–90; Kevin Lewis O'Neill, "Home Security: Drug Rehabilitation Centres, the Devil and Domesticity in Guatemala City," *Journal of Latin American Studies* 52, no. 4 (2020): 785–804; Marianne Schmink, "Women in Brazilian Abertura Politics," *Signs* 7, no. 1 (1981): 115–34.

22. Women's movements in Argentina, Chile, and Brazil have played significant roles in denouncing state violence and demanding justice for victims. Scholarship on women's involvement has emphasized the role of military dictatorships in Argentina (1976–1983) and Chile (1973–1990), as well as authoritarian regimes in Brazil, in perpetrating state violence against women. Marjorie Agosín, *Tapestries of Hope, Threads of Love: The Arpillera Movement in Chile, 1974–1994* (Albuquerque: University of New Mexico Press, 1996); Sonia E. Alvarez, *Engendering Democracy in Brazil: Women's Movements in Transition Politics* (Princeton, NJ: Princeton University Press, 2021); Lisa Baldez, *Why Women Protest: Women's Movements in Chile* (Cambridge: Cambridge University Press, 2002);

Marguerite Feitlowitz, *A Lexicon of Terror: Argentina and the Legacies of Torture* (Oxford: Oxford University Press, 1998); Lynn Stephen, "Gender, Citizenship, and Politics of Identity," *Latin American Perspectives* 28, no. 6 (2001): 54–69.

23. Karen Ortiz Cuchivague, "Las Madres de la Plaza de Mayo y su legado por la defensa de los derechos humanos," *Trabajo Social* 14 (2012): 165–77; Sara Eleanor Howe, "The Madres de La Plaza de Mayo: Asserting Motherhood; Rejecting Feminism?" *Journal of International Women's Studies* 7, no. 3 (2006): 43–50. Abril Zarco, "Maternalismo, identidad colectiva y participación política: Las Madres de Plaza de Mayo," *Revista Punto Género*, no. 1 (2011): 229–47.

24. Marysa Navarro, "The Personal Is Political: Las Madres de Plaza de Mayo," in *Power and Popular Protest: Latin American Social Movements*, ed. Susan Eckstein (Berkeley: University of California Press, 1989), 241–58.

25. Navarro, "The Personal Is Political," 256–57.

26. Kristin A. Goss and Michael T. Heaney, "Organizing Women as Women: Hybridity and Grassroots Collective Action in the Twenty-first Century" *Perspectives on Politics* 8, no. 1 (2010): 27–52; Elva F. Orozco Mendoza, "Las Madres de Chihuahua: Maternal Activism, Public Disclosure, and the Politics of Visibility," *New Political Science* 41, no. 2 (2019): 211–33.

27. This was not the case in the example of Ayotzinapa, where fathers took the lead. See Melissa Wright, "Against the Evils of Democracy: Fighting Forced Disappearance and Neoliberal Terror in Mexico," *Annals of the American Association of Geographers* 108, no. 2 (2018): 327–36.

28. In Janice Gallagher's 2022 book *Bootstrap Justice*, she chronicles the extraordinary lengths to which Juan Carlos went over the years since his first two brothers disappeared in 2008, not only to find his brothers (for whom he still searches) but also to organize and support other victims, which he does through a collective he named after his mother. Janice K. Gallagher, *Bootstrap Justice: The Search for Mexico's Disappeared* (Oxford: Oxford University Press, 2022)

29. Floya Anthias and Nira Yuval-Davis, "Contextualizing Feminism: Gender, Ethnic and Class Divisions," *Feminist Review* 15, no. 1 (1983): 62–75; Kimberlé W. Crenshaw, *On Intersectionality: Essential Writings* (New York: The New Press, 2017); Nira Yuval-Davis, "Intersectionality and Feminist Politics," *European Journal of Women's Studies* 13, no. 3 (2006): 193–209.

30. Isaac Campos, "Mexicans and the Origins of Marijuana Prohibition in the United States: A Reassessment," *Social History of Alcohol and Drugs* 32, no. 1 (2018): 6–37.

31. The BNB links the notion of the "search brigade" directly to the 1968 student brigades in Mexico, the internationalist brigades of the Spanish Civil War, and the free food community kitchens in the United States during the COVID-19 pandemic.

Chapter 2

1. Javier Auyero, *Patients of the State: The Politics of Waiting in Argentina* (Durham, NC: Duke University Press, 2012), 4.

2. Ghassan Hage, "Waiting Out the Crisis: On Stuckedness and Governmentality," *Anthropological Theory* 5 (2009): 463-75.

3. Karine Gagné, "Waiting for the Flood: Technocratic Time and Impending Disaster in the Himalayas," *Disasters* 43, no. 4 (2019): 840-66; Elif Sarı, "Lesbian Refugees in Transit: The Making of Authenticity and Legitimacy in Turkey," *Journal of Lesbian Studies* 24, no. 2 (2020): 140-58.

4. Henceforth referred to as the MP, the Ministerio Público, which exists in all states, is sometimes translated as the Attorney General's Office, though it is an office within the Justice Department that is a much more local and low-level agency than the Attorney General's Office. When a crime is committed or an accident happens, the MP is the office in charge of the first investigations, but the judge's rulings are limited to the specific jurisdiction.

5. The Investigation Agency of Veracruz (AVI) is the state-level agency in charge of doing the fieldwork and investigations for missing persons cases in Veracruz.

6. Akhil Gupta, *Red Tape* (Durham, NC: Duke University Press, 2012), 145. Josiah Heyman, "Deepening the Anthropology of Bureaucracy," *Anthropological Quarterly* 85, no. 4 (2012): 1269-77.

7. Rupert Knox, "Social Movements in Support of the Victims: Human Rights and Digital Communication," in *Beyond the Drug War in Mexico: Human Rights, the Public Sphere and Justice.*, ed. Pansters Wil, Benjamin T. Smith, and Peter Watt (New York: Routledge, 2017), chapter 7.

8. The General Law for Victims made "victim" a legally recognized entity and stipulated a victim's right to respectful treatment, a full investigation of the crime, and the awarding of monetary reparations whenever possible. This was followed by the Law on Enforced Disappearance (2017) which defines and

criminalizes "enforced disappearance" at the national level and requires immediate investigation and search for the missing.

9. Janice K. Gallagher, *Bootstrap Justice: The Search for Mexico's Disappeared* (Oxford: Oxford University Press, 2022).

10. The Collective in Search of Truth and Justice is made up of relatives of disappeared persons from different states of the country. Since 2013, it has been accompanied by the organization Fundar, the Center for Analysis and Investigation, in its dialogue with the Attorney General's Office. The letter is available at "Carta abierta: Familiares de personas desaparecidas piden a Fiscal tomar acciones concretas para la búsqueda e investigación ante el contexto de pandemia," *Fundar, Centro de Análisis e Investigación,* June 15, 2020, https://fundar.org.mx/carta-abierta-familiares-de-personas-desaparecidas-piden-a-fiscal-tomar-acciones-concretas-para-la-busqueda-e-investigacion/.

11. Ximena Antillón, "'¡No más búsquedas, queremos mesas de trabajo!': Políticas de atención a víctimas, administración y resistencia," *SinEmbargo MX,* June 16, 2020, https://www.sinembargo.mx/16-06-2020/3805633.

12. This story also appears in a slightly altered form towards the end of *The Trial.* See Franz Kafka, *The Trial* (New York: Schocken Books, 1999).

13. Kafka, *The Trial.*

14. Auyero, *Patients of the State,* 5; See also Verónica Gago, *Neoliberalism from Below: Popular Pragmatics and Baroque Economies* (Durham, NC: Duke University Press, 2017), 235.

15. Judith Butler and Gayatri Chakravorty Spivak, *Who Sings the Nation-State: Language, Politics, Belonging* (Kolkata: Seagull Books, 2007), 58–61.

16. Auyero, *Patients of the State,* 11.

17. Pierre Bourdieu, *Pascalian Meditations* (Stanford, CA: Stanford University Press, 2000), 228.

18. Anna J. Secor, "Between Longing and Despair: State, Space, and Subjectivity in Turkey," *Environment and Planning D: Society and Space* 25, no. 1 (2007), 42.

19. Invisible Committee, *Now,* Semiotext(e), 23, trans. Robert Hurley (Cambridge, MA: MIT Press, 2018), 16.

Chapter 3

1. Azam Ahmed also chronicles Miriam's life and search in riveting detail in his powerful 2023 book *Fear Is Just a Word: A Missing Daughter, a Violent Cartel, and a Mother's Quest for Vengeance* (London: Hachette UK, 2023). Azam Ahmed, "She Stalked Her Daughter's Killers across Mexico, One by One," *New York Times,* December 13, 2020, https://www.nytimes.com/2020/12/13/world /americas/miriam-rodriguez-san-fernando.html.

2. Los Zetas is a Mexican criminal organization known for its brutality that was formed by former Mexican special forces, initially worked for the Gulf Cartel, and later split and established itself as an independent entity. For an in-depth history and analysis of the formation and function of Los Zetas, see Guadalupe Correa-Cabrera, *Los Zetas Inc.* (Austin: University of Texas Press, 2021).

3. David Agren, "Mexican Woman Who Uncovered Cartel Murder of Daughter Shot Dead," *The Guardian,* May 12, 2017, https://www.theguardian .com/world/2017/may/12/mexican-woman-who-uncovered-cartel-murder -of-daughter-shot-dead-miriam-rodriguez.

4. See for example, Smith's discussion of the popular responses to the murder of a local taxi driver in the 1950s and how both newspapers and civil-society organizations sought justice, leading to the emergence of the Pro-Justice Committee for the Defense of the People (CPJDC) in which women were prominent and in fact outnumbered men. Benjamin T. Smith, "Killing a Cabby: The Press, Civil Society, and Justice in 1950s Chihuahua," *Mexican Studies /Estudios Mexicanos* 36, no. 1–2 (2020): 127–49.

5. María Teresa Villarreal Martínez, "Los colectivos de familiares de personas desaparecidas y la procuración de justicia," *Intersticios Sociales* 11 (2016): 1–28.

6. Villarreal Martínez, "Los colectivos."

7. Collectives are registered in twenty-one Mexican states; there are also three national Mexican collectives and associated collectives based in Honduras, El Salvador, and Guatemala. The collectives based in Honduras, El Salvador, and Guatemala are primarily collectives in search of migrants who have gone missing in Mexico.

8. In Baja California for instance, the Unified Association for the Disappeared of Baja California is a group of twelve search collectives exclusively searching for the disappeared in that state.

9. Daniel Wilkinson, "México: Los Otros Desaparecidos," *Human Rights Watch*, January 14, 2019, https://www.hrw.org/es/news/2019/01/14/mexico-los -otros-desaparecidos#.

10. In 2011, Edgar Huerta Montiel (alias El Wache), a member of Los Zetas cartel, was arrested in Zacatecas for coordinating the kidnapping and disappearances. "Policías federales detienen al coordinador de la masacre en San Fernando," *Expansión*, June 17, 2011, https://expansion.mx/nacional/2011/06/17 /policias-federales-detienen-al-coordinador-de-la-masacre-en-san-fernando. Police are also under investigation for involvement in the deaths, though at this time no conviction or sentence has been made. See "Se cumplen 10 años de masacre de 72 migrantes en San Fernando, y México aceptará que ONU investigue," *Associated Press*, August 24, 2020, https://www.dallasnews.com /espanol/al-dia/mexico/2020/08/24/se-cumplen-10-anos-de-masacre-de- 72-migrantes-en-san-fernando-y-mexico-aceptara-que-onu-investigue/. The incident prompted international condemnation and a migrant shelter in Tenosique, Tabasco, was later named "La 72" in honor of the seventy-two migrants who were killed that day.

11. Jo Tuckman, "Survivor Tells of Escape from Mexican Massacre in Which 72 Were Left Dead," *The Guardian*, August 25, 2010, https://www.theguardian .com/world/2010/aug/25/mexico-massacre-central-american-migrants.

12. Migrants who transit through Mexico, whether from Central America, the interior of Mexico, or from other countries, are vulnerable to the same forms of violence as nonmigrants in Mexico, and more. See Caitlyn Yates and Stephanie Leutert, "A Gender Perspective of Migrant Kidnapping in Mexico," *Victims and Offenders* 15, no. 3 (2020): 295–312. Raúl Diego Rivera Hernández has argued that Central American migrants in Mexico are doubly marginalized, not only for their exploitation in the Mexican and US workforces but also for their vulnerability to the violence and instability caused by the war on drugs. See Raúl Diego Rivera Hernández, *Narratives of Vulnerability in Mexico's War on Drugs* (New York: Springer, 2020), 37. In his book *Deported to Death*, Jeremy Slack argues that US deportation policies place migrants in immense danger and that criminal actors profit from recent deportees' vulnerability after they are returned to Mexican border towns. Slack shows how deported migrants expelled from the United States are sometimes targeted and kidnapped after being pushed back across the Mexican border. Slack argues that migrants, in this case, become an externality of both Mexico's war on drugs and the United

States' war on immigration. See Jeremy Slack, *Deported to Death: How Drug Violence Is Changing Migration on the US-Mexico Border* (Oakland: University of California Press, 2019). On top of these particular vulnerabilities, migrants crossing the border must also survive the violence which the desert landscape itself creates. See Jason De León, *The Land of Open Graves: Living and Dying on the Migrant Trail*, California Series in Public Anthropology, 36 (Oakland: University of California Press, 2015); Ieva Jusionyte, *Threshold: Emergency Responders on the US-Mexico Border* (Oakland: University of California Press, 2018). It's also important to note that drug-related violence has also produced its own forms of displacement, as Séverine Durin's work in Nuevo Leon has shown. See Séverine Durin, "Los que la guerra desplazó: Familias del noreste de México en el exilio," *Desacatos* 38, no. 1 (2012): 29–42. See also Guadalupe Correa-Cabrera, "Security, Migration, and the Economy in the Texas–Tamaulipas Border Region: The 'Real' Effects of Mexico's Drug War," *Politics and Policy* 41, no. 1 (2013): 65–82.

13. Inter-American Commission on Human Rights, "Violence against Lesbian, Gay, Bisexual, Trans and Intersex Persons in the Americas," Organization of American States, Washington DC, 2015, http://www.oas.org/en/iachr/reports/pdfs/violencelgbtipersons.pdf.

14. Elva F. Orozco Mendoza, "Las Madres de Chihuahua: Maternal Activism, Public Disclosure, and the Politics of Visibility," *New Political Science* 41, no. 2 (2019): 211–33; Melissa W. Wright, "Against the Evils of Democracy: Fighting Forced Disappearance and Neoliberal Terror in Mexico," *Annals of the American Association of Geographers* 108, no. 2 (2018): 327–36.

15. Cynthia L. Bejarano, "Las Super Madres de Latino America: Transforming Motherhood by Challenging Violence in Mexico, Argentina, and El Salvador," *Frontiers: A Journal of Women Studies* 23, no. 1 (February 2002): 126–50; Paola Díaz, "Ni vivos ni muertos: El viaje de Las Madres Buscadoras de Sonora," *The Conversation*, January 26, 2020, https://theconversation.com/ni-vivos-ni-muertos-el-viaje-de-las-madres-buscadoras-de-sonora-129603.

16. Emir Olivares Alonso, "Critican ONU y CIDH daños colaterales," *La Jornada*, April 14, 2010, https://www.jornada.com.mx/2010/04/14/politica/007n2pol.

17. Alberto Najar, "'México es una enorme fosa clandestina': Por que la desaparición de personas se convirtió en una grave crisis humanitaria," *BBC News Mundo*, February 6, 2019, https://www.bbc.com/mundo/noticias-america-latina-47126564.

18. X, formerly Twitter, even has a bot dedicated to consolidating posts about disappearances and getting the word out, see https://twitter.com /botDesaparecidx, accessed February 7, 2023.

19. In April 2013, the former Gulf Cartel accountant Jose Carlos Hinojosa testified that the cartel had donated 12 million dollars to support a governor's campaign in Veracruz beginning in 2004, the same year that PRI member Fidel Herrera won the governor's seat in Veracruz, where he served for the next six years (2004–2010). See Elyssa Pachico, "Testimony Describes Zetas' Ties to Mexico Governor," *InSight Crime,* September 11, 2014, https://insightcrime .org/news/brief/testimony-zetas-ties-veracruz-mexico-governor/.

20. Ather Zia, *Resisting Disappearance: Military Occupation and Women's Activism in Kashmir* (Seattle: University of Washington Press, 2019).

21. Zia, *Resisting Disappearance,* 4.

22. Inter-American Commission on Human Rights, "The Human Rights Situation in Mexico," Organization of American States, December 31, 2015, https://www.oas.org/en/iachr/reports/pdfs/Mexico2016-en.pdf, 12, 31.

23. Alejandro Anaya-Muñoz and Barbara Frey, eds., *Mexico's Human Rights Crisis* (Philadelphia: University of Pennsylvania Press, 2019).

24. Some such efforts have emerged from research units, for example, the Center for Mexican Studies at Colombia University formed the Buscadoras Research Unit, which under the direction of anthropologist Claudio Lomnitz has collaborated closely with both family-led and civic society organizations. More attempts to coordinate have also emerged directly from family collectives, such as the National Search Brigade (BNB), which organizes a joint search among hundreds of collectives at rotating sites once a year.

25. Claudio Lomnitz, *Death and the Idea of Mexico* (Brooklyn: Zone Books, 2005), 20.

26. Verónica Gago, *Neoliberalism from Below: Popular Pragmatics and Baroque Economies* (Durham, NC: Duke University Press, 2017); Miyako Inoue, "Language and Gender in an Age of Neoliberalism," *Gender and Language* 1, no. 1 (2007): 79–91; Shannon Speed, "Dangerous Discourses: Human Rights and Multiculturalism in Neoliberal Mexico," *PoLAR: Political and Legal Anthropology* 28, no. 1 (2005): 29–51.

27. Shaylih Muehlmann, *Where the River Ends: Contested Indigeneity in the Mexican Colorado Delta* (Durham, NC: Duke University Press, 2013), chapter 2; Carmen Martínez Novo, *Who Defines Indigenous? Identities, Development,*

Intellectuals, and the State in Northern Mexico (New Brunswick, NJ: Rutgers University Press, 2006).

28. Antonio Fuentes Díaz, "Criminal Violence and Armed Community Defense," in *Organized Violence: Capitalist Warfare in Latin America,* ed. Dawn Paley and Simon Granovsky-Larsen (Regina, Saskatchewan: University of Regina Press, 2019), 196.

Chapter 4

1. The Mexican Secretary of Tourism designates a series of towns around the country that offer visitors a "magical" experience—by reason of their natural beauty, cultural richness, traditions, folklore, historical relevance, cuisine, art, crafts, and hospitality.

2. "Wife of Disgraced Mexican Governor Javier Duarte Held in London," *BBC News,* October 30, 2019, https://www.bbc.com/news/world-latin-america -50219853.

3. Claudia Altamirano, "Un juez gira una orden de aprehensión contra el exgobernador de Veracruz," *El País,* October 18, 2016, https://elpais.com /internacional/2016/10/18/mexico/1476760935_777182.html.

4. "Mexican Official Flies with $1.9 Million Cash in Briefcase and Backpack," *NBC News,* January 31, 2012, https://www.nbcnews.com/id /wbna46200273.

5. "Fugitive Mexican Governor Javier Duarte Arrested in Guatemala," *BBC News,* April 16, 2017, https://www.bbc.com/news/world-latin-america-39612892.

6. Diana Lastiri and Edgar Avila, "Ordenan aprehensión de Javier Duarte por desapariciones," *El Universal,* June 8, 2018, https://www.eluniversal.com .mx/estados/ordenan-aprehension-de-javier-duarte-por-desapariciones.

7. June Beittel, "Mexico: Organized Crime and Drug Trafficking Organizations," Congressional Research Service Report, R41576, Washington DC, July 2022, https://fas.org/sgp/crs/row/R41576.pdf.

8. "Former Mexican Secretary of Public Security Arrested for Drug-Trafficking Conspiracy and Making False Statements," United States Department of Justice, press release, December 10, 2019, https://www.justice.gov /usao-edny/pr/former-mexican-secretary-public-security-arrested-drug -trafficking-conspiracy-and.

9. "Former Nayarit Governor Arrested for Corruption after 8 Months on the Run," *Mexico Daily News,* June 7, 2021, https://mexiconewsdaily.com /news/former-nayarit-governor-arrested-on-corruption-charges-after-8-months-on-the-run/.

10. Luis Astorga, *¿Qué querían que hiciera?: Inseguridad y delincuencia organizada en el gobierno de Felipe Calderón* (Barcelona: Grijalbo, 2015), 158. Benjamin T. Smith, *The Dope: The Real History of the Mexican Drug Trade* (New York: Norton and Company, 2021), 251.

11. Stephen Morris, "Drug Trafficking, Corruption, and Violence in Mexico: Mapping the Linkages," *Trends in Organized Crime* 16, no. 2 (2013): 195–220.

12. Morris, "Drug Trafficking," 195–220.

13. Kate Doyle and Jesse Franzblau, "Archival Evidence of Mexico's Human Rights Crimes: The Case of Aleida Gallangos," *National Security Archive,* Electronic Briefing Book 307, March 9, 2010, https://nsarchive2.gwu.edu /NSAEBB/NSAEBB307/index.htm.

14. Stephen D. Morris, "Fox's Anti-Corruption Campaign in Mexico: A Preliminary Look at Approaches and Strategy," presentation at the Meeting of the Latin American Studies Association, Washington, DC, September 6, 2001.

15. Mark Stevenson and Maria Verza, "Corruption Allegations Long Dogged Ex-Mexico Security Chief," *Associated Press,* December 10, 2019, https://apnews.com/article/54b3d96887d7914b4fbd5b98b9b8408a.

16. Luis Astorga, "The Limits of Anti-Drug Policy in Mexico," *International Social Science Journal* 53, no. 169 (2001): 427–34; Luis Astorga and David Shirk, "Drug Trafficking Organizations and Counter-Drug Strategies in the US-Mexican Context," Center for US-Mexican Studies, working paper 10-01, 2010; Viridiana Ríos, "How Government Coordination Controlled Organized Crime: The Case of Mexico's Cocaine Markets," *Journal of Conflict Resolution* 59, no. 8 (2015): 1–22; Richard Snyder and Angelica Duran-Martinez, "Does Illegality Breed Violence? Drug Trafficking and State-Sponsored Protection Rackets," *Crime, Law and Social Change* 52, no. 3 (2009): 253–73.

17. Ríos, "How Government Coordination Controlled Organized Crime."

18. While President Felipe Calderón officially declared the war on drugs and launched the largest deployment of security forces, Serrano chronicles how the actual militarization of drug policy long preceded his administration. See Mónica Serrano, "A Humanitarian Crisis in the Making," in *Beyond the*

Drug War in Mexico, ed. Wil G. Pansters, Benjamin T. Smith, and Peter Watt (New York: Routledge, 2017), 64.

19. James McKinley Jr., "Mexico's New President Sends Thousands of Federal Officers to Fight Drug Cartels," *The New York Times,* January 7, 2007, https://www.nytimes.com/2007/01/07/world/americas/07mexico.html.

20. "Mexico's Long War: Drugs, Crime, and the Cartels," *Council on Foreign Relations,* September 7, 2022, https://www.cfr.org/backgrounder/mexicos-long-war-drugs-crime-and-cartels.

21. "U.S.-Mexico Security Cooperation: From the Mérida Initiative to the Bicentennial Framework," Congressional Research Service, IF10578, October 9, 2023, https://sgp.fas.org/crs/row/IF10578.pdf.

22. Dawn Paley, "Drug War as Neoliberal Trojan Horse," *Latin American Perspectives* 42, no. 5 (2015): 109–32.

23. Laura Carlsen, "Effects of Militarization in the Name of Counter-Narcotics Efforts and Consequences for Human Rights in Mexico," in *Beyond the Drug War in Mexico,* ed. Wil G. Pansters, Benjamin T. Smith, and Peter Watt (London: Routledge, 2017), chapter 3.

24. Eva Orozco Mendoza, "Punitive Dispossession: Authoritarian Neoliberalism and the Road to Mass Incarceration," in *Organized Violence: Capitalist Warfare in Latin America,* ed. Dawn Paley and Simon Granovsky-Larsen (Regina, Saskatchewan: University of Regina Press, 2019), 238.

25. Malcolm Beith, "A Broken Mexico: Allegations of Collusion between the Sinaloa Cartel and Mexican Political Parties," in *Criminal Insurgencies in Mexico and the Americas,* ed. Robert J. Bunker, 74–93 (London: Routledge, 2013).

26. This was revealed by a now-unsealed indictment. See "Former Mexican Secretary of Public Security Arrested for Drug-Trafficking Conspiracy and Making False Statements," United States Department of Justice, press release, December 10, 2019, https://www.justice.gov/usao-edny/pr/former-mexican-secretary-public-security-arrested-drug-trafficking-conspiracy-and.

27. Smith, *The Dope,* 390.

28. Ley de Seguridad Interior, Diario Oficial de la Federación, December 21, 2017, reformed May 30, 2019, https://www.diputados.gob.mx/LeyesBiblio/pdf/LSInt_300519.pdf.

29. Ximena Suárez-Enríquez and Maureen Meyer, "Nueva Ley de Seguridad Interior enfrenta fuerte rechazo en México," Washington Office on Latin

America, January 26, 2018, https://www.wola.org/es/analisis/cinco-argumentos
-clave-rechazar-ley-de-seguridad-interior-mexico/.

30. Carlsen, "Effects of Militarization."

31. "Mexico: Events of 2019," Human Rights Watch, 2020, https://
www.hrw.org/world-report/2020/country-chapters/mexico#:~:text = In%20
November%202018%2C%20the%20Supreme,and%20violated%20Mexico's
%20international%20obligations.

32. Mary Beth Sheridan, "Mexico's AMLO Putting Civilian-Led National
Guard under Military Control," *Washington Post,* September 9, 2022, https://
www.washingtonpost.com/world/2022/09/09/mexico-national-guard-
army/.

33. Center for Preventative Action, "Criminal Violence in Mexico," Global
Conflict Tracker, Council on Foreign Relations, accessed January 2023,
https://cfr.org/global-conflict-tracker/conflict/criminal-violence-mexico.

34. In fact, Laura Carlsen documents that within the Mexican army there
were strong elements that opposed participation in the war on drugs; see
Carlsen, "Effects of Militarization."

35. Dawn Paley documents that between February and May 2018, twenty-
one people in the state of Tamaulipas disappeared. After an investigation, the
United Nations High Commissioner for Human Rights Zeid Ra'ad Al Hussein
announced that Mexican federal forces were responsible. The next day, the
Nuevo Laredo Human Rights Committee claimed that it had received reports
of fifty-six disappearances in the city of Nuevo Laredo over the same period,
and that it was the Marines who were responsible. Soon after, it was reported by
El País that families of the victims began to be threatened with violence if they
did not withdraw their reports. Paley notes that while the level of impunity char-
acterizing these events is not out of the ordinary for Mexico, the UN corrobora-
tion of state participation in these enforced disappearances was important and
rare in the context of national denial and media censorship over the role of the
military and police in homicide and disappearances. Dawn Paley, "Against Official Discourse," *NACLA Report on the Americas* 50, no. 3 (2018): 311–12.

36. Quoted in Dawn Paley, "Will Mexico's New President Seek Justice for
the Disappeared?" *The Nation,* January 10, 2019, https://www.thenation.com
/article/archive/mexico-drug-war-killings-lopez-obrador/.

37. "Informe del Comité contra la Desaparición Forzada sobre su visita a
México en virtud del artículo 33 de La Convención," UN Office of the High

Commissioner for Human Rights, April 12, 2022, https://hchr.org.mx/wp-content/uploads/2022/04/Informe-de-visita-a-MX-del-Comite-contra-la-Desaparicion-Forzada-abril-2022.pdf.

38. Azam Ahmed, "Salvador Cienfuegos Zepeda, Mexico's Ex-Defense Minister, Is Arrested in L.A.," *The New York Times,* October 16, 2020, https://www.nytimes.com/2020/10/16/us/mexico-general-cienfuegos-dea.html.

39. Christopher Sherman and Mark Stevenson, "Mexico Says US 'Fabricated' Charges, Releases Evidence," *Associated Press,* January 15, 2021, https://apnews.com/article/mexico-elections-crime-arrests-drug-trafficking-a54eb46084fd31fa06f5a840eafafa86.

40. Tim Golden, "Dropping the Charges against General Cienfuegos Was William Barr's Call," *ProPublica,* December 8, 2022, *https://www.propublica.org/article/william-barr-mexico-cartels-cienfuegos-case.*

41. Nicholas Jon Crane and Oliver Gabriel Hernández Lara, "Politicizing Disappearance after Mexico's 'Historic' Election," *Political Geography* 75 (2019), 102025.

42. Peter A. Lupsha, "Drug Lords and Narco-Corruption: The Players Change but the Game Continues," *Crime, Law and Social Change* 16, no. 1 (1991): 41.

43. Ilana Feldman, "Care and Suspicion: Corruption as Definition in Humanitarian Relations," *Current Anthropology* 59, no. S18 (2018): S160–70; Italo Pardo, "Corrupt, Abusive, and Legal: Italian Breaches of the Democratic Contract," *Current Anthropology* 59, no. S18 (2018): S60–71; Arusha Cooray and Friedrich Schneider, "Does Corruption Throw Sand into or Grease the Wheels of Financial Sector Development?" *Public Choice* 177, no. 1 (2018): 111–33.

44. Kregg Hetherington, "Peasants, Experts, Clients, and Soybeans: The Fixing of Paraguay's Civil Service," *Current Anthropology* 59, no. S18 (2018): S173.

45. "Gross Human Rights Abuses: The Legal and Illegal Gun Trade to Mexico," Stop US Arms to Mexico, August 6, 2018, https://stopusarmstomexico.org/gross-human-rights-abuses-the-legal-and-illegal-gun-trade-to-mexico/.

46. Ieva Jusionyte, *Exit Wounds: American Guns, Mexican Lives, and the Vicious Circle of Violence* (Oakland: University of California Press, forthcoming).

47. Peter Andreas, *Border Games: The Politics of Policing the US-Mexico Divide* (Ithaca, NY: Cornell University Press, 2009); Kevin Lewis O'Neill, "Narcotecture," *Environment and Planning D: Society and Space* 34, no. 4 (2016): 672–88.

48. Michelle Alexander, *The New Jim Crow: Mass Incarceration in the Age of Colorblindness* (New York: The New Press, 2010), chapter 2.

49. Every year an average of 250 Customs and Border Protection (CBP) officers are arrested on myriad charges. A.C. Thompson, "Years Ago, the Border Patrol's Discipline System Was Denounced as 'Broken.' It's Still Not Fixed," *ProPublica*, June 20, 2019, https://www.propublica.org/article/border-patrol-discipline-system-was-denounced-as-broken-still-not-fixed. A US Government Accountability Office report found that between 2005 and 2012, 144 CBP employees were arrested or indicted on corruption-related charges. See Clare Ribando Seelke and Kristin M. Finklea, "US-Mexican Security Cooperation: The Mérida Initiative and Beyond," Congressional Research Service, R41349, June 29, 2017, https://sgp.fas.org/crs/row/R41349.pdf, 21. Therefore, while there is less attention to legacies of political actors and government institutions colluding directly with drug traffickers in the United States, there is by now ample, publicly documented evidence of US actors benefiting substantially from both drug trafficking and the war on drugs.

50. This stance also allows the United States to avoid taking responsibility for the poverty of its labor reserve and to maintain a certain level of control over Mexico's economy. See James Ferguson, "Paradoxes of Sovereignty and Independence: 'Real' and 'Pseudo' Nation-States and the Depoliticization of Poverty," in *Siting Culture* (London: Routledge, 2005), 123–41.

51. Smith, *The Dope*, 8.

52. A vivid example that Smith documents was the figure of Esteban Cantú, Baja California's most celebrated governor (1917–1920), who also arranged the first large-scale border narcotics business, establishing the association between local governments and the drug trade. Rather than publicly tax the narcotics business, he created Mexico's first off-the-books drug protection racket. The money from the trade eventually transformed Baja California, which had been one of the most underpopulated, underdeveloped states in Mexico, to one of the richest. Official tax earnings increased fourfold in the five years Cantú was in charge, while individual citizens paid some of the lowest property taxes in the country. See Smith, *The Dope*, 63.

53. BrigadaSolidariaNYC, "¿Qué es la BNBPD: Brigada Nacional de Búsqueda de Personas Desaparecidas?" Spring 2021, available at https://drive.google.com/file/d/1MiBlJbZixwiEoz6CzZTyXwLXB9pBMBrB/view?usp=sharing.

54. Carolina Robledo Silvestre, "Combing History against the Grain: The Search for Truth amongst Mexico's Hidden Graves," in *Beyond the Drug War in Mexico: Human Rights, the Public Sphere and Justice,* ed. Wil G. Pansters, Benjamin T. Smith, and Peter Watt (London: Routledge, 2017), chapter 8.

55. Robledo Silvestre, "Combing History,"183.

56. Issa Cristina Hernández Herrera, "Collaborating with Organized Crime in the Search for Disappeared Persons? Formalizing a Humanitarian Alternative for Mexico," *International Review of the Red Cross* 102, no. 914 (2020): 607–28.

57. Madres Buscadoras de Guaymas, Sonora, "En nombre de las madres que buscan a sus hijos sin descanso, me dirijo respetuosamente a los jefes de los carteles que operan en el Estado de Sonora," video, 2:05, January 2, 2022, https://www.facebook.com/watch/?v=2109324685882968.

58. Hernández Herrera, "Collaborating with Organized Crime," 615.

59. "Veracruz: Fixing Mexico's State of Terror," International Crisis Group, Report no. 61, February 28, 2017.

60. Some of the most vocal activists of drug war violence have petitioned the state and intergovernmental agencies to receive protection. Many of the activists I originally met on the Caravan for Peace in 2012, including María Elena Herrera and her son, were later accompanied everywhere by bodyguards. They had learned the necessity of protection early on in their political organizing. In 2011, Nepomuceno Moreno, a member of the MJPD, was assassinated and while the crime remains unsolved, his murder coincided with the rebuke he made to the then-president, Felipe Calderón, during one of the sessions between the presidency and the MJPD.

61. "Dictamen suspende publicación a Sergio Aguayo por criticar a Javier Duarte," *Plumas Libres,* November 7, 2015, https://plumaslibres.com.mx/2015/11/07/dictamen-suspende-publicacion-a-sergio-aguayo-por-criticar-a-javier-duarte/.

62. See Michel-Rolph Trouillot's essay "Adieu, Culture" for a historical discussion of how this use of the concept of culture came to be hegemonic, and how it has been used in the Haitian context. Trouillot argues that the word *culture* today is irretrievably tainted by both the politics of identity and the politics of blame, including the racialization of behavior that it was meant to avoid. Michel-Rolph Trouillot, "Adieu, Culture: A New Duty Arises," in *Anthropology*

beyond Culture, ed. Richard G. Fox and Barbara J. King (London: Routledge, 2020), 349.

Chapter 5

1. While some citizen-led collectives have taught themselves basic forensics or how to preserve a crime scene, other collectives have worked directly with professional forensic teams. The Equipo Argentino de Antropología Forense (EAAF), for example, is currently working closely with Mexican organizations across many states. The EAAF has also worked with the Centro de Derechos Humanos de las Mujeres (CEDEHM) and government agencies in the state of Chihuahua, for instance on femicides in the state. See Lizzie Wade, "How Forensic Anthropologists Are Helping the Families of Mexico's Disappeared Seek Justice," *Science,* December 14, 2016, https://www.science.org /content/article/how-forensic-anthropologists-are-helping-families-mexicos -disappeared-seek-justice.

2. Jacobo Dayán, "La fosa más grande del país: Colinas de Santa Fe," *Aristegui Noticias,* August 9, 2019, https://aristeguinoticias.com/0908/mexico /la-fosa-mas-grande-del-pais-colinas-de-santa-fe-articulo/.

3. The term *fosa clandestine* ("clandestine grave") is commonly used to refer to this type of burial site. It can, however, be offensive to relatives of the disappeared in Mexico for a number of reasons. It implies illegality, not just for the perpetrators but also for the victims, which can be hurtful to families who knew their loved ones as law-abiding citizens. The term may also avoid acknowledging the full extent of the tragedy, serving as a euphemism that doesn't fully convey the horror of what has happened. It can serve as a painful reminder of the absence of justice for their loved ones, suggesting their deaths were hidden and unacknowledged, rather than investigated and prosecuted. I acknowledge here, however, that there are no good alternatives, as "unmarked" and "undocumented" also fail to convey the severity of the human rights abuse that the existence of such graves embodies.

4. Gabriel Gatti, "The Social Disappeared: Genealogy, Global Circulations, and (Possible) Uses of a Category for the Bad Life," *Public Culture* 32, no. 1 (2020): 30.

5. Melissa Wright, "Epistemological Ignorances and Fighting for the Disappeared: Lessons from Mexico," *Antipode* 49, no. 1 (2017): 249–69.

6. José Abraham Sanz, "Sin cuerpo no hay delito: 'Ya nunca apareció,'" *Quinto Elemento,* January 24, 2022, https://quintoelab.org/project/masterlab -sin-cuerpo-no-hay-delito.

7. Sanz, "Sin cuerpo."

8. Quoted in Julian Resendiz, "Juarez Sees Drop in Homicides in 2021, but Drug and Impunity Issues Persist," *BorderReport,* January 3, 2022, https://www .borderreport.com/immigration/border-crime/juarez-sees-drop-in-homicides -in-2021-but-drug-and-impunity-issues-persist/.

9. Quoted in Jorge Ruiz Reyes, "Fosas clandestinas y su relación con crímenes de lesa humanidad: Propuesta metodológica para la documentación de casos que determinen responsabilidad penal internacional en México," *Historia y Grafía,* no. 52 (2019): 111 (my translation).

10. To see the map, go to https://data.adondevanlosdesaparecidos.org/.

11. "Datos del horror: Hay 3,024 fosas clandestinas en México," *Aristegui Noticias,* August 30, 2019, https://aristeguinoticias.com/3008/mexico/datos -del-horror-hay-3024-fosas-clandestinas-en-mexico/.

12. "Mexico Mass Grave in Abandoned Mine Has 55 Bodies," *BBC News,* June 7, 2010, https://www.bbc.com/news/10260789.

13. Adriana Covarrubias, "Estaban 55 cuerpos en narcofosa de Taxco: PGJE," *El Universal,* June 8, 2010, https://archivo.eluniversal.com.mx/estados /76318.html; Alejandra Guillén, Mago Torres, and Marcela Turati, "El país de las 2 mil fosas," November 12, 2018, https://adondevanlosdesaparecidos.org/2018 /11/12/2-mil-fosas-en-mexico/.

14. Covarrubias, "Estaban 55 cuerpos."

15. "México: Maletas abandonadas, pista para esclarecer asesinatos en Tamaulipas," *Terra,* April 19, 2011, https://web.archive.org/web/20160306200844 /http://www.terra.com.mx/noticias/articulo/1093197/Mexico+Maletas+aban donadas+pista+para+esclarecer+asesinatos+en+Tamaulipas.htm.

16. Omar Granados, "Los misterios de la masacre de San Fernando," *Animal Politico,* September 24, 2011, https://www.animalpolitico.com/2011/09 /los-misterios-de-la-masacre-de-san-fernando/.

17. Guillén, Torres, and Turati, "El país de las 2 mil fosas."

18. Fuentes Díaz, "Criminal Violence and Armed Community Defense," in *Organized Violence: Capitalist Warfare in Latin America,* ed. Dawn Paley and Simon Granovsky-Larsen (Regina, Saskatchewan: University of Regina Press, 2019), 178–200.

19. Natalia Mendoza, "Un día y su noche en Caborca," *Nexos,* August 1, 2020, https://www.nexos.com.mx/?p=49123.

20. Map 1 displays data on covert mass graves in Mexico, spanning from 2006 to April 2023, sourced from the internal database of the National Commission for the Search for Persons (Comision Nacional de Busqueda de Personas). The data, pinpointed to the municipal level, are contributed by the National Prosecutor's Office (FGR) and respective state prosecutors, hence they include only graves acknowledged by these legal entities, excluding findings from local groups, individuals, or other nonofficial entities involved in identifying missing persons and mass graves. The dataset does not disclose the number of bodies per grave or offer precise locations beyond municipal boundaries. Therefore, it likely underrepresents the true extent of mass graves in Mexico, although it remains the most extensive database. Out of 5,329 documented mass graves, 299 lack specific municipal or state data and are thus omitted from the map's aggregation. See Efraín Tzuc, "México rebasa las 5 mil 600 fosas clandestinas," *Quinto Elemento,* October 9, 2023, available at https://quintoelab.org/project/mexico-rebasa-cinco-mil-fosas-clandestinas#:~:text=Al%20aumento%20en%20el%20n%C3%BAmero,guerra%20contra%20la%20delincuencia%20organizada. Map prepared by Caitlyn Yates.

21. Stephanie Nolan, "Unforgotten in Mexico: How the Grieving Searchers of Iguala Have Kept Digging for Answers," *Globe and Mail,* April 15, 2016, https://www.theglobeandmail.com/news/world/unforgotten-in-mexico-searchers-of-iguala-dig-for-answers-about-lost-lovedones/article29642885/.

22. Jo Tuckman, "Bringing Up the Bodies: Mexico's Missing Students Draw Attention to 20,000 'Vanished' Others," *The Guardian,* November 26, 2014, https://www.theguardian.com/world/2014/nov/26/mexico-missing-students-thousands-vanished-grave-diggers.

23. Carolina Robledo Silvestre, "Combing History against the Grain: The Search for Truth amongst Mexico's Hidden Graves," in *Beyond the Drug War in Mexico: Human Rights, the Public Sphere and Justice,* ed. Wil G. Pansters, Benjamin T. Smith, and Peter Watt (London: Routledge, 2017), 164–84. Pau Pérez-Sales and Susana Navarro García, *Resistencias contra el olvido: Trabajo psicosocial en procesos de exhumaciones* (Barcelona: Editorial Gedisa, 2007).

24. Olof Kjell Oscar Ohlson, *Mexico's Rebellious Afterlives: Armed Uprisings and Activism in the Narco War* (Lanham, MD: Rowman and Littlefield, 2022).

25. BrigadaSolidariaNYC, "¿Qué es la BNBPD: Brigada Nacional de Búsqueda de Personas Desaparecidas?" Spring 2021, available at https://drive.google.com /file/d/1MiBlJbZixwiEoz6CzZTyXwLXB9pBMBrB/view?usp=sharing.

26. This perspective mirrors the activism during Argentina's "Dirty War" (1976–1983), where groups like the Mothers of the Plaza de Mayo protested disappearances with the conviction that their loved ones were still alive, embodied in the slogan "Aparición con vida." The practice of naming the disappeared as *presente*, or "present," during roll calls, was a powerful act of resistance, symbolically affirming the ongoing existence of the disappeared in the collective memory and challenging state narratives. This ritual, alongside the demand for the living return of the *desparecidos*, remains a poignant example of hope and defiance against oppressive silence.

27. Quoted in Antonius C. G. M. Robben, *Political Violence and Trauma in Argentina* (Philadelphia: University of Pennsylvania Press, 2005).

28. Kamari Maxine Clarke, "Rendering the Absent Visible: Victimhood and the Irreconcilability of Violence," *Journal of the Royal Anthropological Institute* 28, no. S1 (2022): 135–52.

29. Azam Ahmed, "In Mexico, Not Dead. Not Alive. Just Gone.," *The New York Times*, November 20, 2017, https://www.nytimes.com/2017/11/20/world /americas/mexico-drug-war-dead.html.

30. Guillén, Torres, and Turati, "El país de las 2 mil fosas."

31. Alejandra Guillén, Mago Torres, and Marcela Turati, "2,000 Clandestine Graves: How a Decade of the Drug War Turned Mexico into a Burial Ground," *The Intercept*, December 13, 2018, *https://theintercept.com/2018/12/13 /mexico-drug-war-mass-graves/*.

32. Guillén, Torres, and Turati, "El país de las 2 mil fosas."

33. Guillén, Torres, and Turati, "El país de las 2 mil fosas."

34. Carlos Quintero, "De fosa en fosa, de anfiteatro en anfiteatro, las fiscalías se desentienden de sus cadáveres," *A dónde van los desaparecidos,* October 29, 2020, https://adondevanlosdesaparecidos.org/2020/10/29/de-fosa-en-fosa -de-anfiteatro-en-anfiteatro-las-fiscalias-se-desentienden-de-sus-cadaveres /?fbclid = IwAR1AXTH1Ylwzds5EMx1pBLf5iyeOs7NRfYf28Q71tzuYNAnEv1p _liLFjQg.

35. Guillén, Torres, and Turati, "El país de las 2 mil fosas."

36. For example, in March 2019, Nayarit's State Commission for the Search for Disappeared Persons recovered five sets of remains in Bahia de Banderas fol-

lowing an anonymous source that told them of "hundreds" of victims. See "Hallan predios en Nayarit usados para desaparecer personas," *EFE*, March 9, 2020, https://www.azcentral.com/story/mexico/2020/03/09/hallan-predios-en -nayarit-usados-para-desaparecer-personas/5003550002/. Similarly, in August 2020, the Network of the Disappeared in Colima received an anonymous tip that led to the discovery of thirty-one bodies in mass graves in that state. See Raúl Torres, "Rescatan 31 cuerpos de fosas clandestinas en Tecomán, Colima," *El Universal*, August 17, 2020, https://www.eluniversal.com.mx/estados/colima-rescatan -31-cuerpos-de-fosas-clandestinas-en-tecoman. To confound the issue of how information is relayed across these different networks, there have also been some cases of family members of the disappeared receiving false tips. In one case, Mirna—a leader of the Rastreadoras search collective in Los Mochis—received information about where to find a body but when she arrived at the location, she found a dummy made of sandbags that was clothed and covered in a red liquid that looked like blood. See Ana Karina Zatarain, "Searching with the Mothers of Mexico's Disappeared." *The New Yorker,* August 5, 2020, https://www.newyorker .com/news/dispatch/searching-with-the-mothers-of-mexicos-disappeared.

37. Michael Taussig, *Defacement: Public Secrecy and the Labor of the Negative* (Stanford. CA: Stanford University Press, 1999), 149.

38. Angélica Durán-Martínez, "To Kill and Tell? State Power, Criminal Competition, and Drug Violence," *Journal of Conflict Resolution* 59, no. 8 (2015): 1377–1402.

39. "El Zabe', le llaman. Es el hombre de Los Salazar en Mexicali, donde se libra una guerra sin cuartel," *SinEmbargo.MX*, March 17, 2021, https://www .sinembargo.mx/17-03-2021/3952534.

40. It did not, however, circulate in local media outlets or newspapers, which is not unusual but is worth noting.

41. Emiliano Rodríguez Mega, "An Investigation into Mexico's 43 Missing Students Ends in 'Falsehoods and Diversions,'" *The New York Times,* July 25, 2023, https://www.nytimes.com/2023/07/25/world/americas/mexico-missing -students-investigation.html.

Conclusions

1. *Campos* in this region are clusters of basic houses and campsites where people fish, hunt, and camp.

2. Luis Alejandro Astorga, *El siglo de las drogas: El narcotráfico, del Porfiriato al nuevo milenio* (Cuidad de México: Plaza y Janés, 2005); Ricardo Pérez Montfort, Alberto del Castillo Yurrita, and Pablo Piccato, *Hábitos, normas y escándalo: Prensa, criminalidad y drogas durante el Porfiriato tardío* (Cuidad de México: Plaza y Valdés, 1997); Paul J. Vanderwood, *Juan Soldado: Rapist, Murderer, Martyr, Saint* (Durham, NC: Duke University Press, 2004).

3. Natalia Mendoza Rockwell, *Conversaciones en el desierto: Cultura y tráfico de drogas* (Cuidad de México: CIDE, 2017).

4. Arturo Angel, "Juez sentencia a Javier Duarte a nueve años de prisión por asociación delictuosa y lavado de dinero," *Animal Politico*, September 26, 2018, https://www.animalpolitico.com/2018/09/duarte-se-declara-culpable/.

5. PRI member Flavino Rios was selected as the interim governor in Duarte's absence, but he was later arrested on charges related to helping Duarte escape Veracruz. See Victor Hugo Arteaga, "Juez da un año de prisión preventiva a Flavino Ríos; lo acusan de encubrir a Javier Duarte," *Animal Politico*, March 13, 2017. https://www.animalpolitico.com/2017/03/detienen -flavino-rios-ex-gobernador-veracruz.

6. Manu Ureste, "El PAN gana la elección en Veracruz tras 86 años de gobiernos Priistas," *Animal Politico*, June 6, 2016, https://www.animalpolitico .com/2016/06/el-pan-se-perfila-como-ganador-en-veracruz-en-una-votacion -muy-cerrada.

7. Arturo Angel and Manu Ureste, "Investigan más de 200 desapariciones forzadas por policías de Javier Duarte en Veracruz," *Animal Politico*, February 9, 2018, https://www.animalpolitico.com/2018/02/duarte-veracruz-desaparicion- forzada.

8. Angel and Ureste, "Investigan más de 200 desapariciones forzadas."

9. José Raúl Linares, "Los desaparecidos, cuenta pendiente del exgobernador Javier Duarte," *Proceso*, July 20, 2019, https://www.proceso.com.mx /nacional/2019/7/20/los-desaparecidos-cuenta-pendiente-del-exgobernador-javier-duarte-228282.html.

10. Arturo Angel, "Falta de permiso diplomático impide procesar a Javier Duarte por desapariciones," *Animal Politico*, July 27, 2020, https://www .animalpolitico.com/2020/07/javier-duarte-falta-permiso-diplomatico- desaparicion-forzada.

11. For more on how Winckler Ortíz failed to build more general capacity to address disappearances beyond the targets he pursued through his narrow

political opportunism, see Janice K. Gallagher, *Bootstrap Justice: The Search for Mexico's Disappeared* (Oxford: Oxford University Press, 2022), chapter 5.

12. "AMLO: Órdenes de Aprehensión de Jorge Winckler, Asunto de La Fiscalía," *Milenio*, September 24, 2019, https://www.milenio.com/politica /amlo-ordenes-aprehension-jorge-winckler-asunto-fiscalia.

13. "Permanecerá en prisión Jorge Winckler, ex fiscal de Veracruz," *Gobernantes*, August 16, 2023, *http://www.gobernantes.com/vernota.php?id=415277*.

14. Oscar Lopez, "Mexico Says Disappearance of 43 Students Was a 'Crime of the State.'" *The New York Times*, August 18, 2022, https://www.nytimes.com /2022/08/18/world/americas/mexico-students-disappearance.html.

15. Lopez, "Mexico Says."

16. Judith Butler argues that this question is ultimately about how affect is produced by the frame of "grievability." She contends that specific lives cannot be apprehended as lost if they are not first apprehended as living and that this apprehension is presupposed by certain norms of recognition. Judith Butler, *Frames of War: When Is Life Grievable?* (London: Verso Books, 2016).

17. Benjamin T. Smith also documents how protection rackets and the nature of corruption in Mexico changed in the 1970s as federal police and then traffickers increasingly took control of protection rackets or *plazas*. It is a history that underscores the complexity and historical contingency of what we think of as corrupt systems. Benjamin T. Smith, *The Dope: The Real History of the Mexican Drug Trade* (New York: Norton and Company, 2021), 8.

18. Canadian Mental Health Association, "Preventing Drug-Related Deaths," last modified August 24, 2023, *https://cmha.ca/brochure/preventing-drug-related-deaths/*.

19. Gallagher, *Bootstrap Justice*.

Works Cited

Aburto, José Manuel, Hiram Beltrán-Sánchez, Víctor Manuel García-Guerrero, and Vladimir Canudas-Romo. "Homicides in Mexico Reversed Life Expectancy Gains for Men and Slowed Them for Women, 2000–10." *Health Affairs* 35, no. 1 (2016): 88–95.

Agosín, Marjorie. *Tapestries of Hope, Threads of Love: The Arpillera Movement in Chile, 1974–1994*. Albuquerque: University of New Mexico Press, 1996.

Aguilar, Raquel Gutiérrez. "Porque vivas nos queremos, juntas estamos trastocándolo todo. Notas para pensar, una vez más, los caminos de la transformación social." *Theomai*, no. 37 (2018): 41–55.

Ahmed, Azam. *Fear Is Just a Word: A Missing Daughter, a Violent Cartel, and a Mother's Quest for Vengeance*. London: Hachette UK, 2023.

Alexander, Michelle. *The New Jim Crow: Mass Incarceration in the Age of Colorblindness*. New York: The New Press, 2010.

Alvarez, Sonia E. *Engendering Democracy in Brazil: Women's Movements in Transition Politics*. Princeton, NJ: Princeton University Press, 2021.

Anaya-Muñoz, Alejandro, and Barbara Frey. *Mexico's Human Rights Crisis*. Philadelphia: University of Pennsylvania Press, 2019.

Andreas, Peter. *Border Games: The Politics of Policing the US-Mexico Divide*. Ithaca, NY: Cornell University Press, 2009.

Anthias, Floya, and Nira Yuval-Davis. "Contextualizing Feminism: Gender, Ethnic and Class Divisions." *Feminist Review* 15, no. 1 (1983): 62–75.

Astorga, Luis. "The Limits of Anti-Drug Policy in Mexico." *International Social Science Journal* 53, no. 169 (2001): 427–34.

——. *¿Qué querían que hiciera?: Inseguridad y delincuencia organizada en el gobierno de Felipe Calderón.* Barcelona: Grijalbo, 2015.

——. *El siglo de las drogas: El narcotráfico, del Porfiriato al nuevo milenio.* Cuidad de México: Plaza Y Janés, 2005.

Astorga, Luis, and David Shirk. "Drug Trafficking Organizations and Counter-Drug Strategies in the US-Mexican Context," Center for US-Mexican Studies, working paper 10-01, 2010.

Auyero, Javier. *Patients of the State: The Politics of Waiting in Argentina.* Durham, NC: Duke University Press, 2012.

Azaola, Elena. "El Movimiento por la Paz con Justicia y Dignidad." *Desacatos* 40 (2012): 143–56.

Baldez, Lisa. *Why Women Protest: Women's Movements in Chile.* Cambridge: Cambridge University Press, 2002.

Beith, Malcolm. "A Broken Mexico: Allegations of Collusion between the Sinaloa Cartel and Mexican Political Parties." In *Criminal Insurgencies in Mexico and the Americas,* edited by Robert J. Bunker, 74–93. London: Routledge, 2013.

Bejarano, Cynthia L. "Las Super Madres de Latino America: Transforming Motherhood by Challenging Violence in Mexico, Argentina, and El Salvador." *Frontiers: A Journal of Women Studies* 23, no. 1 (2002): 126–50.

Bertram, Eva, Morris Blachman, Kenneth Sharpe, and Peter Andreas. *Drug War Politics: The Price of Denial.* Berkeley: University of California Press, 1996.

Blancas, Patricia Ravelo, and Héctor Domínguez Rubalcaba. "Ciudad Juárez: asedios a la ciudadanía y cancelación de la vida urbana," *El Cotidiano,* no. 164 (November–December 2010).

Bourdieu, Pierre. *Pascalian Meditations.* Stanford, CA: Stanford University Press, 2000.

Brana-Shute, Rosemary and Gary Brana-Shute. *Crime and Punishment in the Caribbean.* Gainesville: Center for Latin American Studies, University of Florida, 1980.

Butler, Judith. *Frames of War: When Is Life Grievable?* London: Verso Books, 2016.

Butler, Judith, and Gayatri Chakravorty Spivak. *Who Sings the Nation-State?: Language, Politics, Belonging.* Kolkata: Seagull Books, 2007.

Caldeira, Teresa P. R., and James Holston. "Comparative Studies in Society and History Democracy and Violence in Brazil." *Comparative Studies in Society and History* 41, no. 4 (1999): 691–729.

Campos, Isaac. "Mexicans and the Origins of Marijuana Prohibition in the United States: A Reassessment." *Social History of Alcohol and Drugs* 32, no. 1 (2018): 6–37.

Carlsen, Laura. "Effects of Militarization in the Name of Counter-Narcotics Efforts and Consequences for Human Rights in Mexico." In *Beyond the Drug War in Mexico,* edited by Wil G. Pansters, Benjamin T. Smith, and Peter Watt, 76–94. London: Routledge, 2017.

Clarke, Kamari Maxine. "Rendering the Absent Visible: Victimhood and the Irreconcilability of Violence." *Journal of the Royal Anthropological Institute* 28, no. S1 (2022): 135–52.

Cooray, Arusha, and Friedrich Schneider. "Does Corruption Throw Sand into or Grease the Wheels of Financial Sector Development?" *Public Choice* 177, no. 1 (2018): 111–33.

Correa-Cabrera, Guadalupe. *Los Zetas Inc.* Austin: University of Texas Press, 2021.

———. "Security, Migration, and the Economy in the Texas–Tamaulipas Border Region: The 'Real' Effects of Mexico's Drug War." *Politics and Policy* 41, no. 1 (2013): 65–82.

Crane, Nicholas Jon, and Oliver Gabriel Hernández Lara. "Politicizing Disappearance after Mexico's 'Historic' Election." *Political Geography* 75 (2019): 102025.

Crenshaw, Kimberlé W. *On Intersectionality: Essential Writings.* New York: The New Press, 2017.

Cruz-Torres, María L. *Pink Gold: Women, Shrimp, and Work in Mexico.* University of Texas Press, 2023.

Curry, Alexander, and Leonie Ansems de Vries. "Violent Governance, Identity and the Production of Legitimacy: Autodefensas in Latin America." *Journal of International Relations and Development* 23, no. 2 (2020): 262–84.

Dahlin, Miranda. "To Wait amongst Shadows: Violence, Forced Migration, and the Spectral Geography of the Juárez-El Paso Borderlands." PhD diss., McGill University, 2019.

de Barbieri, Teresita, and Orlandina de Oliveira. "Nuevos sujetos sociales: La presencia política de las mujeres en América Latina." *Nueva Antropología* 8, no. 30 (1986): 5–29.

De León, Jason. *The Land of Open Graves: Living and Dying on the Migrant Trail.* California Series in Public Anthropology, 36. Oakland: University of California Press, 2015.

Del Palacio, Celia. *"Porque la lucha por un hijo no termina . . . ": Testimonios de las madres del Colectivo Familias de Desaparecidos Orizaba-Córdoba.* Xalapa: Universidad Veracruzana, 2020.

Diaz-Cotto, Juanita. "Latinas and the War on Drugs in the United States, Latin America, and Europe." In *Global Lockdown: Race, Gender, and the Prison-Industrial Complex,* edited by J. Sudbury, 137–53. London: Routledge, 2005.

Driver, Alice. *More or Less Dead: Feminicide, Haunting, and the Ethics of Representation in Mexico.* Tucson: University of Arizona Press, 2015.

Durán-Martínez, Angélica. "To Kill and Tell? State Power, Criminal Competition, and Drug Violence." *Journal of Conflict Resolution* 59, no. 8 (2015): 1377–1402.

Durin, Séverine. "Los que la guerra desplazó: Familias del noreste de México en el exilio." *Desacatos,* no. 38 (2012): 29–42.

Feitlowitz, Marguerite. *A Lexicon of Terror: Argentina and the Legacies of Torture.* Oxford: Oxford University Press, 1998.

Feldman, Ilana. "Care and Suspicion: Corruption as Definition in Humanitarian Relations." *Current Anthropology* 59, no. S18 (2018): S160–70.

Feldstein, Ruth. "I Wanted the Whole World to See: Race, Gender, and Constructions of Motherhood in the Death of Emmet Till." In *Not June Cleaver: Women and Gender in Postwar America, 1945–1960,* edited by June Meyerowitz, 263–303. Philadelphia: Temple University Press, 1994.

Ferguson, James. "Paradoxes of Sovereignty and Independence:'Real' and 'Pseudo' Nation-States and the Depoliticization of Poverty." In *Siting Culture,* 123–41. London: Routledge, 2005.

Fregoso, Rosa-Linda, and Cynthia Bejarano. *Terrorizing Women.* Durham, NC: Duke University Press Books, 2009.

Fuentes Díaz. "Criminal Violence and Armed Community Defense." In *Organized Violence: Capitalist Warfare in Latin America,* edited by Dawn Paley and Simon Granovsky-Larsen, 178–200. Regina, Saskatchewan: University of Regina Press, 2019.

Gagné, Karine. "Waiting for the Flood: Technocratic Time and Impending Disaster in the Himalayas." *Disasters* 43, no. 4 (2019): 840–66.

Gago, Verónica. *Neoliberalism from Below: Popular Pragmatics and Baroque Economies.* Durham, NC: Duke University Press, 2017.

Gallagher, Janice K. *Bootstrap Justice: The Search for Mexico's Disappeared.* Oxford: Oxford University Press, 2022.

———. "The Last Mile Problem: Activists, Advocates, and the Struggle for Justice in Domestic Courts." *Comparative Political Studies* 50, no. 12 (2017): 1666–98.

Gatti, Gabriel. "The Social Disappeared: Genealogy, Global Circulations, and (Possible) Uses of a Category for the Bad Life." *Public Culture* 32, no. 1 (2020): 25–43.

Gibler, John. *Mexico Unconquered: Chronicles of Power and Revolt.* San Francisco: City Lights Publishers, 2009.

Goss, Kristin A., and Michael T. Heaney. "Organizing Women as Women: Hybridity and Grassroots Collective Action in the 21st Century." *Perspectives on Politics* 8, no. 1 (2010): 27–52.

Grandmaison, Romain Le Cour. "Becoming a Violent Broker: Cartels, Autodefensas, and the State in Michoacán, Mexico." *European Review of Latin American and Caribbean Studies* 112, no. 2 (2021): 137–58.

Gupta, Akhil. *Red Tape.* Durham, NC: Duke University Press, 2012.

Hage, Ghassan. "Waiting Out the Crisis: On Stuckedness and Governmentality." *Anthropological Theory* 5 (2009): 463–75.

Hernández, Raúl Diego Rivera. *Narratives of Vulnerability in Mexico's War on Drugs.* New York: Springer, 2020.

Hernández Herrera, Issa Cristina. "Collaborating with Organized Crime in the Search for Disappeared Persons? Formalizing a Humanitarian Alternative for Mexico." *International Review of the Red Cross* 102, no. 914 (2020): 607–28.

Hetherington, Kregg. "Peasants, Experts, Clients, and Soybeans: The Fixing of Paraguay's Civil Service." *Current Anthropology* 59, no. S18 (2018): S171–81.

Heyman, Josiah. "Deepening the Anthropology of Bureaucracy." *Anthropological Quarterly* 85, no. 4 (2012): 1269–77.

Howe, Sara Eleanor. "The Madres de La Plaza de Mayo: Asserting Motherhood; Rejecting Feminism?" *Journal of International Women's Studies* 7, no. 3 (2006): 43–50.

Inoue, Miyako. "Language and Gender in an Age of Neoliberalism." *Gender and Language* 1, no. 1 (2007): 79–91.

Invisible Committee. *Now*. Semiotext(e), 23. Translated by Robert Hurley. Cambridge, MA: MIT Press, 2018.

Jusionyte, Ieva. *Exit Wounds: American Guns, Mexican Lives, and the Vicious Circle of Violence*. Oakland: University of California Press, forthcoming.

———. *Threshold: Emergency Responders on the US-Mexico Border*. Berkeley: University of California Press, 2018.

Kafka, Franz. *The Trial*. New York: Schocken Books, 1999.

Kaplan, Temma. "Female Consciousness and Collective Action: The Case of Barcelona, 1910–1918." *Signs: Journal of Women in Culture and Society* 7, no. 3 (April 1982): 545–66.

Knox, Rupert. "Social Movements in Support of the Victims: Human Rights and Digital Communication." In *Beyond the Drug War in Mexico: Human Rights, the Public Sphere and Justice.*, edited by Wil G. Pansters, Benjamin T. Smith, and Peter Watt, 126–46. London: Routledge, 2017.

Koven, Seth and Sonya Michel, eds. *Mothers of a New World: Maternalist Politics and the Origins of Welfare States*. London: Routledge, 2013.

Lomnitz, Claudio. *Death and the Idea of Mexico*. Brooklyn: Zone Books, 2005.

Lupsha, Peter A. "Drug Lords and Narco-Corruption: The Players Change but the Game Continues." *Crime, Law and Social Change* 16, no. 1 (1991): 41–58.

Mandolessi, Silvana. "Introduction: Disappearances in Mexico." In *Disappearances in Mexico: From the "Dirty War" to the "War on Drugs,"* edited by Silvana Mandolessi and Katia Olalde Rico, 1–28. London: Routledge, 2022.

Mandolessi, Silvana, and Katia Olalde Rico, eds. *Disappearances in Mexico: From the "Dirty War" to the "War on Drugs."* London: Routledge, 2022.

Martin, Joann. "Motherhood and Power: The Production of a Women's Culture of Politics in a Mexican Community." *American Ethnologist* 17, no. 3 (1990): 470–90.

Massing, Michael. *The Fix*. Berkeley: University of California Press, 2000.

Mendoza Rockwell, Natalia. *Conversaciones en el desierto: Cultura y tráfico de drogas*. Cuidad de México: Centro de Investigación y Docencia Económicas Mexico City (CIDE), 2008.

Monárrez Fragoso, Julia Estela. *Trama de una injusticia feminicidio sexual sistémico en Ciudad Juárez*. Tijuana: Colegio de la Frontera Norte, 2009.

Morris, Stephen. "Drug Trafficking, Corruption, and Violence in Mexico: Mapping the Linkages." *Trends in Organized Crime* 16, no. 2 (2013): 195-220.

Muehlmann, Shaylih. "'*Hasta la Madre!*': Mexican Mothers against 'the War on Drugs.'" *The Social History of Alcohol and Drugs* 31, no. 1 (2017): 85-106.

———. "The Narco Uncanny." *Public Culture* 32, no. 2 (2020): 327-48.

———. *When I Wear My Alligator Boots: Narco-Culture in the US Mexico Borderlands*. California Series in Public Anthropology, 33. Berkeley: University of California Press, 2013.

———. *Where the River Ends: Contested Indigeneity in the Mexican Colorado Delta*. Durham, NC: Duke University Press, 2013.

Navarro, Marysa. "The Personal Is Political: Las Madres de Plaza de Mayo." In *Power and Popular Protest: Latin American Social Movements,* edited by Susan Eckstein, 241-58. Berkeley: University of California Press, 1989.

Novo, Carmen Martínez. *Who Defines Indigenous?: Identities, Development, Intellectuals, and the State in Northern Mexico*. New Brunswick, NJ: Rutgers University Press, 2006.

Ohlson, Olof Kjell Oscar. *Mexico's Rebellious Afterlives: Armed Uprisings and Activism in the Narco War*. Lanham, MD: Rowman and Littlefield, 2022.

O'Neill, Kevin Lewis. "Home Security: Drug Rehabilitation Centres, the Devil and Domesticity in Guatemala City." *Journal of Latin American Studies* 52, no. 4 (2020): 785-804.

———. "Narcotecture." *Environment and Planning D: Society and Space* 34, no. 4 (2016): 672-88.

Orozco Mendoza, Elva F. "Las Madres de Chihuahua: Maternal Activism, Public Disclosure, and the Politics of Visibility." *New Political Science* 41, no. 2 (2019): 211-33.

———. "Punitive Dispossession: Authoritarian Neoliberalism and the Road to Mass Incarceration." In *Organized Violence: Capitalist Warfare in Latin America,* edited by Dawn Paley and Simon Granovsky-Larsen, 237-60. Regina, Saskatchewan: University of Regina Press, 2019.

Ortiz Cuchivague, Karen. "Las Madres de la Plaza de Mayo y su legado por la defensa de los derechos humanos." *Trabajo social* 14 (2012): 165-77.

Paley, Dawn. "Against Official Discourse." *NACLA Report on the Americas* 50, no. 3 (2018): 311-12.

————. "Drug War as Neoliberal Trojan Horse." *Latin American Perspectives* 42, no. 5 (2015): 109–32.

————. *Drug War Capitalism*. Oakland: AK Press, 2014.

————. *Guerra neoliberal: Desaparición y búsqueda en el Norte de México*. San Juan, Puerto Rico: Libertad Bajo Palabra, 2020.

Paley, Dawn, and Simon Granovsky-Larsen. *Organized Violence: Capitalist Warfare in Latin America*. Regina, Saskatchewan: University of Regina Press, 2019.

Pansters, Wil G., Benjamin T. Smith, and Peter Watt, eds. *Beyond the Drug War in Mexico: Human Rights, the Public Sphere and Justice*. London: Routledge, 2017.

Pardo, Italo. "Corrupt, Abusive, and Legal: Italian Breaches of the Democratic Contract." *Current Anthropology* 59, no. S18 (2018): S60–71.

Payne, Leigh, Karina Ansolabehere, and Barbara Frey. "Observatorio sobre desaparición e impunidad: Informe sobre desapariciones en el estado de Nuevo León con información de CADHAC," FLACSO México, Human Rights Program University of Minnesota, University of Oxford, 2017.

Pérez Montfort, Ricardo, Alberto Del Castillo Yurrita, and Pablo Piccato. *Hábitos, normas y escándalo: Prensa, criminalidad y drogas durante el Porfiriato tardío*. Mexico City: Plaza y Valdés, 1997.

Pérez-Sales, Pau, and Susana Navarro García. *Resistencias contra el olvido: Trabajo psicosocial en procesos de exhumaciones*. Barcelona: Editorial Gedisa, 2007.

Ríos, Viridiana. "How Government Coordination Controlled Organized Crime: The Case of Mexico's Cocaine Markets." *Journal of Conflict Resolution* 59, no. 8 (2015): 1–22.

Robben, Antonius C. G. M. *Political Violence and Trauma in Argentina*. Philadelphia: University of Pennsylvania Press, 2005.

Robledo Silvestre, Carolina. "Combing History against the Grain: The Search for Truth amongst Mexico's Hidden Graves." In *Beyond the Drug War in Mexico: Human Rights, the Public Sphere and Justice*, edited by Wil G. Pansters, Benjamin T. Smith, and Peter Watt, 164–184. London: Routledge, 2017.

————. *Drama social y política del duelo: Las desapariciones de la guerra contra las drogas en Tijuana*. Ciudad de México: El Colegio de Mexico, 2017.

Rosa, Jonathan. *Looking like a Language, Sounding like a Race.* Oxford Studies in the Anthropology of Language. Oxford: Oxford University Press, 2019.

Ruiz Reyes, Jorge. "Fosas clandestinas y su relación con crímenes de lesa humanidad. Propuesta metodológica para la documentación de casos que determinen responsabilidad penal internacional en México." *Historia y Grafía,* no. 52 (2019): 97–128.

Sarı, Elif. "Lesbian Refugees in Transit: The Making of Authenticity and Legitimacy in Turkey." *Journal of Lesbian Studies* 24, no. 2 (2020): 140–58.

Schmink, Marianne. "Women in Brazilian Abertura Politics." *Signs* 7, no. 1 (1981): 115–34.

Secor, Anna J. "Between Longing and Despair: State, Space, and Subjectivity in Turkey." *Environment and Planning D: Society and Space* 25, no. 1 (2007): 33–52.

Serrano, Mónica. "A Humanitarian Crisis in the Making." In *Beyond the Drug War in Mexico,* edited by Wil G. Pansters, Benjamin T. Smith, and Peter Watt, 64–86. London: Routledge, 2017.

Slack, Jeremy. *Deported to Death How Drug Violence Is Changing Migration on the US-Mexico Border.* Oakland: University of California Press, 2019.

Smith, Benjamin T. *The Dope: The Real History of the Mexican Drug Trade.* New York: Norton and Company, 2021.

———. "Killing a Cabby: The Press, Civil Society, and Justice in 1950s Chihuahua." *Mexican Studies/Estudios Mexicanos* 36, no. 1–2 (2020): 127–49.

Snyder, Richard, and Angelica Duran-Martinez. "Does Illegality Breed Violence? Drug Trafficking and State-Sponsored Protection Rackets." *Crime, Law and Social Change* 52, no. 3 (2009): 253–73.

Speed, Shannon. "Dangerous Discourses: Human Rights and Multiculturalism in Neoliberal Mexico." *PoLAR: Political and Legal Anthropology* 28, no. 1 (2005): 29–51.

Stephen, Lynn. "Gender, Citizenship, and Politics of Identity." *Latin American Perspectives* 28, no. 6 (2001): 54–69.

Tate, Winifred. *Drugs, Thugs, and Diplomats: US Policymaking in Colombia.* Stanford, CA: Stanford University Press, 2015.

Taussig, Michael. *Defacement: Public Secrecy and the Labor of the Negative.* Stanford, CA: Stanford University Press, 1999.

Taylor, Diana. *Disappearing Acts: Spectacles of Gender and Nationalism in Argentina's" Dirty War."* Durham, NC: Duke University Press, 1997.

Ticktin, Miriam. "What's Wrong with Innocence." *Society for Cultural Anthropology,* June 28, 2016.

Trouillot, Michel-Rolph. "Adieu, Culture: A New Duty Arises." In *Anthropology beyond Culture,,* edited by Richard G. Fox and Barbara J. King, 37–60. London: Routledge, 2020.

Vanderwood, Paul J. *Juan Soldado: Rapist, Murderer, Martyr, Saint.* Durham, NC: Duke University Press, 2004.

Villarreal, Ana. "Domesticating Danger: Coping Codes and Symbolic Security amid Violent Organized Crime in Mexico." *Sociological Theory* 39, no. 4 (2021): 225–44.

Villarreal Martínez, María Teresa. "Los colectivos de familiares de personas desaparecidas y la procuración de justicia." *Intersticios Sociales* 11 (2016): 1–28.

Wright, Melissa. "Against the Evils of Democracy: Fighting Forced Disappearance and Neoliberal Terror in Mexico." *Annals of the American Association of Geographers* 108, no. 2 (2018): 327–36.

———. "Epistemological Ignorances and Fighting for the Disappeared: Lessons from Mexico." *Antipode* 49, no. 1 (2017): 249–69.

Yates, Caitlyn, and Stephanie Leutert. "A Gender Perspective of Migrant Kidnapping in Mexico." *Victims and Offenders* 15, no. 3 (2020): 295–312.

Yuval-Davis, Nira. "Intersectionality and Feminist Politics." *European Journal of Women's Studies* 13, no. 3 (2006): 193–209.

Zarco, Abril. "Maternalismo, identidad colectiva y participación política: Las Madres de Plaza de Mayo." *Revista Punto Género,* no. 1 (2011): 229–47.

Zia, Ather. *Resisting Disappearance: Military Occupation and Women's Activism in Kashmir.* Seattle: University of Washington Press, 2019.

Index

activism: drug war, 59–62; human rights, 170; Leticia, 97–98; maternal, 56–59, 90, 93; naming perpetrators, 188; and presumed innocence, 190–191; women-led, 12–13, 54, 191

activists: Ayotzinapa disappearances, 154, 226n26; Black activists in US, 39; caravan, 33, 34, 42–43, 45; Caravan for Peace, 3, 50; "Collateral Damage," 95; collectives, 110, 111, 170, 193; combating victim blaming, 189; confronted collusion, 143; demands of, 46; disappearances, 38, 74, 115, 148, 158, 159; distinguishing among, 206n1; documentation, 109–110; gendered, 25; government strategy, 77; Javier Sicilia, 32–33, 34; legislative changes, 75; make connections with drug traffickers, 138; María Elena Herrera, 205n31, 222n60; on mass graves, 153, 157, 193; murdered, 137; network of, 5, 17, 195; politicization among, 40, 118; politics of, 51; reporting to

police, 104; researching among, 20–21; roles, 11; and waiting, 64, 80

Alejandro Solalinde, Padre, 153

Anaya-Muñoz, Alejandro, 110

Annabel, 72–73

Antillón, Ximena, 77–78

Antonia, 47–48, 58

Attorney General's Office (PGR), 126

Auyero, Javier, 80–81

Ayotzinapa disappearances: case, 154–156, 187, 209n27; killings, 130; names listed, 226n26; students, 91–92, 93, 153, 157, 186

Baena, Nabor, 151

Beltrán Leyva Organization Cartel, 122, 126

Black Americans, 44–45; police brutality, 41–42

Black Lives Matter, 62

Bourdieu, Pierre, 81

Calderón, Felipe, 2, 16, 94–95, 113, 124–127, 150

Camarena, Kiki, 123–124

California Series in Public Anthropology

The California Series in Public Anthropology emphasizes the anthropologist's role as an engaged intellectual. It continues anthropology's commitment to being an ethnographic witness, to describing, in human terms, how life is lived beyond the borders of many readers' experiences. But it also adds a commitment, through ethnography, to reframing the terms of public debate—transforming received, accepted understandings of social issues with new insights, new framings.

SERIES EDITOR: IEVA JUSIONYTE (BROWN UNIVERSITY)

FOUNDING EDITOR: ROBERT BOROFSKY (HAWAII PACIFIC UNIVERSITY)

ADVISORY BOARD: CATHERINE BESTEMAN (COLBY COLLEGE), PHILIPPE BOURGOIS (UCLA), JASON DE LEÓN (UCLA), LAURENCE RALPH (PRINCETON UNIVERSITY), AND NANCY SCHEPER-HUGHES (UC BERKELEY)

Founded in 1893,
UNIVERSITY OF CALIFORNIA PRESS
publishes bold, progressive books and journals
on topics in the arts, humanities, social sciences,
and natural sciences—with a focus on social
justice issues—that inspire thought and action
among readers worldwide.

The UC PRESS FOUNDATION
raises funds to uphold the press's vital role
as an independent, nonprofit publisher, and
receives philanthropic support from a wide
range of individuals and institutions—and from
committed readers like you. To learn more, visit
ucpress.edu/supportus.

www.ingramcontent.com/pod-product-compliance
Lightning Source LLC
Chambersburg PA
CBHW020849270326
41928CB00006B/618